Data Bank Applications in Archaeology

Data Bank Applications in Archaeology

Sylvia W. Gaines, editor

CONTRIBUTORS
Louis Bourrelly
James A. Brown
Robert G. Chenhall
Eugene Chouraqui
Stanley Clayton
Thomas Genn Cook
Sylvia W. Gaines
Jacques Le Maitre
W. Fredrick Limp
Charles W. McNett, Jr.
Michael G. Million
Fred Plog
Anne Rieger
Sandra C. Scholtz
Timothy Wendt
Bernard Werner
John D. Wilcock

The University of Arizona Press
Tucson, Arizona

About the Editor . . .

Sylvia W. Gaines has been interested in computerized data bank applications in archaeology since the early 1960s. She has supervised the design and implementation of the computerized site survey files and excavation file data banks at Arizona State University, as well as the ADAM I and ADAM II information retrieval systems for remote field use. Since 1973 she has been the Data Bank Coordinator for the Southwestern Anthropological Research Group and has served as editor of the *Newsletter of Computer Archaeology.* Dr. Gaines received her Ph.D. degree from Arizona State University and became Assistant Professor of Anthropology there in 1975.

The cover illustration is a partial reproduction of an early microcomputer design. The actual circuit dimensions were reduced to fit onto a silicon chip approximately one-half centimeter square.

THE UNIVERSITY OF ARIZONA PRESS

This book was set in 10/12 Geneva on an Autologic APS-5 phototypesetter.

Library of Congress Cataloging in Publication Data

Data bank applications in archaeology.

    Includes index.
    1. Archaeology—Data processing—Addresses, essays,
lectures. I. Gaines, Sylvia W. II. Bourrelly, Louis.
CC80.4.D37   930.1'028'5   81-901

ISBN 0-8165-0686-8   AACR2

Contents

TABLES

FIGURES

Preface

The advent of electronic computers has had far reaching implications for human society, and the trend is accelerating and rapidly spreading into ever increasing new roles. Archaeology, like many disciplines, is experiencing the impact of this new technology. Historically, archaeology followed closely in the footsteps of the physical and natural sciences in exploiting the power of the computer in mathematical and statistical applications. Within the last decade, a new role of computer use, broader in scope, has begun to evolve—the automating of data bank management.

This new focus is due in part to the increased availability of large-scale computers and inexpensive data storage facilities. However, the major impetus has been the theoretical and methodological concerns that have evolved within archaeology itself. Archaeologists are faced with an expanding base of information and are interested in a complexity of questions that necessitate inquiry and selective extraction of logically related items from a large and diverse body of information.

The role of data management may appear as an extension from earlier ad hoc applications. In one sense this is so, but the attendant problems, both technical and methodological, have made this a slow, and often painful process. We are still faced with some of the earlier problems: What data should be computerized? What are the functions and uses of data banks? Should descriptions be standardized and compatible? Perhaps two of the most critical problems of the late 1970s, and ones that will have long term implications, concern the procedural and administrative questions of data access and data safeguards.

In many respects, archaeology is in its adolescence in terms of computerized data management and information systems. Hopefully, we have progressed from the "nuts and bolts" infancy into more effective approaches. The road has been long and filled with trials and errors. We are still experimenting but one thing is clear—we are on the right track and the computer offers a solution to the tedious manual approaches to data bank applications. With the growing awareness by archaeologists of the vast potential that computerized information systems hold, coupled with the ever increasing technical advances in the computer industry itself, this book is a timely effort to draw together the current "state of the art" of data bank applications in archaeology. It must be viewed as a starting point for future trends and applications.

The terms "data bank" and "data base" often are used interchangeably in the literature. Historically, the term data bank became associated with archaeological applications, while data base is more general in other disciplines. In this book, "data bank" refers to collections of multiple record types, containing relationships between records and data items.

The authors herein are concerned with more than the simple storing of vast quantities of data. It is the *management* of the data so that these can be used for a wide variety of applications that is the important consideration. Ad hoc designs are wasteful and tend to discourage cross correlations that are critical to many areas of research. Ideally, data should be independent of the programs using them so that they can be added to or restructured without changing the programs. Additionally, it should be possible to interrogate and search the data bank without the lengthy operation of writing programs in conventional program languages. There are many different ways in which a data bank can be structured, and each has particular advantages and disadvantages. Archaeologists require many distinct kinds of data that require unique structures. The optimum data bank organization and management techniques are not always obvious. It is this uncertainty that makes the problem controversial and amenable to different approaches, some of which are discussed in this book.

Since it is the purpose of this book to present a range of current data bank applications, the chapters contain a wide variety of examples in archaeology. Chapters 1 and 2 are general in scope and provide background material for better understanding the basic approaches to computerized archaeological information. The remaining chapters describe specific approaches used for various projects in the United States and Europe.

In Chapter 1, Chenhall presents an overview of the history of data banks in archaeology as well as a detailed discussion of the kinds of systematic analyses that are desirable prerequisites to any computerization. Anyone concerned with building a useful record system will find this chapter a valuable starting point. Chapter 2 by Wilcock provides an overview of information retrieval systems for archaeology and discusses applicable techniques, according to their development in Britain.

The next two chapters describe the functions of information retrieval systems for statewide applications. Although both chapters are oriented toward cultural resource management goals, research aspects also are stressed. The AMASDA system utilized for the Arkansas Archeology Survey (Chapter 3 by Scholtz and Million) includes a number of files for site inventories, land use, and projects. The AZSITE system employed at the Arizona State Museum (Chapter 4 by Rieger) similarly functions as a repository of state computerized site information.

Chapters 5 through 9 provide project-specific examples of computerized data bank applications. Plog (Chapter 5) describes how a computerized data bank is utilized by the cooperative investigations of the Southwestern Anthropological Research Group. Computerized files provide both management and research capabilities on a pan-regional level of the American Southwest. Chapter 6 (by Limp and Cook) is an overview of the uses of the ORACLE system developed at Indiana University for research and cultural resource management purposes. Data bank organization, processing procedures, and examples of various projects that utilize the system are presented. Brown and his associates (Chapter 7) discuss the role of computerized information for the Koster Project, a large scale, long term excavation. Because of the project's remote site, research requirements necessitate a variety of unique approaches, and these are reflected in the entire processing procedure. Gaines (Chapter 8) offers an example of how a computerized data bank system can be utilized from a remote field site that includes both survey and excavation. Problems relating to technical and organizational aspects and to field strategies are addressed. Computer graphics are playing an increasingly important role in archaeological research, and Chapter 9 (by McNett) presents the integration of graphic techniques with a computerized information retrieval system.

The final three chapters deal with computerized information systems currently in use in Europe. Chapter 10 (by Wilcock) provides a comprehensive review of archaeological data banks in Britain. It is both a historical presentation, following the thinking and developments on a national scale, as well as a review of current techniques, applications, and attendant problems that confront users of computerized information systems. SOFIA (Chapter 11 by Le Maitre) is a general purpose system used in France that provides an exchange format into which data expressed in other input formats can be translated. Data organization, file organization, data handling, and procedural operations of SOFIA are discussed, as well as a number of examples of how this system is currently utilized. Chapter 12 (Bourrelly and Chouraqui) departs from the foregoing chapters with a discussion of automatic documentation as produced by the SATIN I system. A detailed report on the data description language of the system and its organization is offered with examples of its use with documents in France.

The future of data bank applications in archaeology is challenging. The vast majority of information is not yet computerized. The cost of computer storage is dropping more rapidly than other costs in data processing and soon it will become cheaper to store data on computer files than to store them on paper. Not only printed information will be stored, but also line drawings, data in facsimile form, and even photographs. Clearly, data banks will continue to play a major role in future advances in the field of archaeology.

ACKNOWLEDGMENTS

Throughout this entire endeavor, Dr. Raymond H. Thompson has offered continuing support and encouragement and made available the necessary technical processing. Without his effort this book would not have become a reality. I am also indebted to Carol Gifford, whose skill at editing translated this manuscript into the current form. Jill Neitzel assisted in the technical production of many of the figures. My appreciation is directed to all the authors who had to endure my many memos and constant demands for meeting schedule deadlines. I am especially grateful to the personnel at the University of Arizona Press who made this publication possible. Finally, my husband Warren, the "real" computer expert, provided constant expertise and support.

Sylvia W. Gaines

About the Authors

LOUIS BOURRELLY holds a position at the Laboratoire d'Informatique pour les Sciences de l'Homme (Centre National de la Recherche Scientifique, Marseille). Since the early 1970s his work has been directed toward the design and development of computerized data base systems for prehistory, art history, and classical archaeology.

JAMES A. BROWN, Professor of Anthropology since 1979, began his faculty association at Northwestern University in 1971. He has been Director of Research for the Koster Project since 1971. Brown's computer data bank applications include both data management and statistical analyses.

ROBERT G. CHENHALL began his present position as Director of the Buffalo Museum of Science in 1979. He chairs the American Association of Museums Documentation Committee (1977-present) and is a member of the Board of Directors, ICOM International Documentation Committee (1971-present). Chenhall served as Chairman of the Museum Data Bank Committee (1974-1977), as the Executive Director of the Museum Data Bank Coordinating Committee from 1972-1974 and as a member of the Board of Directors, Museum Computer Network, Inc. from 1971-1977. In 1965, Chenhall founded the *Newsletter of Computer Archaeology* and was editor until 1971.

EUGENE CHOURAQUI holds a position at the Laboratoire d'Informatique pour les Sciences de l'Homme (Centre National de la Recherche Scientifique, Marseille). Since the early 1970s his work has been directed toward the design and development of computerized data base systems for prehistory, art history, and classical archaeology.

STANLEY C. CLAYTON was a student at Northwestern University where he assisted in the design of the Koster Retrieval System from 1975 to 1976.

THOMAS GENN COOK has held a split position as Research Associate, Indiana University and Senior Research Archaeologist at Northwestern University since 1972. He has been active in the design and development of five computerized archaeological data banks and has a number of monographs and manuscripts relating to these.

JACQUES LeMAITRE began his present position as an engineer at the Centre de Recherches Archéologiques, Centre National de la Recherche Scientifique (Paris) in 1973. Since the early 1970s he has been active in computerized data base applications with emphasis on compatibility between data management systems and data base translation.

W. FREDRICK LIMP became Assistant Director of the Arkansas Archeological Survey in 1979. Previous positions include Co-director of Contract Archeology for the Northwestern University Archeological Program at Kampsville (1978-79) and the Director of the ORACLE Project at Indiana University from 1976-1978. He has worked with a number of computer data base applications in the ORACLE Project, including a regional overview study, a site location and predictive model analysis and the development of a storage/retrieval system for ceramic data.

CHARLES W. McNETT, JR. is Professor of Anthropology at The American University and Director of the Potomac River Archaeology Survey. He has participated in computer data bank applications for the past decade as well as pioneering in the use of graphic techniques for use with information retrieval systems.

MICHAEL G. MILLION is a Research Assistant with the Arkansas Archeological Survey. His area of specialization is the computerized management of archaeological sites in Arkansas, with emphasis on ceramic analyses.

FRED PLOG is Professor of Anthropology and Chairman, Department of Anthropology, Arizona State University. As President of the Southwestern Anthropological Research Group since 1976, he has participated in the computerization of the data for this organization. Other computer assisted data base projects include an investigation for the United States Forest Service (1979) and the Chavez Pass Project application (1978-81).

ANNE RIEGER was an Assistant Archaeologist with the Arizona State Museum for several years. During that time she helped to refine the AZSITE site computerization file and directed the work on this project.

SANDRA C. SCHOLTZ is a statistician and computer specialist with the Arkansas Archeological Survey at the University of Arkansas. She is Vice President of the Museum Computer Network, Inc. and a member of the Museum Data Bank Coordinating Committee. Scholtz is author of a number of publications on statistical applications and the use of computers in museums and for archaeological data bases.

TIMOTHY A. WENDT, a computer specialist, contributed to the design of the Koster Retrieval System at Northwestern University from 1973 to 1975.

BERNARD WERNER has been active in commercial computerized data processing and applications since 1973. He was a contributor to the design of the Koster Retrieval System at Northwestern University from 1971 to 1973.

JOHN D. WILCOCK entered the computer industry in 1961 and has worked in both engineering and archaeological capacities. In 1969 he became Senior Lecturer in Computing at North Staffordshire Polytechnic and Head of the Research Centre for Computer Archaeology in 1974. He also holds the position of Lecturer in Archaeology at the University of Keele. Wilcock is Managing Editor of *Science and Archaeology* and is the author of numerous books and articles on data bank applications in archaeology. He is a member of the Council for British Archaeology and has worked as consultant for many museums and archaeological projects.

1. Computerized Data Bank Management

Robert G. Chenhall
Buffalo Museum of Science

INTRODUCTION

The feasibility of utilizing a computer to store large quantities of archaeological data was demonstrated as early as 1967 (for example, see Chenhall 1967), but no one had actually used a computerized data bank on an archaeological project. In 1971 the first archaeological data bank conference was held at the University of Arkansas (Gaines 1971), and the following year a similar conference was held in France (Gardin 1974). Since then the situation has changed considerably. Computerized data banks have now been used on a number of research projects. The utilization of computers in archaeological research is not yet common, perhaps, but it is no longer in the experimental stage, and several trends can be observed that indicate it will be a great deal more common in the future than it has been up to now.

The entire climate for the use of computers to store archaeological data has changed dramatically during the decade of the 1970s. Three things are happening at the same time to bring this about and they are all world-wide in scope. Any one of them would be important, but together they have an impact that is not fully appreciated by most archaeologists.

First, we must recognize that a virtual revolution has been taking place in the development of computers and computer programming systems. In the last chapter of a book published in the mid 1970s, there was a section on "Catalogs of the Future" (Chenhall 1975: 250–56). In this section the use of cathode-ray-tube (CRT) terminals was described as an important future development because it provided a means of economically obtaining the large computing capacity required on an occasional basis for an effective computerized catalog. By the late 1970s many of us were regularly using CRT and other types of terminals in just this way. Already some institutions are using their own mini-computers to do things that, until recently, could only be done with larger equipment. In the long run, these are more economical than even the use of terminals, and the mini-computer is already being out-dated by the micro-computer; with every step both computer size and processing cost go down.

In the mid 1960s a computer containing 4,096 bits of memory required approximately 200 square feet of floor space, but by 1978 a 14-pin "Bubble Package" was available that permitted the storage of 92,304 bits of memory in a 1-by-1.2-by-0.4 inch space. This does not mean, of course, that we have large computer capacity we can put in our vest pockets, but it does mean that extremely powerful computers are now available that are no larger than the desk-top adding machines sold as recently as 1960.

Miniaturization, though, is not the entire story. The 14-pin Bubble Package could be purchased in 1979 for $37. A complete desk-top computer providing virtually unlimited storage on small flexible discs sold for $6,250 in 1978. Both in terms of size and cost, the revolution that is taking place in computers is exactly comparable to the revolution we have experienced in the last few years with electronic calculators.

Along with the technical development of computers, another phenomenon has been taking place that few people have noticed—the gradual maturing of knowledge about how to effectively use computers in archaeological work. Maturing is always a slow and painful process. We make mistakes and, hopefully, we learn from our mistakes. Because the process is so slow it is difficult for us to predict when the learning curve will begin accelerating by geometric proportions, but this is now happening in our knowledge of how to use computers effectively. Let me briefly mention some of the things we have learned.

1. All potentially useful information does not need to be stored in the computer; the computer can be used effectively along with, or as an adjunct to, various kinds of manual records.

2. The most efficient computer files often are cross-indexes to records, objects, and photographs; they are not replacements for records, objects, and photographs.

3. Computers can be worthwhile purely for inventory control purposes; they may also aid in research projects, but the two objectives must be handled separately.

4. Any computerized record has to be purpose-oriented and the purposes have to be defined in specific terms. There is no such thing as a general-purpose computer file; a file serves defined purposes or it does not serve any worthwhile end.

5. Data categories ("data elements" to the computer scientist) have to be carefully defined in terms that are consistent both with the purposes of each file and with the way the files are structured.

6. The data itself (the content of what is recorded within each data category) has to be carefully controlled, specifying well-defined formats for each category of information and developing word lists, lexicons, or thesauri that can be effectively used as authority files.

This is not an exhaustive list of what we have learned but it is enough to indicate that there has been a gradual maturing of our knowledge as computers have become more readily available.

Finally, it is important to recognize that there is an ever increasing demand for more detailed, more precise, and more reliable information about all kinds of archaeological phenomena. This information explosion is at least as great in the field of prehistory as it is in other aspects of our complex society. In part, it is the result of the national awareness developing within Third World countries. The developed nations at one time felt free to remove cultural objects to their own countries for purposes of study and enjoyment. Importing archaeological items is now illegal, so there must be adequate records of objects that are discovered within the developing nations or there will be nothing available for study elsewhere. Despite this oversimplification of a complex phenomenon, the fact remains that, for a variety of reasons, there is a greater demand for information than there has ever been before.

In contrast with the remaining material in this book, this introductory chapter is not a report on a specific data bank project, nor is it a discussion of application questions such as forms design or the relative merits of different computer systems. Rather it is an exposition of the kinds of analyses that are desirable *prerequisites* to any computerized data bank. Included are the preliminary processes necessary in order for a computerized data bank to be a *useful* archaeological tool. The systematic analysis of our information needs usually is worthwhile, even if there is no contemplated use of a computer. A great deal of time and energy can be lost, and sometimes complete chaos can result, when an attempt is made to build an archaeological data bank without first undertaking such analyses. Specifically, I discuss the procedures that are involved in the creation of an *integrated record system* for an archaeological project. This is defined as a system of interrelated data files, manual or computerized or both, in which: (a) each file contains well-defined and delimited sets of data pertinent to a particular kind of activity, and (b) each file contains at least one data category that may be used as a connecting link or pointer to data stored in other files.

Computer technology can be of significant value on an archaeological project. However, the precision necessary to create and utilize adequate computer records requires a thorough examination of several items: (a) the activities to be undertaken; (b) the present and future demands for information that will emanate from those activities; (c) the data files that are necessary or desirable in order to provide that information; (d) the categories of data that must be identified, defined, and controlled in the records in one or more of the files; and (e) the interrelationships between the files that satisfy the information needs of the project in the most efficient manner possible. Each of these topics is considered in the following paragraphs, and the question of when it is worthwhile to use a computer is discussed.

ANALYSIS OF ARCHAEOLOGICAL ACTIVITIES

The first step in designing an integrated record system is to analyze the activities to be undertaken and the needs for various record files. In these paragraphs we are dealing only with those activities that are common to most archaeological projects. As many people have pointed out (for example, Smith 1977), the computer can also be useful for such things as the administration of expense accounts, probability sampling, mathematical modeling, mapping computer graphics, and so on, but these applications are not considered here.

Archaeological activities may be conveniently grouped into three categories on the basis of where and when they are performed (see Fig. 1.1).

Project Field Activities

Field activities consist of either archaeological site surveying or site excavation, and both of these activities do involve the need for records. In addition, field

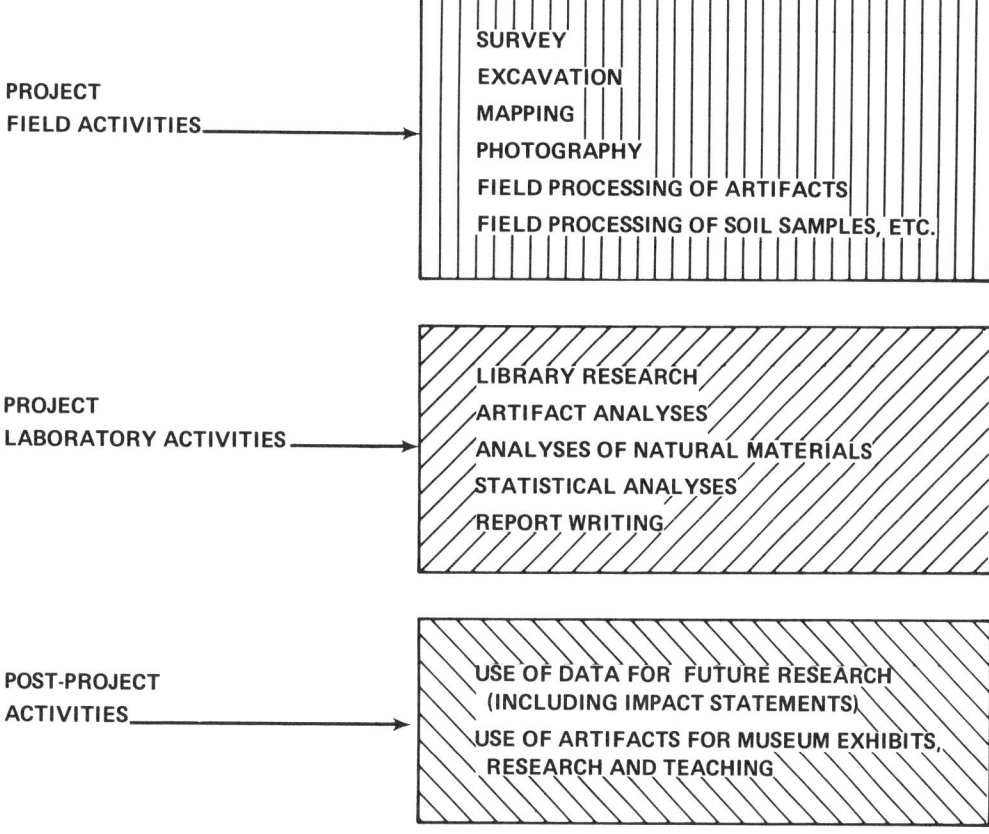

PROJECT
FIELD ACTIVITIES

SURVEY
EXCAVATION
MAPPING
PHOTOGRAPHY
FIELD PROCESSING OF ARTIFACTS
FIELD PROCESSING OF SOIL SAMPLES, ETC.

PROJECT
LABORATORY ACTIVITIES

LIBRARY RESEARCH
ARTIFACT ANALYSES
ANALYSES OF NATURAL MATERIALS
STATISTICAL ANALYSES
REPORT WRITING

POST-PROJECT
ACTIVITIES

USE OF DATA FOR FUTURE RESEARCH
(INCLUDING IMPACT STATEMENTS)
USE OF ARTIFACTS FOR MUSEUM EXHIBITS,
RESEARCH AND TEACHING

Fig. 1.1. Archaeological activities.

activities also include the creation of maps, photography, the preliminary processing of artifacts, and the recording and packing of samples of natural materials such as soils and pollens.

Project Laboratory Activities

The real labor of archaeology begins after the field season is completed. There are many kinds of activities performed in the lab, including: analyses of all the artifacts and natural materials collected, statistical summaries and analyses of various kinds, library research, and, finally, the preparation of the report. It has often been pointed out that the difference between the "real" professional and the dilettante is not a matter of advanced degrees but rather a willingness to carry each project to its completion by performing the project laboratory activities. In a very real sense, the essential work of archaeology is performed in the lab.

Postproject Activities

After an archaeological project has been completed, it is a temptation to turn the boxes of artifactual material and, perhaps, a more-or-less finalized report over to "someone" in the laboratory or museum and assume that "somehow" information will automatically be made available if it is ever needed again. In an integrated record system that information is preserved for specific, definable purposes. The system (which, of course, encompasses the records from a multiplicity of archaeological projects) must include files and indexes that will make the artifacts and the data from each previous project available for future research, for museum exhibits, and for teaching purposes. These postproject activities cannot be ignored in any kind of integrated record system.

FILES TO SUPPORT THE DEFINED ACTIVITIES

Viewed from the broad perspective of a system analyst, archaeological field activities, laboratory activities, and postproject activities become three independent but connected subsystems. When the essential activities within each subsystem have been defined, the next step in the analysis is to develop a clear and precise statement of what is needed in order for those activities to be performed most efficiently. "What is needed" always means having all of the information required for each defined activity available at the right time and place for the person who is to perform the activity, and to accomplish this as cheaply as possible.

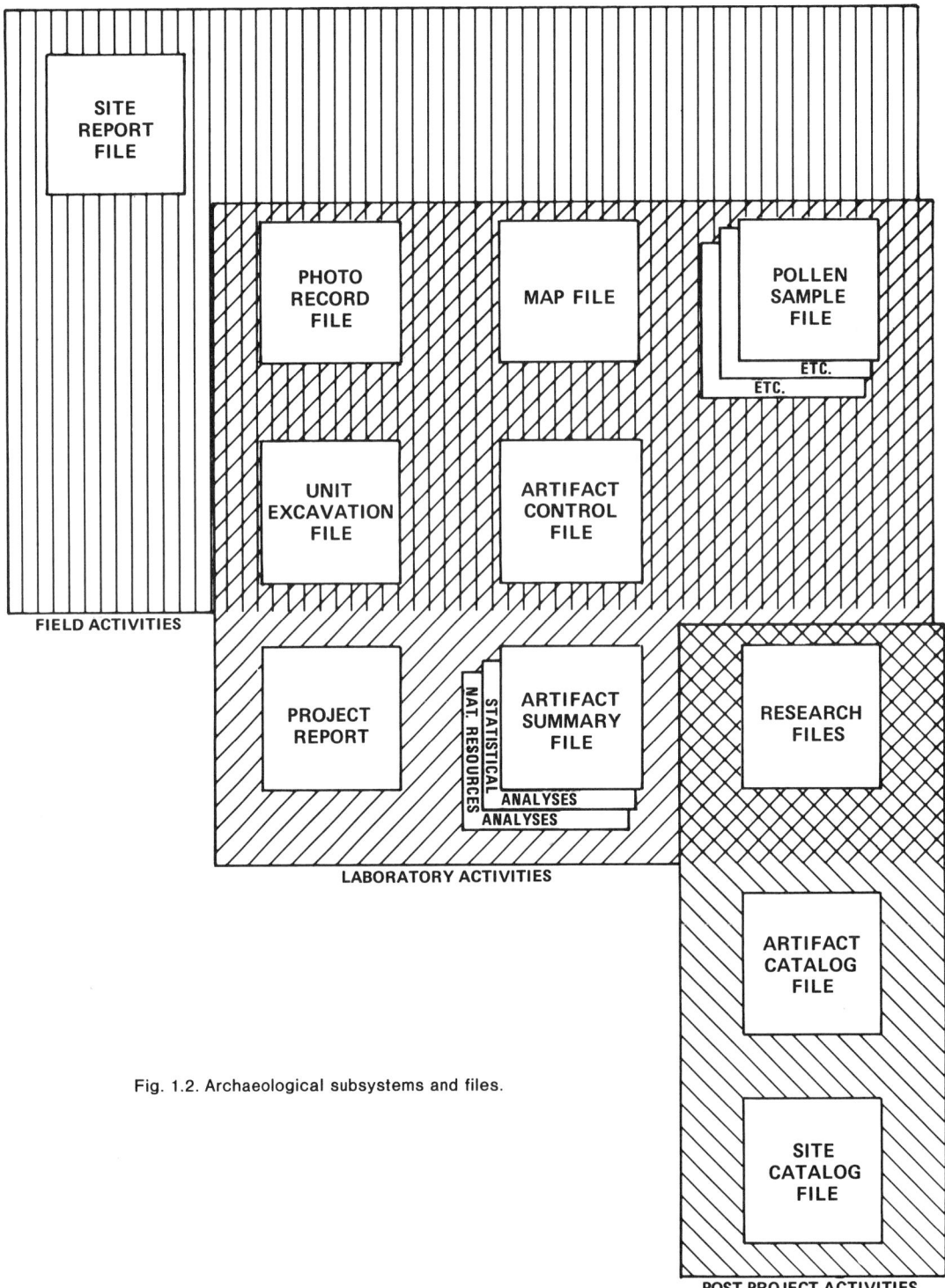

Fig. 1.2. Archaeological subsystems and files.

After examining the activities that are to be performed, it is possible to define the various data files that appear to be necessary in order to satisfy the present and future demands for information that will emanate from those activities. It should be kept in mind that these files can be any desirable combination of manual and computerized files, but that decision is not important at this stage. What is important is that the individuals involved in the analysis understand how the various files relate to each other, how each file is organized, and how it must be accessed.

Figure 1.2 shows the relationships among the three subsystems and the files that might be needed to carry on the activities within each subsystem. The subsystems overlap and, as a consequence, some of the files have multiple uses.

The following list indicates files designed primarily for use in field activities.

   a. Site Report File, containing on each record information about the site that developed during the survey activity.
   b. Photo Record File, the catalog of all photographic negatives exposed during either the survey or the excavation.
   c. Map File, maps prepared during survey or excavation.
   d. Catalogs of various natural materials sampled during either the survey or excavation activity.
   e. Unit Excavation File, descriptive and control data recorded as each site unit (such as room, square, burial pit) is excavated.
   f. Artifact Control File, the catalog of containers (such as bags, boxes) in which artifacts are stored through the initial field processing and shipment to the laboratory.

Files designed primarily for use in the laboratory include the following.

   a. Artifact Summary File, data concerning numbers of artifacts of each type and variety recovered from each excavation unit.
   b. Statistical Analyses, as appropriate to the objectives of the particular project.
   c. Natural Resource Analyses, as appropriate to the particular project.
   d. Research Files, a library catalog organized by subject and, perhaps, subdivided into a separate Natural Resource Research File, an Artifact Research File, and a Cultural Research File.
   e. Project Report, containing the final analysis of all the field and laboratory work.

Two files are designed primarily for use in post-project activities.

   a. Artifact Catalog File, essential data about each artifact such as might be required by a museum in order to locate appropriate objects for an exhibit, a research project, or some other educational activity.
   b. Site Catalog File, essential information about each recorded site for use in future impact statements or other types of research.

As the specific needs of each project and the controlling organizational entity are more closely defined, and later as specific data categories necessary for each file are specified, the connections among these files will be indicated. Once the interrelationships among the files are specified, it is possible to visualize how various files might be used together or even combined if the information recorded in more than one file will be regularly required in order to perform any of the ongoing activities.

DETERMINATION AND CONTROL OF DATA CATEGORIES

Once the files that are part of the total system have been described, it is necessary to determine (that is, to identify and define) the data categories to be contained within each file. Identification and definition of data categories are closely interrelated. First, one must determine what information is required on each particular record, based on the purpose the record is to serve. The various elements of that information can then be identified and dispersed into various data categories. Each data category must be defined in precise, unambiguous terms that enable anyone to distinguish it from all other categories.

In the following discussion, an assumption is made that it is necessary to record a specific data category only in files where that information is needed. Every pertinent data category must be recorded in at least one place but informational categories, other than those required to cross-reference the files, should be recorded only once. In an integrated record system, any data category can serve as a pointer to some other file where additional pertinent information exists. The final configuration of the record system will determine whether data can easily be located in another file with minimum effort by the record system user. There must be a balance between the ease of using the files and the expense and effort required to record the data, and this balance is always achieved as a tradeoff. If a data category is not regularly required to perform the primary activities that the file in question is designed to serve and the information is available in another accessible file, then the information should not be duplicated in both files.

In the specification of data categories required for any particular file, we should always keep in mind several questions: Who needs to use this file? What data categories are essential in this file? What additional data categories are desirable to facilitate accurate communication? What other records are related to this data category? How is this data category uniquely separate from other data categories?

As an example, consider the Site Catalog File in Figure 1.2. We probably cannot define precisely who will be using the file. However, we can state that the user of the file will most often be looking for records concerning: (a) the physical location of archaeological sites; (b) sites with particular cultural characteristics; or (c) the physical location of sites with particular cultural characteristics. These needs dictate that we must have the ability to locate records in this file according to a number of specific parameters, and this in turn means that each record must contain the following data categories.

   a. Site number, as a means of cross-referencing the Site Catalog File to other files.
   b. Site location (geophysical), in order to locate the site precisely within a standardized system or systems such as Township-Range-Section, Latitude and Longitude, or Universal Transverse Mercator Grid.

c. Site location (political), in order to locate the site within a county and, perhaps, by street or rural route address.

d. Site classification (cultural), in order to locate groups of sites that are culturally related.

e. Site classification (physical), in order to locate sites that are situated in similar settings (such as caves, bluff shelters, south facing).

f. Site reporter and date reported, in order to access the probable validity of the data.

Each of these data categories or data category groups contains information that probably will be necessary for anyone using the Site Catalog File in the future. Note, however, that the records in this file do not have to be complete duplications of the records in the Site Report File. Presumably, in an integrated system, the user of the Site Catalog File can go back to the Site Report File and from there back to the Photo-Record File, the Map File, and so on, for the detailed information that probably is needed only rarely. Likewise, the Site Catalog File does not need to contain a complete listing of artifacts or even the types of artifacts recovered from every site. In an integrated record system, this information can be accessed through the Artifact Catalog File or through the Artifact Summary File that presumably is prepared as a regular part of the laboratory work on each project.

The concept of an integrated record system demands that the content of certain data categories be carefully controlled. These are the "descriptor" categories used for sorting, searching, indexing, and retrieving information from the files, as opposed to "free-text" categories used to complete the description of an object but not as a basis for sorting and searching for information. The content of free-text categories does not need to be controlled except in a general way, but the content of descriptor categories must be precise and unambiguous. The only way this can be accomplished is by carefully controlling what is initially recorded.

With some descriptor categories content can be controlled by delimiting the format of the data; with other descriptor categories data entries must be selected from lists of acceptable content words, that is, from previously approved authority files. "Format" means the rules used for recording data: the order of words, the number of characters required or allowed, the division of segments, the use of upper or lower case, the use of singular and plural terms, the meaning of special characters, and so on. For example, format means specifying the structure to be used for recording a date, such as year-month-day, with a 4 digit year, 2 digit month, and 2 digit day. With descriptor categories where it is necessary to use a controlled list of acceptable content words, format rules must also be specified (such as the order of multi-word phrases), but format alone is not sufficient. For example, if pottery type names or cultural designations are going to be recorded in a computerized data bank, they must always be spelled the same way and, as nearly as possible, they should always have the same precise meanings.

It is important for archaeologists to recognize that authority files are simply tools that enable one to consistently order and find records within a given file. They should be based on reality as it is known at the time the record system is created, of course, but they do not have to be changed to accommodate every new structuring of available knowledge. For example, a data category often maintained within the group that defines "Site Location, Political," is a county designation. County designations are, in a sense, arbitrary subdivisions of state boundaries, but by convention they do have an empirical reality. In the same sense, a system for designating the geophysical location of a site (for example, the Universal Transverse Mercator Grid) is also arbitrary but empirically meaningful. The classification of archaeological sites according to cultural and physical taxonomies should be viewed from this same broad perspective. Cultural and physical designations tend to be more localized in usage than the other categories mentioned but content control within these data categories is equally important and, for these purposes, equally arbitrary.

The process of accurately defining and controlling each data category for a given file is a vital step in the design of an integrated record system. It does not matter whether the file under consideration is to be a manual or a computer file. The determination and then the defining of the data categories always leads to more accurate communication because it makes it possible for users of the files to understand the structure and the consistency of the records.

DESIGN OF FILE RELATIONSHIPS

An analysis of the entire system in the manner discussed above should lead to the answering of questions such as: What data files are needed? How should the files be separated? Which files are used together frequently and can be combined? We have yet to consider, however, the questions of which files need to be interrelated and what data categories can be used to relate them.

The integration of multiple files into a single system requires the use of "pointers"—common data categories that permit us to move conveniently from the records in one file to the records in another file, regardless of the form of the files (manual or computerized, graphic or verbal) and regardless of the order in which the records are stored. For example, one common data category in several files is often Site Number. This number can be used as a convenient pointer

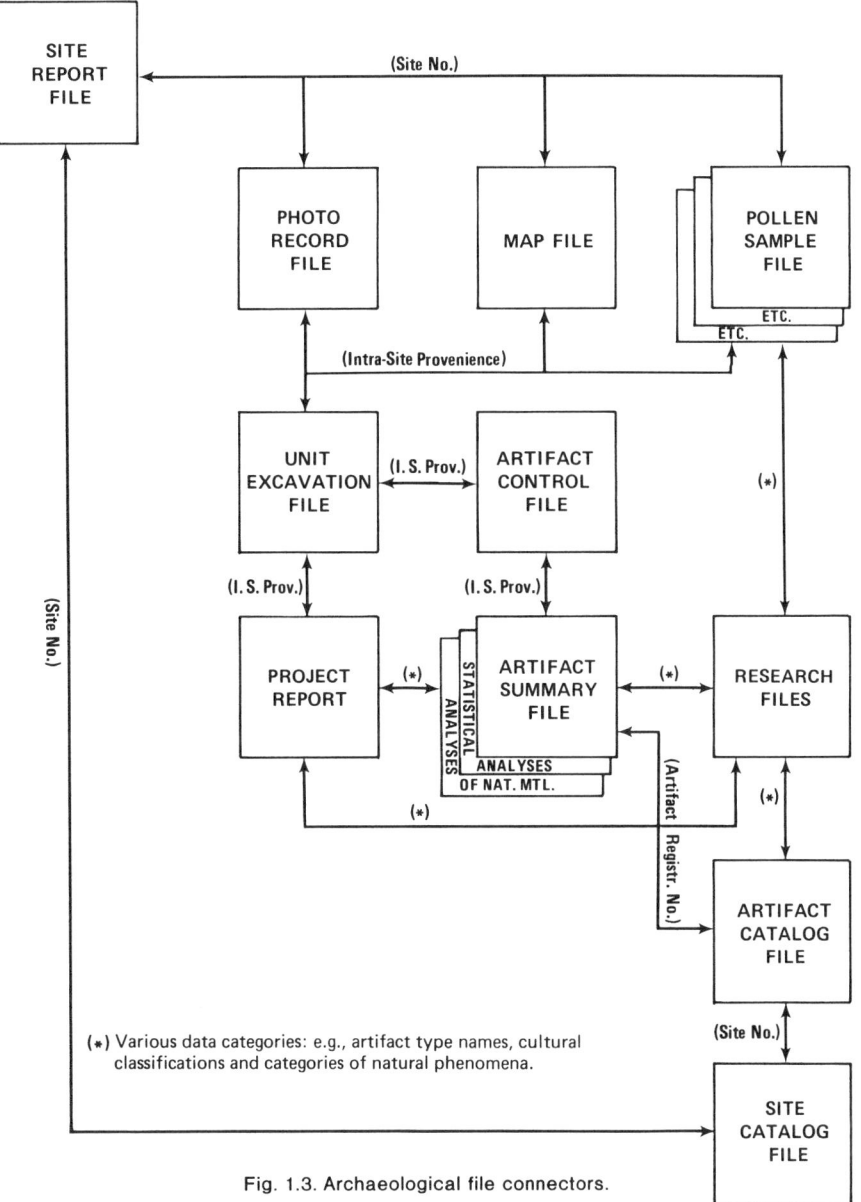

Fig. 1.3. Archaeological file connectors.

to direct the user from any file where it exists into any other file that is sortable by that number—from the Site Catalog File back to the Site Report File, or to the Photo-Record File, or to the Map File, or perhaps to the Artifact Catalog File.

The numerous files that are a part of the total system in some cases are considered separately because of their physical distinctiveness (for example, a Photo-Record File and a Map File). In other cases, the files are separated into the three subsystems discussed above (see *Files to Support the Defined Activities*) on the basis of when they are prepared and how they are used. However, it is usually most efficient to maintain separate files for each definable activity and to control access from one file to another by means of pointers such as the data categories shown in paren-

theses in Figure 1.3. Developing the integrated record system in this manner allows us to create each file so that it will serve a carefully defined purpose in the most efficient manner possible. Consideration must be given to the simplicity of preparing the records initially and to making the information readily available in carrying out several different later activities.

REASONS FOR USING A COMPUTER

This lengthy consideration of integrated record systems has not been presented in order to provide a formula for computer usage, but rather to illustrate the types of analyses that are essential prerequisites to the systematic utilization of the computer for data banking purposes. It is only after all of these data systems analyses have been completed that a person is in a position to consider how to gather the data and how to process it. This material has been presented in order to direct attention to the careful structuring of data that computerized data banking demands. Only then is it possible to discuss when to use a computer.

There are only two rational reasons for storing a file of information on a computer: (a) if the file can be maintained less expensively on the computer than it can by any other manual or semimechanical means; or (b) if analyses can be performed on the computer that, from a practical standpoint, cannot be accomplished any other way.

It has seldom been possible to justify the use of a computerized data bank entirely on the grounds of economics. No situation has come to my attention where anyone has claimed that he has saved money by maintaining an archaeological data bank on a computer. The justification for computerized data bank management of archaeological information at present must be found in the kinds of analyses that are possible with a computer and not possible by any other means. The use of a computer can be justified on these grounds, but such usage does not apply equally to all of the files of information that must be maintained by archaeologists.

The clearest justification for utilizing a computer to maintain an archaeological data bank can be found in those situations where access to the file will regularly be required according to a number of different data categories or a number of different ways of hierarchically structuring the data categories. The justification is most convincing with those files associated in this chapter with postproject activities, for instance the Site Catalog File, Artifact Catalog File, and, possibly, one or more of the Research Files. In order to illustrate why this is true, let us consider the Site Catalog File again. Normally this file is maintained in site number sequence. However, the need for information from the file will usually consist of a listing of sites selected from the file according to some criterion (some data category) other than site number, and often in a hierarchical arrangement such as, perhaps, a given list of politically determined locations by counties, within each county an arrangement of the sites by cultural classification, and within each cultural classification an arrangement by the type of physical terrain on which the site is located. On another occasion, retrieval of information from the Site Catalog File may be according to some other hierarchical structuring of the data categories and some other parameters. A Site Catalog File, though maintained in site number sequence, is seldom searched in that sequence. Therefore, it is one file that most often can be kept more efficiently on a computer than by any other means.

The most important feature that computerized data bank management offers to an archaeologist is the ability to search a file of information according to a variety of parameters. The use of a computer can be justified whenever it is anticipated that this situation will occur frequently. The use of a computer can also be justified for such things as statistical analyses of various kinds, but statistical analyses are quite different from data bank management of information. Whenever a single data category is the logical means both of arranging the individual records within a file *and* searching for the records in that file, then computerized data bank management of the file is seldom justified. For example, the various records maintained as a part of project field activities, even though they involve a number of different files, always have the same logical basis for the arrangement of the records and the searching for the records: namely, a site number and within that a hierarchical structure that proceeds from an excavation unit to a specific location within that unit and then, perhaps, to a vertical level. The hierarchical structuring of the information remains the same whether a person is recording in the field or searching for data later as part of preparing the project report.

In the final analysis, it is essential that archaeologists be able to clearly define the activities they are going to perform, the data that will emanate from those activities, the kinds of files that must be kept in order for that data to be controlled in a logical manner, and the data categories and the control of data categories that is necessary to accomplish the desired objectives. If these activities are just a matter of accumulating, storing, and retrieving information, then a computerized data bank is probably not justified. On the other hand, the computer does permit one to accomplish various analyses, particularly with the ongoing, postproject activities that are not possible by any other means.

REFERENCES

Chenhall, Robert G.
    1967   The description of archaeological data in computer language. *American Antiquity* 32: 161–67.
    1975   *Museum Cataloging in the Computer Age.* Nashville: American Association for State and Local History.
Gaines, S. W., editor
    1971   *Newsletter of Computer Archaeology* 6(4).
Gardin, J. C.
    1974   *Les Banques de Données Archéologiques.* Paris: Centre National de la Recherche Scientifique.
Smith, Landon D.
    1977   Programmable pocket calculators: some archaeological applications. *Newsletter of Computer Archaeology* 12(3): 1–26.

2. Information Retrieval for Archaeology

J. D. Wilcock
Research Centre for Computer Archaeology, Stafford, England

INTRODUCTION

Considered against a background of the proliferation of computer applications in most aspects of everyday life, such as industry, commerce, banking, transport, power supplies, welfare, defense, and government, it was inevitable that the computer should be applied to the problem of information retrieval in archaeology. Every excavation produces large amounts of information, and yet usually only a small "representative" sample of these data ever gets published. The high costs of conventional publication methods mean that the remainder is stored in the form of site books, lists, and research notes, perhaps in a museum with the items resulting from the original excavation. Here it may be cross-indexed on a card file if the museum staff have the time and energy required; otherwise the documentary evidence for the excavation will receive only a single accession number. Such information is effectively inaccessible to all but the dedicated research worker who can visit the museum in person.

Historically, computer applications in British archaeological studies were heavily weighted toward statistical analyses, as they were in the United States. From these beginnings in the late 1950s, however, evolved a development of data banks by the mid 1960s, and by the mid 1970s there was full appreciation that integrated software systems comprising information retrieval, statistics, and graphics could offer great advantages to the archaeologist. Such systems provided: (a) data base management; (b) routine data processing (for example, the production of site location maps from numerical readings provided by resistivity meters or magnetometers, the sorting of archaeological contexts to produce correct phase diagrams showing time relationships, the presentation of data by means of histograms and piecharts); (c) statistics (such as seriation, cluster analysis, multidimensional scaling); and finally, (d) computer graphics to produce publishable maps, plans, diagrams, and lists. It is within this comprehensive systems background that computerized information retrieval in Britain should be viewed.

Objectives and Functions

Three different areas of application may be distinguished. First is the excavation record. Items are recorded on the computer as they emerge from the ground, perhaps even from the site office itself, using a remote computer terminal connected by telephone line to the computer, which may be many miles away. Such schemes were developed in the late 1960s, and in the middle 1970s had still not proved financially viable. The extra expense involved in obtaining an on-line immediate service as opposed to a few days' visit to the computer center was not justified within the strictures of a limited budget.

Second, a museum may place its catalog on the computer. Some museums in Britain began to do this in the early 1970s using the formats proposed from 1965 by the Information Retrieval Group of the Museums Association (IRGMA), a body financed jointly by the national and area museum councils. The group changed its name in 1977 to the Museums Documentation Association (MDA).

Third, any large body of specialist information may be placed on the computer such as individual files for petroglyphs, inscriptions, pottery types, clay pipes, masons' marks, projectile point types, and the like.

Systems Selected

Before looking at computer information retrieval in detail, it is wise to consider possible alternative systems and to act as one's own devil's advocate. Hollerith and edge-punched cards have long been used for information retrieval—may not they be an alternative? Such systems are perfectly satisfactory for small bodies of data. For large bodies of data, however, they become extremely cumbersome and bulky, and only a limited amount of information may be recorded on each card. Computer storage, on the other hand, may be made large indeed by the use of magnetic tapes and magnetic discs. Also the performance of logical functions for retrieval becomes tedious and time-consuming beyond a simple level of complexity using edge-punched cards, but the arithmetic and logical powers of the computer will allow complex relationships to be examined extremely quickly.

Any computer system will bring with it many practical difficulties. Who will pay for it? How may the items be described, and how are questions to be formulated? It is clear that considerable thought and care must be expended on such matters. If we accept that open access to archaeological information by computer is a good thing, then we must consider who is to prepare the data for the machine and how the whole operation is to be managed. Will it not be a "dangerous intrusion of the machine into the humanities" as some would have us believe? Certainly, an overhasty stipulation of requirements and data formats is likely to prove more a methodological straightjacket to the archaeologist than an advantage. The different modes of use on the archaeological site, in the museum, and for large files of specialist data or for area surveys have different sets of requirements and often quite different emphases. A summary of the various applications that have been attempted in Britain is given below.

TECHNIQUES FOR THE RECORDING AND RETRIEVAL OF ARCHAEOLOGICAL DATA

Types of Files

First, let us consider how the information may be marshalled so that we know where to look for a required item.

Normal Files

A collection of data for a specific purpose is usually referred to in computer parlance as a *file*. A *normal* file consists of *records,* each of which describes an item using a selection of previously-defined descriptive terms. This is called a *term-on-item* classification scheme, and is nothing more than the conventional procedure of describing an object.

A common procedure is to record all items sequentially as they emerge from the ground, or in accession number order in a museum context; this is called a *serial* or *sequential* file. In computer terms this has a disadvantage, for in retrieving records from a reel of magnetic tape, for example, it is necessary to read or skip over all previous blocks on the tape before the required item may be read, perhaps taking several minutes. Magnetic tape recording by tape unit or cassette, however, is relatively cheap.

An improvement is to organize the data by cross-indexing. A descriptive term is selected and the records are sorted according to the values they have for the term, so that all records with the same term value occur together; thus a record with a specific value for the term is quickly found. The records sorted in this way form a major block on the tape, and there is a major block sorted on each term.

Finally, if all the information is recorded on a device such as a replaceable disc unit, the magnetic heads may be moved to any desired area of the disc recording surfaces, and any item is accessible as quickly as any other, within about one-quarter of a second. The amount of data that can be recorded on a single replaceable disc unit (or disc pack) is often less than can be recorded on a single reel of magnetic tape, and disc packs are far more expensive. However, there is the advantage that a randomly-selected item may be obtained quickly, and hence this type of file is called *random-access.*

Inverted Files

Alternatively an *item-on-term* classification scheme or *inverted* file may be used (mnemonic: *i*nverted, *i*tem-on-term); here each record refers to a particular *keyword,* and all items for which this keyword is appropriate have their accession numbers placed in the record. Thus to find all Roman bronze objects from layer 3 we need only look at the records for keywords ROMAN, BRONZE, and LAYER 3 and determine which item numbers they have in common. Keywords are previously defined, and may refer to any category of information in the chosen classification scheme: date, material, provenience, and form are frequent types of keyword.

Types of Information

Each archaeologist uses unconsciously a wide range of types of data in his description of artifacts. Since the various types of data have different properties it is important to define these properties in order that comparisons between items may be made. This is particularly necessary if the information is to be placed on the computer, for although a person recognizes instinctively the difference between, for example, a string of letters and a numerical quantity, and accepts that a comparison is impossible between them, all data are recorded as numbers in the computer and the machine must be told how the numbers are to be interpreted and what comparisons are valid.

Alphanumeric Data

Probably the most common type of data in archaeological descriptions consists of strings of letters of the alphabet, numerals, punctuation signs, and spaces in any desired combination ranging from brief codes to full-length natural language sentences. Since such information is variable in length it becomes necessary to tell the computer what the maximum length of an item can possibly be. Room must be left in storage for the longest item, and in comparisons we need to know how far to go in the search for letters belonging to the item. Sometimes it is necessary to compare the item as a whole, involving a pattern match along the complete word, phrase, or sentence. Often only a partial match is required, consisting of a keyword or syllable. For instance, the records (a) ROMAN POTTERY and (b) IRON AGE POTSHERDS will both be retrieved if the keyword POT is used. On the contrary, if the keyword POTS is used, record (b) will be retrieved but not (a). In the natural language sense we can see that (a) should be retrieved, but the machine will not recognize this. The problem of synonyms immediately arises, and it can be resolved only by archaeologists agreeing to use one synonym exclusively in preference to another, or by having elaborate dictionaries of synonyms, adding considerably to the cost of the retrieval process.

Quantitative Data

Numerical quantities to which some significance may be attached have several different properties or scales of measurement as follows:

Ratio scale data. Some familiar measurements such as length, weight, or butt angle of a stone axe are examples of *ratio scale* quantities. In these quantities some meaning may be attached to differences between two measurements, and the origin or zero point is also real and unambiguous in its meaning.

Interval scale data. In other measurements, like the firing temperature of a pot, it is still possible to attach meaning to differences between quantities, but the origin is entirely arbitrary. The Celsius, Fahrenheit, and Kelvin scales of temperature all have different zero points, and are examples of *interval scale* quantities.

Ranked or Ordinal data. While numerical in appearance, ranked or ordinal data may not be compared by arithmetic processes in any meaningful sense, nor is their origin meaningful. It is possible to arrange the observations in rank order, but nothing more. An example is the Moh scale of hardness applied to geological materials, ranging from hardness 1 for talc to hardness 10 for diamond. The steps in this *ordinal* scale are not equal, nor do the numbers mean anything other than a relative order of hardness.

Qualitative or Nominal Data

Another very common archaeological classification concerns qualitative judgment. One of a number of distinct values, all named, may be attached to an object: color may be described in terms of traditional color names (red, green) or using a Munsell chart; material may be listed in terms of metal or stone (iron, bronze, flint, glass, ceramic). These observations may not be compared; comparing "red" with "green" is meaningless other than to say that they are different. In general, qualitative observations are expressed by alphanumeric data, but not always. A special case is the *Boolean* type of data that is also common in archaeology. First defined by the mathematician George Boole working with Aristotelian logic, items may be *true* or *false,* never carrying any other shades of meaning. In archaeology items are recorded as *present* or *absent,* and may be represented in the computer by 1 and 0 respectively. This presence/absence observation for a given feature (a decorative motif, for instance) is a special case of a qualitative dichotomy, where the *presence* observation carries much more significance than the negative *absence* observation. A more normal dichotomy is sex observation on skeletons in a cemetery, where *male* and *female* are of equal weight.

To Code or Not to Code?

It is a common misconception that the computer requires data to be coded, that is, expressed in combinations of letters and figures, or abbreviated in some way. Data may be in natural language, subject only to practical limitations on storage. Archaeologists are usually quick to insist that any computer information retrieval scheme used by them must allow natural language items. Faced with the prospect of writing out their information on computer data sheets, however, they happily invent numerous abbreviations and codes. This is entirely as it should be, for the computer is a servant and not a master.

Comparison of Data

The kinds of comparisons that are possible between items will depend on how the data type has been defined. As a general rule it is important that the data type be appropriate to the observation. Detail should not be missed by using a qualitative scale where a quantitative one would be more appropriate, nor should an illusory sophistication be indicated by using quantitative observations for essentially qualitative data. The usual comparisons available are shown in Table 2.1.

Computer Data Bases

General Remarks

Card systems (for example, box file cards, edge-punched cards, PEEKABOO cards), while a practical solution for a small data base, are bulky, easily damaged, and difficult to store. Instead all the records may be put on magnetic tape or disc and then handled by a computer. The amount of storage available is effectively unlimited; magnetic tape is far cheaper than magnetic discs as a storage medium. Recently the cassette (replacing magnetic tape) and the "floppy disc" (replacing magnetic discs) have become available. These are cheap, exceedingly portable, and may be sent through the mail without damage. Microcomputer-based intelligent terminals will probably be the answer to data capture problems for many archaeologists. Files of data recorded in this way may be normal or inverted files, and in addition the high speed of the computer may be used to analyze the records and retrieve information.

Desirable Features of a Data Base Management System

It is relevant at this stage to consider the features desirable in any system designed to handle archaeological records. The system should be independent of the data format, handling a particular data base by referring to a subsidiary file that gives a description of the data format in use and where to find each category of information. It should have flexible input capabilities, allowing data to be read from cards, punched paper tape, magnetic tape, magnetic discs, and any other media the archaeologist wishes to use. In the future it will be possible to read written documents and microfilms, and even to allow voice entry of the data.

Data validation is an important feature. Unfortunately the computer cannot spell, so spelling mistakes will go undetected, but at least numerical values may be checked to be within specified ranges.

There must be a capability for the building of files, and for the editing of existing files by amendment, insertion, and deletion of records. Other useful features are the expansion of short codes and abbreviations (designed by the archaeologist) to full-length natural language statements, and sorting of records by any desired keyword or value (the Keyword-in-Context or KWIC list is a common form of output, where the keywords appear in alphabetical order in a centrally-aligned column, surrounded by their contexts).

The next requirement is for logical search of any desired complexity, and retrieval of the records that satisfy the criteria. Card systems are limited to simple intersection (logical AND) operations. The computer may use several other logical concepts, notably INCLUSIVE OR and NOT, and these may be joined to any degree of complexity. The logical operations involved are given in Table 2.2. Note that while AND and OR both operate on two variables or values, NOT operates only on one. If very few records are found to satisfy the request, there must be some means of relaxing the criteria. As an example, consider a retrieval request for burials of Roman or Iron Age date containing bronze implements not of military character. Representing "Roman" by R, "Iron Age" by I, "bronze" by B and "military character" by M, the request may be defined logically as:

$$(R \; OR \; I) \; AND \; B \; AND \; NOT \; M$$

or in symbols as:

$$(R_v I) . B . \overline{M}.$$

TABLE 2.1
Comparison of Data

Alphanumeric	Complete or partial pattern match
Quantitative	
Ratio	Arithmetic comparisons
	$= \neq < \leq > \geq$
	Detection of origin
Interval	Arithmetic comparisons only (see Ratio above)
Ranked	None, other than alphanumeric match, or detection of higher or lower rank
Qualitative	
Multiple (i.e., >2 values)	None, other than complete or partial pattern match if alphanumeric (i.e., detection whether the "same" or "different")
Dichotomy	Pattern match if alphanumeric; Boolean detection for presence/absence

TABLE 2.2
Common Boolean Operations

		AND	INCLUSIVE OR	NOT	
Value a	Value b	a.b	$a_v b$	"NOT a" written $\overline{a}$	$\overline{b}$
F	F	F	F	T	T
F	T	F	T	T	F
T	F	F	T	F	T
T	T	T	T	F	F

F = false, T = true.

The types of records that will satisfy this request are given in Table 2.3.

Security is essential in three separate areas. The system must be robust in the sense that if files are corrupted they may be regenerated correctly. File names must be checked so that the correct file out of several is accessed. Finally, unauthorized users must be denied access; this is usually achieved by the use of passwords.

The control of the whole data base management system must be easy; that is to say, the control language must be natural and readily learned by archaeologists. There are several specially-designed applications languages for this purpose.

Finally, the output is of prime importance. Most archaeological systems will produce printed lists, sorted by keyword-in-context or by any other desired item such as material, date, or accession number. It is common to add headings and page numbers on all pages of the printout. But perhaps the most useful features are the by-products of the information retrieval process. If grid references of finds are included in the data, then it is an easy matter to produce distribution maps automatically, with map outline, north point, scale, border, legends, and a range of symbols, thus saving the archaeologist many hours of work. It is also desirable that the data base management system should be linked with a statistical package of programs, and ultimately with graphic programs. We may note here that a simple counting process during the information retrieval operation yields data on the statistical distribution of the parameters, which may be portrayed on bar charts, histograms, and piecharts. Furthermore, if locational information is also extracted an automatic distribution map may be produced at the time of the information retrieval run (for example, see Fig. 2.1).

TABLE 2.3
Truth Tables
Expression is (R OR I) AND B AND NOT M

Full Truth Table (16 combinations of the variables)

Roman	Iron Age	Bronze	Military Character	Request Satisfied?
R	I	B	M	
F	F	F	F	no
F	F	F	T	no
F	F	T	F	no
F	F	T	T	no
F	T	F	F	no
F	T	F	T	no
F	T	T	F	YES
F	T	T	T	no
T	F	F	F	no
T	F	F	T	no
T	F	T	F	YES
T	F	T	T	no
T	T	F	F	no
T	T	F	T	no
T	T	T	F	YES
T	T	T	T	no

T = true, F = false.

Sparse Table (simplified, with only 5 entries)

Roman	Iron Age	Bronze	Military Character	Request Satisfied?
R	I	B	M	
T	—	T	F	YES
—	T	T	F	YES
F	F	—	—	no
—	—	F	—	no
—	—	—	T	no

T = true, F = false, — = unspecified or don't care.

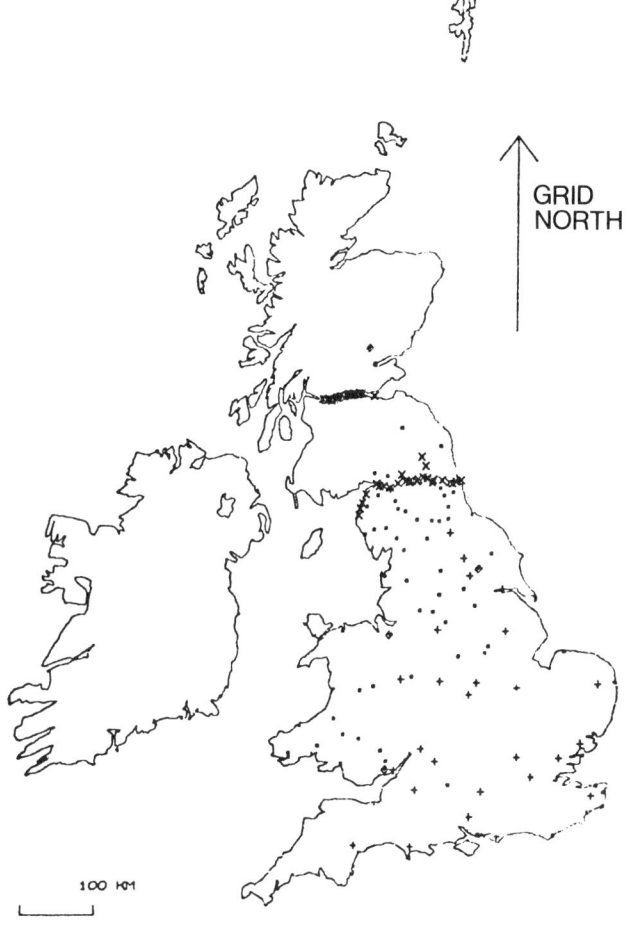

GRID NORTH

100 KM

Fig. 2.1. Distribution map for the chief Roman settlements in Britain, a by-product of an information retrieval run. The + symbols indicate civil settlements; diamonds, legionary fortresses; X, Hadrian's wall, outlier forts, and the Antonine wall; and dots, other major forts. The map outline is obtained from magnetic tape, and the border, north point, scale, and title are added automatically.

The Role of the Computer Scientist

The problem remaining is mainly one of communication and education. The computer scientists have moved at least half-way toward the archaeologists, and it remains for the archaeologists to reciprocate. In their effort to be helpful to all, the computer scientists have evolved monumental data classification schemes (see Chapter 10) that can be just the reverse of helpful, for only a small number of the categories are in general applicable to a given record. The reaction of the archaeologists is to throw up their hands in horror at the large number of categories of information, saying that they will never have the time to record their data in such fashion. But all the proposed categories are useful in some circumstances, or they would not have evolved. It should be realized that if an information category is irrelevant for a given record, is unknown, or cannot be completed without a great deal of research, then the category may be cheerfully left blank. Archaeologists will only expend energy on the completion of such records if they can see real benefit appearing from the exercise such as improved research facilities or aids to publication. The responsibility is on the computer scientists to provide resilient, well-designed and well-proven systems to fulfill these aims.

3. A Management Information System for Archaeological Resources

A Recent Computer Application by the Arkansas Archeological Survey

Sandra C. Scholtz and Michael G. Million
Arkansas Archeological Survey

INTRODUCTION

The use of the computer in archaeological applications by the Arkansas Archeological Survey and the University of Arkansas Museum covers a broad spectrum. Both organizations support ongoing research and collections management computer applications. The collections management information system of the Museum, described elsewhere (Scholtz 1976), includes an accession file that serves as a general level inventory of all archaeological materials accessioned by the Museum. There are more than 20 professional archaeologists on the Survey staff, all of whom are engaged in research projects which, from time to time, are expedited by the use of the computer for organizational and analytical purposes. This chapter, however, addresses the current effort being supported by the Survey to design and put into operation a management information system for archaeological site data that will encompass information about sites, their distributions, and efforts to locate sites.

THE NEED FOR A MANAGEMENT INFORMATION SYSTEM FOR ARCHAEOLOGICAL RESOURCES

The need for such an information system is based on the data requirements of a cultural resource management program and its interrelated managerial and research functions. A brief description of the development and operation of such programs helps to explain these data requirements.

During the late 1960s and early 1970s a strong conservation philosophy has developed in American archaeology. Archaeologists have become keenly aware of the increasing rate of destruction of their nonrenewable resource base due to both positive and negative human activities, including construction and vandalism. Recent legislation such as the National Historic Preservation Act of 1966, the National Environmental Policy Act of 1969, Executive Order 11593 of 1971, and the Archaeological and Historic Preservation Act of 1974 (McGimsey and Davis 1977: 8–15) has supported the conservation philosophy. The legislation has also included authorization for the expenditure of federal funds to carry out archaeological work as a part of the mitigation of the impact on cultural resources of federally funded or licensed projects that involve disturbance of the earth's surface. A significant result of the legislation has been the involvement of archaeologists in the planning stage of projects, when it is still possible to evaluate the impact of alternative plans on the archaeological resource base. Effective consultation with archaeologists during the early planning stages of a given project will not only reduce the amount of future research costs necessitated by the project, but will also permit more effective *avoidance* of what may be considered "prime" archaeological resources, thereby playing a major role in their conservation.

The growth of cultural resource management has nurtured the planning and management process for projects involving land surface alterations (Lipe 1977: 26). With this increased involvement in planning has come an increased responsibility for control and management of archaeological data. The archaeological advisor must be in a position to communicate with the land alteration agency, and is under increasing pressure to provide information relative to known cultural resources in a project area. The ability of the archaeologist to rapidly and effectively summarize and present this current knowledge of archaeological resources in the project area to the planners is a necessary part of the communication.

At the 1974 Cultural Resource Management Conference, Thompson (1974: 20) recognized our responsibility for developing ". . . management information systems to provide access to and the means of dealing with the data." A cultural resource management program must have effective control over and access to the growing body of archaeological site information in order to meet the needs of the planner and manager of archaeological resources. Several writers (cf. Canouts 1977) stress the importance of a cumulative resource base on which to build subsequent research. The data base itself is a very important part of this resource base, and once sites are destroyed, the information and materials from the site serve as our only means of utilizing that site in research.

Canouts (1977: 122) outlines the stages of project research and describes the process of using site survey files in planning a research project. The files furnish information about expected site types and densities in the area of interest. Schiffer and Gumerman (1977: 132) urge "that research designs for field studies make use of up-to-date knowledge of the area." In a cultural resource management program the functions of research and management are not independent; current knowledge is necessary for good research designs, and the better our understanding of the archaeological resources becomes, the more accurate our explanatory models will be, thus improving our ability to manage the resource base.

The need to give priority to producing good site inventories in cultural resource management programs is well recognized. However, traditional site inventories accumulate knowledge about where sites are located and not about where they are *not* found. Lipe (1977: 27) states that "useful inventories must . . . provide data about where sites are not as well as where they are." MacCord (1977: 3) suggests that site surveys should result in the plotting of negative areas as well as locations of sites found. A proposal set forth by the Interagency Archaeological Services (King and Cole 1977) discussed the problem of interpreting incomplete site inventories. The authors proposed the accumulation of information about site surveys with the resulting materials and reports organized by "geographical units of some convenient size" such as "quadrangles matching the 7.5 minute USGS maps or squares 10,000 meters on a side designated by UTM references" (King and Cole 1977: 3). The need for a data base about site surveys is desirable

for meaningful interpretation of site inventory information about site densities; without such knowledge accurate distinctions are not easily made between areas that were actually sparsely populated in the past and areas that simply have not been surveyed. It is debatable, however, whether geographical units of either size suggested by King and Cole are of sufficiently refined resolution to be used effectively in archaeological resource management.

THE ROLE OF THE COMPUTER IN A CULTURAL RESOURCES MANAGEMENT INFORMATION SYSTEM

To be useful in planning, the data base of a resource management program must be readily accessible. A computerized resource data base that can be accessed by a data base management system provides this accessibility, as well as the reporting capabilities of the computer for organizing and presenting the desired information to the planners. Not only is speed frequently necessary in the initial planning phases of projects, but also by relegating the records search and report function to the computer, we are aided in an attempt to maximize research potential by freeing some time that can be used in other research activities.

Computerized archaeological site inventories have been utilized before by various agencies. The Arizona State Museum has converted into machine readable form site information from the State Museum files (Thompson 1974: 20). The State of Florida Division of Archives, History and Records Management, has begun a similar project (M. Kathrine Jones, personal communication), as undoubtedly have a number of other agencies that collect archaeological site information (see Chapters 4, 6, and 10). This is not meant to be an exhaustive list of projects computerizing archaeological site information, but some other examples are the New York Archaeological Council (Trubowitz 1976), North Carolina Department of Cultural Resources (Thomas E. Scheitlin, personal communication), the Glenn A. Black Laboratory of Archaeology at Indiana University (Limp 1977a, 1977b), and the Illinois State Museum (Benchley 1975). The Southwestern Anthropological Research Group (SARG) devised a plan for computerizing information about sites in the southwestern United States (see Chapter 5); their interest was in explaining site distributions (Plog and Hill 1971). The Arkansas Archeological Survey experimented with computerizing site records in the early 1970s, and the resulting recommendation was that such computerized data bases should be designed with specific applications in mind (Scholtz and Chenhall 1976). It is with this approach that we have developed our current plan for implementing a data management system for cultural resource management.

AUTOMATED MANAGEMENT OF ARCHEOLOGICAL SURVEY DATA IN ARKANSAS (AMASDA)

Any effective management information system must be designed to serve particular purposes. An information system that will serve the needs of conservation archaeology must address the interrelated functions of management and research. The information needs of both cultural resource management and research can be viewed in terms of two levels of information assessment, a general level and a specific level.

The general level information assessment needs of management are: (a) the internal organization, maintenance, and preservation of information sources such as proposals, reports, and maps; (b) the accumulation and maintenance of information regarding the history of archaeological investigations in the area of interest to management; and (c) the ability to generate reports that summarize activities in terms of administrative parameters as well as archaeological parameters.

The fulfillment of these general information assessment needs of management contributes to the fulfillment of management's detailed information assessment needs, including (a) the ability to generate reports and/or maps communicating site characteristics, locations, and densities for particular areas of interest; and (b) the identification of environmental zones with low, medium, or high probabilities of cultural resources.

Cultural resource managers need both general and detailed information assessment capabilities to communicate effectively with planners and researchers as well as to practice conservation archaeology. The information needs of researchers may be viewed also at a general level and a detailed level. The researcher's general information assessment needs are related to the functions of synthesizing past archaeological work and generating hypotheses to test. Information needs required to support the deductive mode of scientific activity include: (a) information regarding the history of archaeological investigations in the area of interest to the researcher; and (b) information concerning the research designs and results of past archaeological projects in the perspective of the environmental characteristics of the project areas.

The detailed information assessment needs of the researcher are dependent on a particular problem orientation, and thus are impossible to enumerate. The design for a management information system can in-clude the information needs for some specific research problems. The present design supports an inductive approach by allowing associations of environmental characteristics with site characteristics and locations. This kind of information is necessary for a basic settlement pattern problem orientation. Research studies of this nature feed information back to management, improving the ability to manage the cultural resources.

In consideration of management and research functions, an information system must include data categories, files, and output capabilities which serve these functions. A comprehensive plan for the management of archaeological site information should include the following characteristics: (1) a machine-readable standardized data base of site inventory information; (2) any additional data bases necessary for the interpretation of the growing site inventory; (3) the ability to assess these data bases with relation to diversified types of land modification projects; (4) computer programs for manipulation of the data; and (5) preferably a map format for analysis and presentation of distributional site information.

The management information system we have designed to meet some of the needs of conservation archaeology in Arkansas is called *Automated Management of Archeological Survey Data in Arkansas* (AMASDA). Although AMASDA has not been fully implemented, its design includes archaeological site information organized into three basic files, each with a different unit of organization: (1) the site inventory file records are organized by site and include data items chosen carefully for their value in a management and research program; (2) the land use file contains information organized by square kilometer; and (3) the project file organizes information about archaeological projects, those involving contracts as well as those funded locally or even unfunded, that have resulted in the location of sites or attempts to locate sites.

Site Inventory File

The Survey in 1979 had on record about 10,000 site reports, and this number was increasing at a rate of about 1000 per year. The present plan for handling site information is to scan the notebook file manually, extract the desired information when it is present, and locate the site on the appropriate USGS quadrangle. Other sources of information will be studied as each site is processed to obtain environmental data for the site. The data thus obtained are captured on a specially designed form on which data items for each site are coded on both sides of one page. Appendix 3.A is a list of data categories for the site inventory file.

Some data items, such as site number, are written directly on a recording form in the provided space. Other data items are checked to indicate their presence or left blank to indicate a lack of evidence implying absence. A "Q" designation allows the recorder to code the associated data item as questionable or unreliable information.

Coded data will be input via a CDC cathode ray tube terminal and will be stored both in a coded form as well as in an extended version for report generation. Data concerning each site is processed by a computer program that translates it into the appropriate English language word, or phrase, and places it into the extended site file.

As each of the USGS Quad maps is processed, the Universal Transverse Mercator (UTM) coordinates for each site are obtained with the assistance of the Computing Center's digitizing tablet. The tablet is somewhat similar to a tabletop, on which a map can be secured in position. A device with crosshair precision can be located at any point on the map, and the coordinates of that point recorded by pressing a button. With proper programming, the device will allow the user to define UTM coordinates for several known points on the map and then to compute the coordinates for any other points on the map simply by aligning the crosshairs on the point in question. The coordinates for each site can be added by an appropriate computer program to the site file. This information can be used also to update the land use file, a function explained below.

The actual data items included on the op-scan form and translated into machine-readable form were selected with regard to several criteria. One prime consideration was that the data items should be useful for preliminary evaluation of the archaeological resources of an area being considered for a land alteration project. A second rationale for selection was an attempt to anticipate future research needs by collecting information that could be gathered relatively easily from maps and other documentary sources. Important notations are environmental variables for each site, including such items as physiographic and soils information, elevation, and drainage data.

A coordinate system such as UTM is necessary for efficient retrieval of sites located in the project area, although sites will be indexed also by township and section designations because occasionally requests for information do come phrased in that manner. Categories of data such as size and configuration, features, general artifact categories, and cultural affiliation will aid in the evaluation of the known resources in the defined project area. The environmental information to be included in the file will provide the basis for correlational analyses aimed at improving our ability to predict site locations. Current research indicates the value of such variables in understanding site distributions. For example, Klinger (1976a) has shown a particular soil type to be a significant predictor of site locations in the Village Creek project area (a 316 square-mile area in lowland eastern Arkansas).

A preliminary examination of the portion of this data base that applies to a defined project area can be useful in the early planning stages of a project, perhaps suggesting desirable alternatives and certainly in planning effective surveys of the area to gather more information systematically about the resources of the area.

The plan for the electronic storage of the site inventory is designed to maximize the efficiency with which the data can be accessed for multipurpose use. A data base management system called GRIPHOS (General Retrieval and Information Processor for Humanities Oriented Studies) is being used. The site inventory file is a direct access file—a record in the file can be accessed directly by its file address for the purposes of retrieval, adding information to an existing record, or correcting previously added information. Importantly, the entire file does not have to be processed to retrieve information from a portion of the records. The data categories to be coded with standardized data values will be indexed in an inverted file storing, along with the data value, the addresses of all the records in which the data value appears. This index to the site inventory file will be built along with the inventory itself so that it will be available from the beginning in accessing the inventory. The categories to be included in the index are locational, environmental, and descriptive (materials and features), so that any of these characteristics, or any combination of them, may be the basis for an efficient retrieval. Locational categories of county and USGS Quad will allow preliminary file reductions within which more refined locational searches on the basis of UTM or township and section designation can be made. The site numbers themselves will be indexed and it will not be necessary to know the file address of the site record in order to add new information or retrieve stored information. Given the appropriate indexing, direct access files should be efficient to process, and the categories to be indexed are sufficiently wide in character to allow multipurpose retrieval of the data.

Land Use File

At the request of a number of Arkansas State Governmental agencies, chiefly the Department of Local Services, a computerized land use file was structured and stored at the University's Computing Center. Stored in this file in 1979 were a few categories of data about each square kilometer in the state, including the UTM coordinates necessary for locating each square, a land use code (urban, agriculture, forest, water, wet lands, barren lands), a county code, and a drainage subbasin code. For the latter code, the state has been divided into 39 subbasins with boundaries agreed on by the state agencies involved. The land use file was designed with the capability of expansion for the addition of variables. One variable that will be added by the Survey is the number of archaeological sites per square kilometer. This data will be added automatically with the UTM coordinates output from the digitizing tablet; that is, a computer program will use each set of site coordinates for updating the number of sites in the appropriate square kilometer. There are a number of graphic output programming systems available at the Computing Center to process this kind of data file. Square kilometers can be selected for output onto a map on which codes are represented by up to seven colors or several symbols, a color or symbol to fill in each square. The map can be prepared on white paper or different portions of it on acetate overlays. This file can be processed also by a surface trend approach, and contours can be drawn to reflect site density in an area of interest. We plan to develop the capability to deal with certain areas with a finer resolution than a square kilometer, a critical need in areas of high site density, just as the Department of Local Services found it to be in urban areas. A square 100 meters on a side would nearly correspond to a city block and would probably be an adequate unit to express site density in areas of relatively high site concentration.

Additional plans are being made to use this file for refinement of all archaeological sites in a square kilometer. Separate variables could be structured to represent the tally of site components in broad general time periods, or other classification schemes could be used. Climatic variables, such as mean annual rainfall, length of growing season, mean seasonal temperatures, or mean annual runoff, will be added to the land use file. This organization of information should provide an invaluable data set for increasing our understanding of site location-settlement pattern questions.

Project File

A file of information is being accumulated concerning any project that has resulted in the location of or the attempt to locate archaeological sites. The file is designed to provide data in three basic categories.

1. Each project is identified by name, number, report, supervisor, and locational information.

2. Several categories of data prepared for administrative purposes include accounting material, information regarding the nature and source of contracts, and dates regarding the work.

3. A number of data items describe the project area and the fieldwork, including methods of sampling and collecting, and intensity of survey as indicated by subsurface testing techniques and walking procedures.

The primary reason for creating a field survey project file is so that interpretations of the *recorded* distribution of archaeological resources can be performed with information available about *how* the data were gathered. Without systematic accumulation of this kind of information, one is left without any real basis for interpreting the accumulating data in a site inventory file. The inventory is designed to handle positive site information—if a site is found, it is added to the inventory. A survey locating no sites, however, makes no imprint on the inventory at all. The knowledge that an area was intensively surveyed and resulted in many site locations, is much more informative than a mere list of known sites in the area. The project file data categories and the ability to retrieve projects by locational characteristics improves our ability to interpret the information in the expanding site inventory. An added incentive for the project file is that it is a beginning toward the accumulation of information that will be useful in fitting academic problems to already existing data sets. Archaeological work itself represents one kind of site destruction that should be avoided if possible. The desirability of using an existing data set to answer a research question instead of initiating new fieldwork is obvious for conservation of money and time as well as the archaeological resources, but the traditional mode of operation for archaeology has not made this kind of information readily available.

Finally, the project file will be invaluable for sample selection from the entire site inventory for analyses of a statistical nature that require a probabilistic sample design. A retrieval from the project file can indicate which surveys were done with a sampling design adequate to meet the needs of a particular statistical procedure. Actual statistical correlations can be limited to those portions of the information in the site inventory file and the land use file that have a probabilistic basis for selection.

Base Maps for Graphic Display

Graphic display as a mode of output is not essential to the use and interpretation of the information in the AMASDA files, but it does offer convenient techniques for summarizing information retrieved from the files. Graphic displays provide visually interpretable data summaries, and frequently they are preferable to lists or reports of the same information. With this in mind, we are attempting to develop the graphic capabilities within AMASDA. With the UTM coordinates in the site inventory file, it is possible to plot a retrieved set of sites on a map or map overlay. The graphic output possible in the analysis of information in the land use file was discussed above. Several other graphic capabilities are either available or are planned.

A number of base maps have been digitized, and the resulting coordinate information is stored and can be drawn to any scale by a CalComp Plotter at the Computing Center. Base maps can be produced on white paper or on acetate overlays. The maps already available include 75 county outlines, 39 subbasin outlines, and the state outline. We will expand this list in time and plan to digitize a base map for each project in the project file. The ability to overlay project outlines on maps of archaeological site densities will be essential in interpreting the density maps.

RESULTS AND EVALUATION

Integration of File Information

The site inventory, land use, and project files are separate entities, each of which can be processed independently. But the ultimate goal in the design of AMASDA is the integrated use of not only these files of information but also any other source of useful information as well. The land use file represents a useful mode of organization of site information and from it we can determine meaningful interpretations over and above those from a simple site inventory. The project file, on the other hand, accumulates descriptive information about surveys that can be used for more meaningful interpretations of data in both the site inventory and land use files.

It is our contention that simple site inventories alone will not suffice to meet the needs of an effective cultural resource management program. The information needs of conservation archaeology are forcing us to innovate ways of improving our abilities to interpret survey information. If, in a resource management program, we are not building a cumulative data base that is readily accessible, is easily manipulated, and dynamically increases our understanding of the cultural resources, then we are not fulfilling our obligation to the archaeological consumer and the land altering agency that seeks our assistance and advice, nor are we fulfilling our obligation toward the conservation of archaeological resources. It is with this goal in mind that we have designed AMASDA.

Evaluation of the Project

It is difficult to evaluate a project such as AMASDA when it is hardly past the design phase, but we will make a few statements about the reliability of the information we are to amass as well as its projected use. The site inventory data category list, appearing in Appendix 3.A, could still change but certainly only minimally. The project file has received less attention than other aspects of the plan, but it, too, is expected to change no more than minimally. In addition to the designing and planning aspects, efforts have been directed toward plotting the sites on a set of quad maps for the state.

The site plotting phase of the project is of utmost importance because locational accuracy is crucial. If the locational information is such that the site cannot be plotted accurately on a 7.5 minute quad map, then it is not to be entered into the inventory of the land use files. Instead it is handled through an amendment procedure in an attempt to get accurate locational information. The amendment procedure identifies the site with questionable locational information for the Survey Archaeologist in whose area it is located; the state is divided into seven such areas. As time permits, the survey station archaeologist or assistant will, if possible, amend the locational information by virtue of records and field checks. Only when this process is completed is the site added to the computerized inventory. Initial work indicates that only 50 to 65 percent of the sites can be immediately plotted. This figure may seem at first discouraging; however, initial efforts to amend locational information for the remaining 35 to 50 percent seem to be meeting with reasonable success. The project may not result in the plotting of 100 percent of the sites reported in Arkansas over the past 40 years, but a valuable outcome will be the knowledge of what proportion of the data base does have locational control.

The quality of nonlocational information in a site inventory also is a concern, and seems increasingly so when an inventory is computerized. The information about a site in our inventory may have come from several sources, with the possibility of conflicting data. When a data item is questionable for whatever reason, our coding allows it to be flagged as questionable. We are attempting to control, therefore, information of minimal reliability by obviously identifying it as such.

Once the managerial, cultural, environmental, and survey information concerning known archaeological sites and related field surveys has been entered into the data files, it can be utilized *at minimum* to supply an appraisal of the cultural resources in any given area based on two interdependent factors: (1) the distribution of sites on record for the area, and (2) the intensity and nature of archaeological investigations in the area. Although individual site locations will not be provided in a preliminary evaluation, the general nature and distribution of the known sites in a project area will be made available in conjunction with data regarding the level of previous archaeological investigations that have taken place.

In many cases, a general characterization of site distributions may be most effectively and accurately stated in relation to one or more environmental factors. Indeed, at this point there are examples where certain ecological variables such as soils, topographic setting, water associations, and vegetation zones do correlate—either individually or in some combination—with certain site densities as well as specific types of sites (see Klinger 1976b, 1977; Roper 1974). It is here that management and research concerns interface with no perceptible distinction. While even relatively strong correlations do not necessarily imply a casual relationship between site placement and its physical setting, the objectivity of such an approach will lend itself to continued re-evaluation and should be capable of generating testable propositions, if only on a rudimentary level. The potential for refinement in these propositions resulting from feedback data seems considerable.

Furthermore, once the system is operating, the initial approach will be to concentrate analysis in those localities that have already been intensively surveyed,

such as transect surveys, thereby enhancing the reliability of the results. One other major factor that should be incorporated in the analysis is artifact variability. Ideally, specific artifact types collected in a controlled manner from sites in an intensively surveyed area are important factors to integrate in the analysis. Functional interpretations of artifacts would be considered, of course, when reasonable assumptions seem permissible. It should be emphasized, however, that functional assumptions about artifacts are not a necessity for analysis at this level. Rather, strong correlations between almost any two environmental and cultural variables will suggest, in at least some cases, relatively specific site or artifact functions.

Caution and objectivity will certainly have to be exercised in evaluating and interpreting the results of this approach in explaining past human behavior. Even so, the potential of automated manipulation of cultural and environmental data appears considerable in its ability to generate predictive statements that will be amenable to objective re-evaluation and refinement. Further hesitation in the application of such a method seems unjustifiable, especially considering the flexibility of the system and its capacity for restructuring.

APPENDIX 3.A
AMASDA: DATA CATEGORIES FOR SITE INVENTORY FILE

STATE SURVEY NUMBER

PROJECT SITE NUMBER

DATE SITE NUMBER ASSIGNED - Month and Year.

DATE SITE FORM RECEIVED BY SURVEY REGISTRAR - Month and Year.

DATE OF LAST FIELD VISIT - Day, Month, and Year.

FLAG:
    THIS SITE HAS BEEN VISITED BY SURVEY OR POST-1957 U of A MUSEUM PERSONNEL
    1- definite
    2- probable

ASSOCIATED INFORMATION SOURCES
Code =
    1- The information source is referenced.
    2- The information source is referenced as the only source of information for the site.
    BLANK- The information source is not referenced.

____	General Land Office (GLO) Township Map	Q
____	Other Map(s)	Q
____	Archival Source	Q
____	Library Source (Publ. Ref.)	Q
____	Recorded Interview	Q
____	Archeological Report, Manuscript (Publ. or Unpubl. Ref.)	Q
____	Informant	Q
____	AA Survey or post-1957 U of A Museum Personnel	Q
____	Other	Q

MAP REFERENCE -The three digit code of each USGS Quadrangle the site lies upon; up to four quads can be en-

tered. If the quad is an advanced or orthophoto quad series, this can be noted also.

LOCATIONAL RELIABILITY -For now, we are only entering into the site file sites that have reasonably consistent locational information. A code of 1 is used for such sites. Later other codes may be defined for entering sites with less reliable locational information.

NAME AND CLASSIFICATION OF INVESTIGATING PROJECT(S) -Up to six individual projects can be associated with each site. The master list of projects plus a classification scheme have yet to be finalized.

TOWNSHIP-SECTION DATA -Any given site may be associated with up to four townships and four land survey numbers; four sections accompany each of the first two townships and two sections may be coded with the last two. This permits *all* townships and sections that a site may lie in to be entered. Quarter/quarter section data is not being automated.

MIDDEN DEPTH -In centimeters.

MAXIMUM SITE DISPERSION -Six digits may be coded and the unit of measure can be square meters or square kilometers, coded M or K; the latter will be used only when necessary, probably for historic districts and other expansive entities. Archeological sites will be measured in square meters.

AREA OF MATERIAL CONCENTRATION(S) -In square meters. This category is to be used only when there is a definite area of material concentration, surrounded by a less dense scatter of artifacts.

FLAG: ESTIMATE OF MAXIMUM SITE DISPERSION KNOWN

TO BE INCOMPLETE -Use with size, class, or maximum dispersion.

SITE SIZE CLASS -This category is to be used primarily with the presently recorded sites where more precise information may not be available.

01	< 1	Q
02	1 - 10	Q
03	11 - 100	Q
04	101 - 500	Q
05	501 - 1,000	Q
06	1,001 - 5,000	Q
07	5,001 - 10,000	Q
08	10,001 - 20,000	Q
09	20,001 - 30,000	Q
10	30,001 - 40,000	Q
11	40,001 - 60,000	Q
12	60,001 - 80,000	Q
13	80,001 - 100,000	Q
14	100,001 - 200,000	Q
15	> 200,001	Q
16	Unknown	Q

SITE CONFIGURATION

1- Linear
2- Elliptical
3- Circular
4- Rectanguloid
5- Irregular
6- Crescentic
7- Unknown
8- Other

MEAN ELEVATION -Measured in feet, above Mean Sea Level.

GENERAL CULTURAL AFFILIATION

Paleo-Indian	Q
Dalton	Q
Archaic	Q
Early Archaic	Q
Middle Archaic	Q
Late Archaic	Q
Terminal Archaic	Q
Poverty Point	Q
Woodland	Q
Early Woodland	Q
Middle Woodland	Q
Late Woodland	Q
Tchula	Q
Fourche Maline	Q
Early Fourche Maline	Q
Middle Fourche Maline	Q
Late Fourche Maline	Q
Marksville	Q
Barnes	Q
Baytown	Q
Coles Creek	Q
Mississippi	Q
Early Mississippi	Q
Middle Mississippi	Q
Late Mississippi	Q
Caddo	Q
Early Caddo	Q
Middle Caddo	Q
Late Caddo	Q

Plaquemine	Q
Early Plaquemine	Q
Late Plaquemine	Q
Gran Marais	Q
Contact Historic	Q
Pre-AD 1800 Contact Historic	Q
Post-AD 1800 Contact Historic	Q
Euro-American Historic	Q
French	Q
Spanish	Q
British	Q
American	Q
Afro-American	Q
Asian	Q
Unknown Prehistoric	Q
Pre- or Non-Ceramic Site	Q
Ceramic Site	Q
Unknown Historic	Q
Multiple Prehistoric	Q
Unknown	Q

OVERALL RELIABILITY ASSESSMENT OF CULTURAL AFFILIATION(S)

1- Good: All available evidence indicates that the cultural affiliation(s) assigned to this site is (are) reliable.
2- Fair: Some insufficient or conflicting evidence making the reliability of the assignment(s) questionable.
3- Poor: Little or no evidence.

ARCHEOLOGICAL PHASE ASSIGNMENT -Up to ten separate phase assignments can be recorded, each consisting of a three digit code plus a '?' capability.

CLASS OF STATE SITE NUMBER ASSIGNMENT

01 Single artifact
02 Artifact scatter ≤ 10 m^2
03 Artifacts exposed in a shovel test or test excavation
04 Artifacts exposed in a highly restricted eroded area
05 Artifact scatter > 10 m^2
06 Artifact scatter/midden
07 Historic structure w/associated debris
08 Bluff Shelter
09 Pictograph/petroglyph only
10 Mound/mound group
11 Lithic quarry/extraction site
12 Other

SPATIAL RELATIONSHIP(S) OF MATERIAL CONCENTRATIONS

_____ Single locus; discontinuous
_____ Single locus; continuous
_____ Multiple loci; discontinuous; No. of loci _____
_____ Multiple loci; continuous; No. of loci _____
_____ Continuous
_____ Indeterminate

HISTORIC SITE FUNCTION

1- Isolated Artifact	Q
2- Domestic	Q
3- Craft	Q
4- Commercial	Q
5- Military	Q

6- Transportation and Communication	Q
7- Cemetery	Q
8- Religious	Q
9- Other	Q
10- Unknown	Q

GENERAL OBSERVATIONS ON SITE MATERIALS

Lithics	Q
Aboriginal Lithics	Q
Historic Lithics	Q
Ceramics	Q
Aboriginal Ceramics	Q
Historic Ceramics	Q
Metal	Q
Aboriginal Metal	Q
Historic Metal	Q
Human Skeletal Remains	Q
Aboriginal Human Skeletal Remains	Q
Historic Human Skeletal Remains	Q
Faunal Remains	Q
Aboriginal Faunal Remains	Q
Historic Faunal Remains	Q
Floral Remains	Q
Aboriginal Floral Remains	Q
Historic Floral Remains	Q
Other Perishables	Q
Other Aboriginal Perishables	Q
Other Historic Perishables	Q
Building Materials	Q
Aboriginal Building Materials	Q
Historic Building Materials	Q
Other Materials	Q
Other Aboriginal Materials	Q
Other Historic Materials	Q
Glass	Q
None on Record	Q

GENERAL OBSERVATIONS ON SITE FEATURES

____ Mound(s)/Number of ____	Q
Conical	Q
Truncated	Q
Other	Q
____ Other Earthworks	Q
____ Other Aboriginal Earthworks	Q
____ Historic Earthworks	Q
____ Subsurface Features	Q
____ Aboriginal Subsurface Features	Q
____ Historic Subsurface Features	Q
____ Visible Stratigraphy	Q
____ Visible Prehistoric Stratigraphy	Q
____ Visible Historic Stratigraphy	Q
____ Prehistoric Structure(s)	Q
____ Historic Structure(s)	Q
____ Primary	Q
____ Standing ____ Not Standing	Q
____ Abandoned ____ In Use	Q
____ Secondary	Q
____ Standing ____ Not Standing	Q
____ Abandoned ____ In Use	Q
____ Other Historic Surface Structural Feature(s)	Q
____ Midden	Q
____ Aboriginal Midden	Q
____ Historic Midden	Q
____ Shell Midden	Q
____ Petroglyph	Q

____ Pictograph	Q
____ Burial(s)	Q
____ Aboriginal Burial(s)	Q
____ Historic Burial(s)	Q
____ Chimney	Q
____ Well	Q

MOUND DESTRUCTION CODE

1- No mound still standing
2- Some mound(s) standing with only minor damage
3- Mound still standing with only minor damage
4- Some mound(s) standing with major damage
5- Mound still standing but with major damage
6- No serious mound damage apparent
7- Unknown

DEGREE OF SITE DESTRUCTION

01 Relatively Undisturbed
02 Minor
03 Moderate
04 Major
05 Totally Destroyed
06 Unknown

SITE DISTURBANCES

01 Natural Causes
02 Scientific Excavation
03 Non-Scientific Excavation
04 Extensively Surface Collected
05 Construction
06 Road/Highway
07 Drainage Improvement/Channelization
08 Agriculture
09 Clear Cut
10 Land Leveled/Graded
11 Periodically Inundated
12 Indefinitely Inundated
13 Buried Site
14 Re-deposited Site
15 Unknown
16 See Additional Comment

PHYSIOGRAPHIC SUBDIVISION -Up to four physiographic subdivisions can be associated with each site. The first association entered upon the keypunch form is defined as the primary subdivision upon which the site, or most of it, lies. The remaining slots are to record other subdivisions that are transitional—within 2.5 km—to the site.

01 Salem Plateau
02 Springfield Plateau
03 Boston Mountains
04 Arkansas River Valley, undifferentiated
05 Fourche Mountains
06 Central Ouachita Mountains
07 Athens Piedmont Plateau
08 Gulf Coastal Plain, undifferentiated
09 Southwestern Arkansas
10 Mississippi Alluvial Plain, undifferentiated
11 Boeuf Basin
12 Arkansas River Lowlands
13 Lower White River Basin
14 White River Lowlands
15 Grand Prairie
16 Western Lowlands
17 Eastern Lowlands

PHYSIOGRAPHIC SUBDIVISION *(cont.)*
  18 Malden Plain
  19 Macon Ridge
  20 Crowleys Ridge, undifferentiated

GEOLOGIC SUBDIVISION -Up to three geologic subdivisions can be associated with each site. The first is considered the primary association upon which the site, or most of it, lies. The two remaining slots are to be used to note other geologic deposits on which the site may also lie.

  01 Qcm: Alluvium
  02 Qso: Alluvium
  03 Qt: Terrace Deposits
  04 Qds: Dune Sand
  05 Qss: Silt and Sand
  06 Ql: Loess
  07 Qsg: Sand and Gravel
  08 Tj: Jacson Group
  09 Tc: Caiborne Group
  10 Tw: Wilcox Group
  11 Tm: Midway Group
  12 Qal: Alluvium
  13 Kad: Arkadelphia Marl
  14 Kn: Nacatoch Sand
  15 Ks: Saratoga Chalk
  16 Km: Marlbrook Marl
  17 Ka: Annona Chalk
  18 Ko: Ozan Formation
  19 Kb: Brownstown Marl
  20 Kto: Tokio Formation
  21 Kw: Woodbine Formation
  22 Kkg: Kiamichi Formation and Goodland
             Limestone
  23 Kt: Trinity Group
  24 Kde: De Queen Limestone
  25 Kdi: Dierks Limestone
  26 Ke: Igneous Rocks
  27 Pzi: Soapstone-Serpentine
  28 Qat: Alluvium and Terrace Deposits
  29 Tg: Gravel
  30 Ksc: Sand and Clay
  31 Kr: Cretaceous Rocks
  32 Pa: Atoka Formation
  33 Pbh: Boyd Shalde, and
             Prairie Grove Member
  34 Phc: Cane Hill Member of the Hale Formation
  35 Mpfb: Pitkin Limestone, Fayetteville Shale, and
             Batesville Sandstone
  36 Mr: Ruddell Shale
  37 Mm: Moorefield Formation
  38 Mb: Boone Formation
  39 MDcp: Chattanooga Shale, Clifty Limestone, and
             Penters Chert
  40 Slsb: Lafferty, St. Clair, and Brassfield
             Limestones
  41 Ocj: Cason Shale and Fernvale Limestone and
             Kimmswick Limestone, Plattin Limestone,
             and Joachim Dolomite
  42 Ose: St. Peter Sandstone and Everton
             Formation
  43 Op: Powell Dolomite
  44 Ocjc: Cotter and Jefferson City Dolomite
  45 Pby: Boggy Formation
  46 Psu: Savanna Formation

  47 Pma: McAlester Formation
  48 Phs: Hartshorne Sandstone
  49 Pau: Atoka Formation, upper
  50 Pam: Atoka Formation, middle
  51 Pal: Atoka Formation, lower
  52 Pjv: Johns Valley Shale
  53 Pj: Jackfork Sandstone
  54 Ms: Stanley Shale
  55 MDa: Arkansas Nocavulite
  56 Smb: Missouri Mountain Shale and Blaylock
             Sandstone
  57 Opb: Polk Creek Shale and Bigfork Chert
  58 Ow: Womble Shale
  59 Ob: Blakely Sandstone
  60 Om: Mazarn Shale
  61 Ocm: Crystal Mountain Sandstone
  62 Oc: Collier Shale

SPECIFIC TOPOGRAPHIC SETTING -Up to six different terms can be used to describe the setting of any given site; each can be questioned individually. The terms vary considerably in their specificity.

  01 Upland Plateau/Flat
  02 Hill Top
  03 Mountain Top
  04 Ridge Top
  05 Ridge Saddle/Gap
  06 Prominence on Ridge Crest
  07 Ridge Spur
  08 Bluff Top
  09 Bluff Overhang
  10 Cave
  11 Hillslope
  12 Upper Hillslope
  13 Middle Hillslope
  14 Lower Hillslope
  15 Bench
  16 Upland Glade
  17 Apron Wash
  18 Alluvial Fan or Cone
  19 Talus
  20 Hillslope-Floodplain Junc.
  21 Floodplain
  22 Alluvial Terrace
  23 Terrace Surface
  24 Minor Terrace Relief
  25 First Terrace
  26 Second Terrace
  27 Third Terrace
  28 Terrace Edge
  29 Point on Terrace Edge
  30 Primary Alluvial Flat
  31 Minor Floodplain Relief
  32 Natural Levee
  33 Sand Dune
  34 Prairie/Pimple Mound
  35 Meander Scar
  36 Active Stream Channel
  37 Active Stream, Bank of
  38 Relief Channel
  39 Relief Channel, Bank of
  40 Natural Lake Bed
  41 Natural Lake Shore
  42 Artificial Lake Bed

43 Artificial Lake Shore
44 Abandoned Meander Channel
45 Abandoned Meander Channel, Bank of
46 Oxbow Lake
47 Oxbow Lake, Bank of
48 Serpentine Lake
49 Serpentine Lake, Bank of
50 Oxbow Swamp
51 Oxbow Swamp, Bank of
52 Serpentine Swamp
53 Serpentine Swamp, Bank of
54 Cutoff Channel
55 Cutoff Channel, Bank of
56 Nip (Outer) Bank of Meander Loop
57 Slipoff Slope (Inner) Bank of Meander Loop
58 Backswamp/Floodplain
59 Minor Backswamp Relief
60 Relict Braided Stream Channel
61 Relict Braided Stream, Bank of
62 Point Bar
63 Island

CODE AND DISTANCE OF NEAREST STREAM -Each stream which is named on the AHD County Maps has been given a unique four digit code. Additional streams can be placed on the master list as needed.

Distance Scale: 01 Within 100 meters of site
02 Within 500 meters of site
03 Within 1.0 kilometer of site
04 Within 5.0 kilometers of site
05 Within 10.0 kilometers of site

CODE AND DISTANCE OF LARGEST STREAM -Largest stream within 10.0 km is entered; if nearest is also largest, enter only once in above category. Same distance scale as above is used.

OTHER WATER ASSOCIATION(S)

01 Spring w/distance
02 Intermittent Stream
03 Oxbow Lake/Swamp
04 Other Natural Lake
05 Backswamp/Floodbasin
06 Relict or Abandoned Meander Channel
07 Other Relict Stream Channel
08 Other Water Association

ASSOCIATION WITH STREAM CONFLUENCE -Codes of the two streams comprising the largest confluence within 10.0 km of the site are entered here.

ELEVATION OF NEAREST STREAM -In feet.

SUB-BASIN ASSOCIATION -Up to three sub-basins can be associated with any given site. The first entered is considered the primary watershed within which the site, or most of it, lies. A transitional corridor is defined as 1.0 km either side of boundary centerline; site must touch or lie within this.

SUBSURFACE INVESTIGATION(S) -Enter as many of the following that are applicable; only professional investigations qualify.

01 Shovel Test
02 Test Excavation
03 Test Excavation for Determination of Significance
04 Extensive Excavation
05 Auger Test
06 Coring Sample
07 Metal Detector
08 Other
09 None on Record
10 Unknown

GENERAL SOIL ASSOCIATION (CURRENT) -Up to six soil associations can be entered for any given site; each association has a three digit code. The first association entered is to be the primary soil association upon which the site, or most of it, lies. The remaining five slots are to be used for those soil associations which lie within a 2.5 km radius of the site center. Published SCS county soil manuals are to be used for the areas where they are available; if unavailable, the 'advanced' county soil association maps are to be used. A flag is to be marked if the advanced series is used.

GENERAL SOIL ASSOCIATION (EARLY 20TH CENTURY) - The same procedure related above applies here also, except that only one set of maps pertain.

SPECIFIC SOIL TYPE -Up to three specific soil types may be associated with a given site. Category intended to record soil type(s) that the site actually lies upon.

FOREST TYPE -Taken from map in *Arkansas Natural Area Plan* (1974)

1 Loblolly - shortleaf pine - hardwood
2 Upland hardwood
3 Bottomland hardwood
4 Prairie or non-typed areas

FLAG: SITE INCLUDED IN INTENSIVELY SURVEYED TRANSECT

FLAG: SITE INCLUDED IN ANOTHER CONTROLLED INTENSIVELY SURVEYED UNIT

ACCESSION NUMBER(S) -All accession numbers associated with the site are to be recorded; each should be treated as a six digit number.

SITE NAME(S) -All site names associated with the site should be recorded.

SITE ADDRESS -Generally applicable only to historic structures in an urban setting.

SITE DISPOSITION -This category is to be used to record semi-standardized phrases and comments pertaining to the status of the site's official survey number and any confusion between it and other sites or site numbers.

REFERENCES

Benchley, Elizabeth
  1975 An overview of the archeological resources of the metropolitan St. Louis area. Report submitted to the National Park Service. Springfield: Illinois State Museum Society.

Canouts, Veletta
  1977 Management strategies for effective research. In *Conservation Archaeology: A Guide for Cultural Resource Management,* edited by M. B. Schiffer and G. J. Gumerman, pp. 121-27. New York: Academic Press.

King, Thomas F., and Wilford P. Cole
  1977 Automated management of data in archeological surveys and research results: a proposal for discussion. Unpublished manuscript, 5 pp. University of Arkansas.

Klinger, Timothy C. (assembler)
  1976a Village Creek: An Explicitly Regional Approach to the Study of Cultural Resources. Draft report submitted to and on file with the USDA Soil Conservation Service, Little Rock.

  1976b The problem of site definition in cultural resource management. *Proceedings of the Arkansas Academy of Science* 30: 54-56.

  1977 New Hope: an archeological assessment of a proposed strip mine tract in the gulf coastal plain of southwest Arkansas. Draft report on file with the Arkansas Archeological Survey, Fayetteville.

Limp, W. Fredrick
  1977a Oracle system user's manual. *Glenn A. Black Laboratory of Archaeology, Research Report* 2. Indiana University.

  1977b Oracle system survey manual. *Glenn A. Black Laboratory of Archaeology, Research Report* 3. Indiana University.

Lipe, William D.
  1977 A conservation model for American archaeology. In *Conservation Archaeology: A Guide for Cultural Resource Management,* edited by M. B. Schiffer and G. J. Gumerman, pp. 19-42. New York: Academic Press.

MacCord, Howard A., Sr.
  1977 Cultural resource management: site inventories should have higher priorities. *American Society for Conservation Archaeology Newsletter* 3(5): 2-5.

McGimsey, Charles R., III, and Hester A. Davis (editors)
  1977 *The Management of Archeological Resources: The Airlie House Report.* Special publication of the Society for American Archaeology.

Plog, Fred, and James N. Hill
  1971 Explaining variability in the distribution of sites. In The Distribution of Prehistoric Population Aggregates, edited by G. J. Gumerman, pp. 7-36. *Prescott College Anthropological Report* 1.

Schiffer, Michael B., and George J. Gumerman (editors)
  1977 *Conservation Archaeology: A Guide for Cultural Resource Management Studies.* New York: Academic Press.

Scholtz, Sandra C.
  1976 A management information system design for a general museum. *Museum Data Bank Research Report* 12. Rochester: Margaret Woodbury Strong Museum.

Scholtz, Sandra C., and Robert G. Chenhall
  1976 Archaeological data banks in theory and practice. *American Antiquity* 41: 89-96.

Roper, Donna C.
  1974 The distribution of middle Woodland sites within the environment of the lower Sangamon River, Illinois. *Illinois State Museum Reports of Investigation* 30.

Thompson, Raymond H.
  1974 Institutional responsibilities in conservation archaeology. In Proceedings of the 1974 Cultural Resource Management Conference, Federal Center, Denver, Colorado, edited by W. D. Lipe and A. J. Lindsay, Jr., pp. 13-24. *Museum of Northern Arizona Technical Series* 14.

Trubowitz, Neal L.
  1976 New York Archaeological Council site recording system: instruction manual. *New York Archaeological Council, Studies in Cultural Resource Management* 2.

4. AZSITE: The Arizona State Museum Site Survey Data Base

Anne Rieger
Arizona State Museum

INTRODUCTION

AZSITE computerized data base represents a long term effort by Arizona State Museum (ASM) personnel to design, implement, and maintain a file of archaeological site survey records. Assessment of data needs and project planning began in 1970. Data entry activities were initiated by the Museum staff in 1976 and by the end of 1980 the AZSITE file should contain all site record data in the Arizona State Museum archaeological site survey card file (see Vogler 1980 for a complete description of the ASM site survey system).

The Arizona State Museum staff has been involved in active archaeological site survey in Arizona since 1915. Site information was recorded in the field or at the Museum following fieldwork and then stored at the Museum. In 1937 new systematic archaeological survey techniques were implemented to collect data, and an archaeological site survey file became an important part of this new approach to survey. This file, developed by Emil W. Haury, consisted of index cards (5 by 9 inches) printed with a minimum set of site data categories. The site survey cards were organized by site number, and data categories included site location, cultural affiliation, type of site, architectural features, portable artifacts, general surroundings and environment, and a plan view drawing of the site. Survey data were recorded while in the field in a notebook or written directly on the cards, as no standardized site survey form had been developed. Wasley (1964) and Vogler (1980) have described the basic format of the ASM site survey cards and provided instructions on completing data categories.

The site survey card file continued in use for more than twenty years as the primary source of site information in the Museum. During this time the use of the ASM site survey file increased as archaeological data needs proliferated. By the late 1940s archaeological survey information had become an important research tool (Danson 1946, Frick 1954), and file use broadened. The development of a Highway Salvage program at the Museum in 1955 stimulated concern for improved file data, and several years later Raymond H. Thompson, Director of the Museum, encouraged investigation of a computerized archaeological site survey file. Software was developed (FORTRAN IV) for use with an IBM 1130 computer, and the file contained nine categories of information (Lisckha 1968). Data were transcribed into numerical codes while site designation was alphanumeric.

By the early 1970s environmental legislation required more thorough investigation of cultural resources, and a Cultural Resource Management Section was organized in the Museum to provide the archaeological expertise needed by government agencies and private industry for complying with this legislation. However, changes in the ASM site survey system were needed to meet new data requirements of archaeological research. Contract research strategies, based on known cultural resources in a study area, were often developed under stringent time and funding constraints, and a quick method of obtaining site information was desirable. It was recognized that computerization of the site survey file could provide immediate printouts of site inventories and enable extraction of specific types of site information in an organized and easy-to-read format.

AZSITE, a computer site file, was developed in response to this need and to complement the manual site survey card file. To insure more standardized data for AZSITE a new field recording form for archaeological site survey was prepared, with data categories that corresponded closely with those of AZSITE to facilitate entry procedures. The site survey card, previously the only site "record," was also updated to reflect standardized data categories. All of these steps were taken to develop a Museum-wide integrated information system.

EVALUATING THE NEED FOR A COMPUTERIZED FILE OF SITE SURVEY DATA

The need for a computerized site survey file resulted from the inability of the manual system to efficiently meet increasing information requests from ASM archaeologists, University of Arizona faculty and students, other institutions, and project sponsors. The large size of the card file (over 12,000 sites) made it time consuming to retrieve site information, and contract research was adding sites to the file at a considerably increased rate. AZSITE was designed with two primary objectives: (1) to provide a more efficient system of data storage and retrieval for site survey records, and (2) to create a repository of archaeological survey information for Arizona. Both objectives would facilitate research and cultural resource management goals of the Museum.

The ASM archaeological site card file was only one source of archaeological survey data housed at the Museum. Copies of some site survey records from the Museum of Northern Arizona, the University of California at Los Angeles, the Bureau of Land Management, the Bureau of Indian Affairs, and the Amerind Foundation were filed at the Museum. In addition, the Museum maintained all of the site survey records from the Gila Pueblo Foundation, which closed in 1950, and some records from archaeological survey work by archaeologists at Prescott College (the College ceased to operate in 1974). Standardization of the information contained in these records for incorporation into AZSITE was crucial to efficient data retrieval.

AZSITE was developed as one file in a Museum-wide computerized information system. Other files at ASM include artifact collection inventories, bibliographic information, and photographic collections (Table 4.1). These files are all integrated through a single information category, the ASM site survey number. When computerization of these files is completed, the total range of information available at the Museum on a particular archaeological site will be accessible by computer (see Fig. 4.1 for an example based on site AZ U:13:1, Snaketown).

The advent of new environmental legislation calling for the conservation and protection of archaeological sites significantly increased the importance of the ASM archaeological survey file as a primary data source. Federal agencies have been directed by laws, Executive Orders, and procedural guidelines (E.O. 11593, NHPA 1966, and ACHP Part 800) to prepare complete state site inventories. These inventories aid management of cultural resources and archaeological research by indicating the distribution of archaeological sites in relation to surveyed and unsurveyed portions of the state. Thus, a computerized file increases effective management of archaeological resources as it can provide a comprehensive inventory of sites for geographic units of study.

AZSITE was also designed to provide a means for evaluating the archaeological significance of a site or group of sites. Determining site significance has become the basis for decision making when cultural resources are threatened by proposed land modification projects. Thompson (1978) has pointed out that archaeologists must have input in the planning stages of such projects to protect sites and that they must establish the validity and credibility of their professional judgements to their clients by documentation.

> In the final analysis, though, the real basis of judgement is some form of comparison. Several writers and speakers have referred to the relative character of significance, so if we are to be successful in documenting our judgements we need to have a framework for making essential comparisons—a framework with which the process of comparison may take place (Thompson 1978: 7).

With computerization site data can be manipulated so that inter-site comparisons, based on one or more variables, can be quickly formed for large numbers of

TABLE 4.1
Arizona State Museum Computer Files
(From Lominac and Jacobs 1979)

ANP	Inventory of and index to cataloged archaeological nonperishable collections.
ARCHIV	Index to the Arizona State Museum Library Archives.
ASMETH	Inventory of and index to cataloged ethnographic collections.
AZSITE	Research file and index to the Arizona State Museum Archaeological Survey.
DRYMAT	Inventory of and index to cataloged archaeological perishable collections.
FOTOINV	Inventory of and index to photographic collections.
POTYPE	Inventory of and index to cataloged collections of prehistoric pottery vessels.
TEXTIL	Research file and index to cataloged Southwestern ethnographic textile collections; this file is a subset of ASMETH.

AZSITE
MASTER LIST

DATE 00800908

SERIAL	CATEG	LINE	CAT-DEFINITION	DATA
U 13001A	010	01	STATE-	ARIZONA
	020	01	COUNTY-	PINAL
	025	01	USGS TOPO NAME, SERIES-	GILA BUTTE NW
	027	01	USGS TOPO YR, ASM NUM-	1967 024477
	030	01	LOCATION-	03N 04E 11 NE SW
	070	01	UTM REFERENCE, SPECIFIC-	12 414060 3671000
	080	01	ASM SITE SURVEY NUMBER-	AZ. U:13.001
	090	01	NUMBER OF SITE COMPONENTS-	002
	100	01	PROPERTY TYPE-	SITE
	105	01	SITE NAME-	SNAKETOWN
	107	01	SITE DATES-	R BC00300 R AD01100
	110	01	ELEVATION-	01170
	115	01	NEAREST NAMED DRAINAGE-	GILA RIVER
	120	01	DRAINAGE BASIN-	GILA RIVER
	125	01	PERMANENT DRAINAGE-	GILA RIVER
	130	01	BIBLIOGRAPHIC REFERENCES-	HAURY, E. 1976 THE HOHOKAM:DESERT FARMERS AND CRAFTSMAN. U OF A
	130	02		GLADWIN, H.,HAURY AND SAYLES 1937 EXCAVATIONS AT SNAKETOWN.
	135	01	CARD DATE-	110138
	137	01	REPORTES(S) OR RECORDER(S)-	HAURY, E.
	140	01	RECORDING INSTITUTE (OTHER THAN ASM-	GP GILA BUTTE 101
	143	01	PROJECT NAME AND FIELD NUMBER-	ASM ARCHAEOLOGICAL SITE SURVEY
	145	01	PHOTOGRAPHS-	YES ON FILE AT ASM
	150	01	OWNERSHIP-	FED DOI BIA GILA RIVER INDIAN RESERVATION
	200	01	MAJOR PHYSIOGRAPHIC PROVINCE-	DESERT
	210	01	BIOTIC COMMUNITIES-	1 SOUTHWESTERN DESERTSCRUB
	215	01	NATURAL VEGETATION-	3631200 CREOSOTE-BURSAGE COMMUNITIES
	220	01	CONTEMPORARY FLORAL OBSERVATIONS-	3 SALTBUSH/3 MESQUITE
	250	01	TOPOGRAPHIC SETTING-	VALLEY
	270	01	DOMINANT SUBSTRATE TYPE-	ALLUVIUM
	280	01	SOIL TYPE-	SAND
U 13001B	500	01	COMPONENT NUMBER AND TYPE-	1OF 2 HABITATION
	501	02	COMPONENT FEATURES-	001 VILLAGE/MLT BALLCOURT/MLT PITHOUSES/001CANAL/
				001 SHERD SCATTER/001 LITHIC SCATTER/MLT BURIALS
	505	01	COMONENT IDENTIFICATION-	TEMPORAL
	510	01	AREA OF COMPONENT-	IND
	515	01	GREATEST DEPTH OF COMPONENT-	STR
	520	01	COMPONENT'S DEPOSITIONAL INTEGRITY-	EXCAVATED
	522	01	ENDANGERED-	IND
	525	01	TIME CONTROL-	PREHISTORIC
	530	01	COMPONENT DATES-	R BC00300 R AD01100
	535	01	CULTURAL AFFILIATION-	HOHOKAM
	540	01	PERIOD-	PIONEER/SEDENTARY
	545	01	PHASE-	VAHKI/SWEETWATER/ESTRELLA/GILA BUTTE/SANTA CRUZ/SACATON
	550	01	NATIONAL REGISTER STATUS-	LISTED
	557	01	NAT'L REG. AREAS OF SIGNIFICANCE-	ARCHAEOLOGY-PREHISTORIC
	560	01	STATE REGISTER STATUS-	LISTED
	630	01	CERAMIC WARE AND TYPE-	HOHOKAM BUFFWARE, SWEETWATER RED ON GREY/

Fig. 4.1. Examples from Snaketown (AZ U:13:1) of five Arizona State Museum computerized files: MASTER LIST, ARCHIV, FOTOINV, DRYMAT, POTYPE.

DATE 00800908

SERIAL	CATEG	LINE	CAT-DEFINITION	DATA
U 13001B	630	02		HOHOKAM BUFFWARE, GILA BUTTE RED ON BUFF/
		03		HOHOKAM BUFFWARE, SANTA CRUZ RED ON BUFF/
		04		HOHOKAM BUFFWARE, SACATON RED ON BUFF/
		05		PIMERIA BROWNWARE, VAHKI PLAIN/
		06		PIMERIA BROWNWARE, GILA PLAIN/
		07		MOGOLLON BROWNWARE, IND/
		08		ROOSEVELT REDWARE, IND/
		09		TUSAYAN WHITEWARE, IND
	631	01	CERAMIC SAMPLING METHOD-	YES 07
	650	01	LITHIC MATERIAL-CHIPPED-	CHIPPED STONE-GENERAL
	651	01	LITHIC(CHIPPED) SAMPLING METHOD-	YES 07
	660	01	LITHIC MATERIAL-GROUND-	GROUND STONE-GENERAL
	661	01	LITHIC(GROUND) SAMPLING METHOD-	YES 07
	680	01	OTHER MATERIAL ITEMS-	SHELL/FIGURINES/SPINDLE WHORLS/SHELL BRACELETS
	681	01	OTHER MATERIAL ITEMS SAMPLING METHO-	YES 07
	900	01	ADDITIONAL COMMENTS-	SEE ADDITIONAL SITE INFORMATION FILE.
U 13001C	500	01	COMPONENT NUMBER AND TYPE-	2OF 2 HABITATION
	501	01	COMPONENT FEATURES-	001 VILLAGE
	505	01	COMPONENT IDENTIFICATION-	TEMPORAL
	510	01	AREA OF COMPONENT-	IND
	515	01	GREATEST DEPTH OF COMPONENT-	STR
	520	01	COMPONENT'S DEPOSITIONAL INTEGRITY-	EXCAVATED
	522	01	ENDANGERED-	IND
	525	01	TIME CONTROL-	TRANSITIONAL
	530	01	COMPONENT DATES-	IND
	535	01	CULTURAL AFFILIATION-	PIMA
	540	01	PERIOD-	IND
	545	01	PHASE-	IND
	550	01	NATIONAL REGISTER STATUS-	LISTED
	557	01	NAT'L REG. AREAS OF SIGNIFICANCE-	ARCHAEOLOGY-HISTORIC
	558	01	APB THEMATIC ANAYLIS OF SIGNIFICANC-	A1
	560	01	STATE REGISTER STATUS-	LISTED
	630	01	CERAMIC WARE AND TYPE-	PIMA WARE, IND
	631	01	CERAMIC SAMPLING METHOD-	YES 07
	900	01	ADDITIONAL COMMENTS-	SEE ADDITIONAL SITE INFORMATION FILE.

DATE 00800908

SERIAL	CATEG	LINE	CAT-DEFINITION	DATA
00079400	001	01	SUBJECT HEADING--	ARIZONA SITES (ASM) -U=13=1 - SEE SNAKETOWN
01007700	001	01	SUBJECT HEADING--	SNAKETOWN EXCAVATIONS, 1934-1935 -ETHNOBOTANY, SHELLS, GRID MAP, STRATIGRAPHY, ARTIFACTS, ETC. NOTES AND CORRESPONDENCE
	002	01	FOLDER NUMBER--	A-0742

Fig. 4.1. (cont.)

SERIAL   CATEG   LINE   CAT-DEFINITION

0790070A   010   01   REGIS REGIST. NO.--
           015   01   REGIS ACCESS. NO.--
           025   01   DEPOSITOR NAME--
                 02   DEPOSITOR ORGAN.--
                 03   DEPOSITOR ADDRESS--
                 04
           030   01   TRANSACTION DATE--
           037   01   DEPOSITOR (CODED)--
           106   01   REGIS SERIAL NO.--
           127   01   RESTRICTIONS--
           132   01   SOURCE TYPE--
           148   01   PROJECT NAME--
           149   01   PHOTOGRAPHER NAME--
                 02   PHOTOGRAPHER ORGAN.--
                 03   PHOTOGRAPHER ADDRESS--
                 04

0790070B   326   01   ACCESS. LOT STATS.--
           405   01   CULTURE--
           459   01   PHOTO. DATES--
           599   01   LOCATION REMARKS--
           600   01   PUBLICATIONS--
           651   01   ACC. LOT NO.--

DATE 00800908
SERIAL   CATEG   LINE   CAT-DEFINITION

PM013963   100   01   CATALOG NO.--
           120   01   STORAGE LOC.--
           200   01   OBJECT NAME--
           215   01   GENUS-SPECIES--
           305   01   MATERIAL--
           310   01   TECHNIQUE--
           322   01   CONDITION--
           510   01   GEOGRAPHIC LOC.--
           515   01   SITE NAME--
           520   01   ASM SITE NO.--
           525   01   INTRASITE PROV.--
           688   01   REMARKS--

DATE 00800908
SERIAL   CATEG   LINE   CAT-DEFINITION

PT005723   100   01   CATALOG NO.--
           120   01   STORAGE LOC.--
           200   01   OBJECT NAME--
           209   01   POTTERY TYPE--
           322   01   CONDITION--
           510   01   GEOGRAPHIC LOC.--
           515   01   SITE NAME--
           520   01   ASM SITE NO.--

DATA
1111222222222233333333334444444444555555555566666666667777777777
6789012345678901234567890123456789012345678901234567890123456789

AP-79-0070
79-0070
HELGA TEIWES
ARIZONA STATE MUSEUM
UNIVERSTIY OF ARIZONA
TUCSON, ARIZONA 85721
19790424
TEIWES, HELGA
01001401
0
20
MIMBRES AND HOHOKAM CERAMIC SPECIMENS-ASM
HELGA TIEWES
ARIZONA STATE MUSEUM
UNIVERSITY OF ARIZONA
TUCSON, ARIZONA 85721

10 30 00004 1 19790530 000 19790530 13 UNKNOWN
HOHOKAM
19790424
AZ. U.13.001 SNAKETOWN
MARUMOTO 1980*
0790070B

DRYMAT
MASTER LIST
DATA
1111222222222233333333334444444444555555555566666666667777777777
6789012345678901234567890123456789012345678901234567890123456789

A 48790
APM   NT03.AZ. U.13.001-DR02
BEAD
PROSOPIS JULIFLORA
07 SEED
PLANT PROCESSING (CUT; DRILLED)
3
GILA RIVER
SNAKETOWN
AZ.U.13.001
BLOCK 9F/CACHE 2
BURNT

POTYPE
MASTER LIST
DATA
1111222222222233333333334444444444555555555566666666667777777777
6789012345678901234567890123456789012345678901234567890123456789

A 27878
125-R 5-E 4
BOWL
SNAKETOWN RED ON BUFF
3
GILA RIVER
SNAKETOWN
AZ. U.13.001

Fig. 4.1. (cont.)

sites. For example, evaluation of site significance may be assisted by using an index of the AZSITE file sorted on cultural affiliation (Fig. 4.2) to provide cultural-historical information. Such indices are an efficient way to synthesize a large volume of data for decision making in the earliest planning stages of proposed construction projects.

Another important consideration in the development of the AZSITE file was to increase the ability to statistically manipulate data for archaeological research. Thus, the categories of data in AZSITE include most of those recorded on the standard ASM site survey field recording form that was designed to fulfill these research needs. AZSITE could also be used to aid excavation planning by providing data retrieval on other sites with similar characteristics. As statistical tests become more essential to archaeological research, adoption of a computerized site survey file will broaden use of ASM site survey information by structuring data in such a way that they are more easily amenable to statistical analysis.

In summary, AZSITE was initiated to resolve problems in using the manual card file, to provide a standard format for future data entry, to facilitate contract research through rapid, efficient, and accurate data retrieval, and to establish a centralized file system.

SOFTWARE SELECTION

Once the need for computerized data management was established for Museum files, a program package was sought that would meet ASM archaeological data requirements. The objectives for the system selected included the ability to: (1) allow the user to establish a set of "qualifications" or "conditions" that would determine whether an item should be retrieved; (2) provide a listing of all or certain parts of the information on an item if it were qualified for listing; (3) sort the output list on any combination of retrieval keys; and (4) provide tabulations of categories or cross-tabulations of two or more categories or levels within categories. Since the file would be used by individuals with minimal computer expertise (archaeologists and other Museum personnel), the system also needed the following characteristics: (1) input and output should be in English words, not numerical codes, and be capable of interpretation without the aid of codesheets; and (2) requests for retrieval of information should be user oriented.

The University of Arizona Computer Center did not have software available with these characteristics. A number of program packages were considered but only two of those examined were found suitable for the complex data structures typical of archaeological site survey information. These two program packages,

GRIPHOS and SELGEM, were frequently used by museums. GRIPHOS (see Chapter 3), written in IBM-specific computer language PL/1, had to be rejected because it was not available at the University of Arizona Computer Center. SELGEM (see Chapter 9) is written in COBOL, a widely used computer language available on the University computers.

The SELGEM (SELf-GEnerating Master) program package, developed by the Information Systems Division of the Smithsonian Institution, was found suitable for the Museum's objectives. SELGEM's capabilities included masterfile maintenance, updating, retrieval, multiple sorting, indexing, the ability to handle large information sets, some tallying capabilities, and report production. SELGEM allows both free-format and fixed-format entries. This kind of data formatting flexibility enables a maximum amount and variety of data to be encoded for each site. Two other decisive factors for using the SELGEM package were that SELGEM was offered without charge to the Museum, and it had already been successfully used by the National Museum of Natural History and other affiliates of the Smithsonian Institution. (For a complete discussion of SELGEM, see Chenall 1975.)

THE AZSITE FILE

File Structure

The AZSITE file is a modified hierarchical file containing 65 categories of information. It is not a true hierarchy because all categories of information are present for each record. The file structure is predicated on a hierarchical arrangement of site data, and information categories are divided into two levels of data. First level categories (categories 010–280) include primarily environmental, jurisdictional, and locational site information. Second level data (categories 500–900) contain component specific archaeological site information (Fig. 4.3). The varied types of data recorded in the file reflect the multipurpose application anticipated. The categories were derived from the ASM site survey form and site card and incorporated suggested additions from the State Historic Preservation Officer (SHPO). Most data categories are specific to manifestations common to the Greater Southwest.

Encoding Procedures

The majority of the categories in the AZSITE file are free-format entries. To ensure standardized encoding of data, many categories have a list of legal entries from which the appropriate term must be selected. The use of vegetation maps and established vegeta-

ARIZONA STATE MUSEUM
SITE SURVEY FILE
CULTURE X TYPE
09/09/80

TIME	CULTURE	TYPE	ADDITIONAL INFORMATION

HISTORIC   ANGLO   COMMERCIAL/HISTORIC/HABITATION

```
                          COMPONENT:                  10F  1
                          COMPONENT DATE:             R AD01851 R AD01900
                          PERIOD:                     LATE 19TH/EARLY 20TH CENTURY
                          COMPONENT FEATURES:         001 HOUSE
                          COMPONENT ID:               SINGLE COMPONENT
                          AREA OF COMPONENT:          0000005400  M
                          DEPTH OF COMPONENT:         SUR
                          DEPOSITIONAL INTEGRITY:     ABS
                          HISTORICAL INTEGRITY:       ABS
                          SITE NAME:                  JACK RABBIT HOUSE
                          SITE NUMBER:                AA05005
```

HISTORIC   PAPAGO   HABITATION

```
                          COMPONENT:                  10F  1
                          COMPONENT DATE:             R AD01891 R AD011906
                          PERIOD:                     LATE 19TH/EARLY 20TH CENTURY
                          COMPONENT FEATURES:         001 VILLAGE/MLT HEARTHS
                          COMPONENT ID:               SINGLE COMPONENT
                          AREA OF COMPONENT:          ABS  M
                          DEPTH OF COMPONENT:         SUR
                          DEPOSITIONAL INTEGRITY:     ERODED
                          HISTORICAL INTEGRITY:       ORIGINAL SITE-ALTERED
                          SITE NAME:                  ABS
                          SITE NUMBER:                AA05002
```

HISTORIC   PAPAGO   HABITATION

```
                          COMPONENT:                  10F  1
                          COMPONENT DATE:             R AD011890 R AD01922
                          PERIOD:                     LATE 19TH/EARLY 20TH CENTURY
                          COMPONENT FEATURES:         001 VILLAGE/001 ARTIFACT SCATTER/001 MISSION
                          COMPONENT ID:               SINGLE COMPONENT
                          AREA OF COMPONENT:          ABS  M
                          DEPTH OF COMPONENT:         SUR
                          DEPOSITIONAL INTEGRITY:     ERODED
                          HISTORICAL INTEGRITY:       ORIGINAL SITE-ALTERED
                          SITE NAME:                  VIAVA VO
                          SITE NUMBER:                AA05003
```

Fig. 4.2. AZSITE index sorted on cultural affiliation.

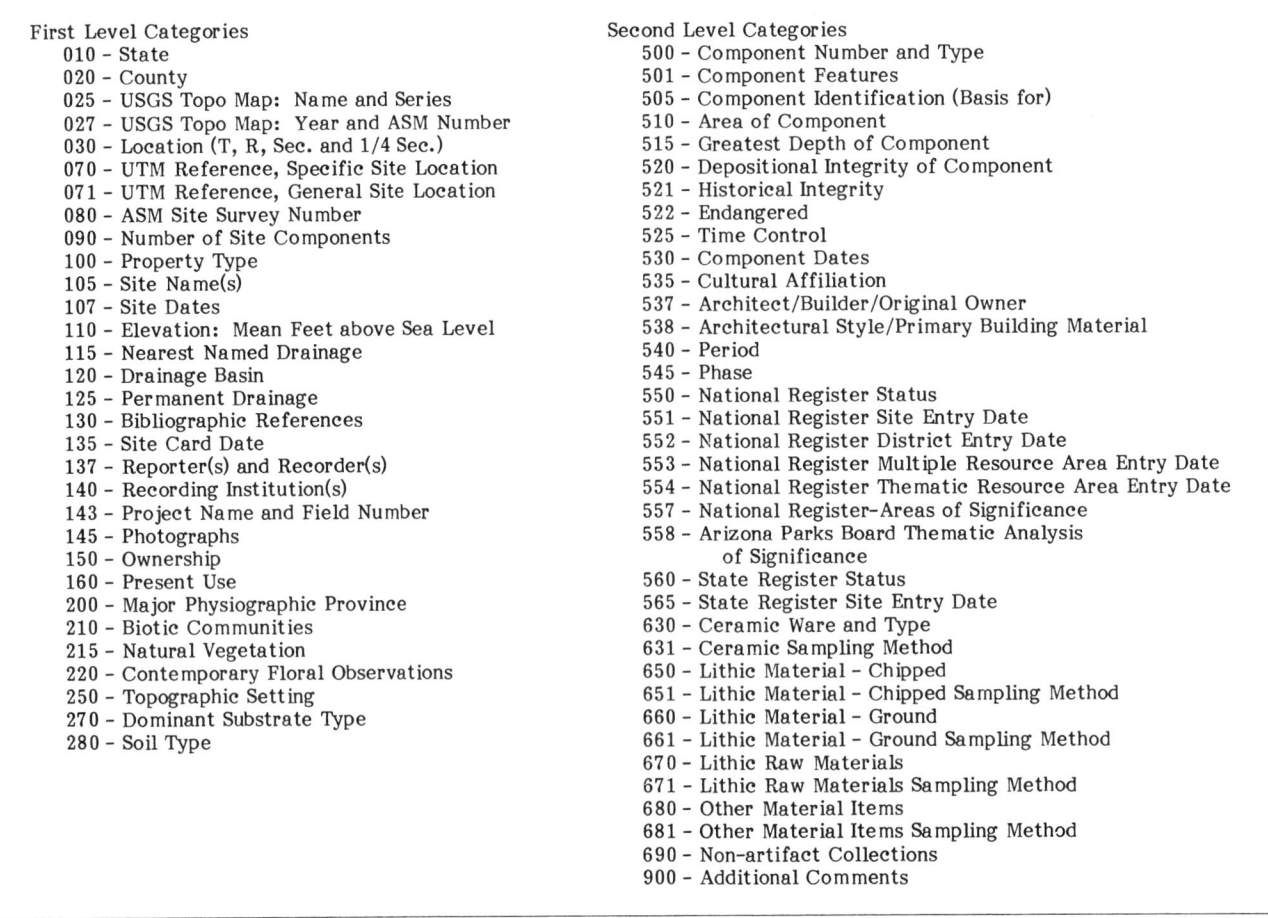

First Level Categories
010 - State
020 - County
025 - USGS Topo Map: Name and Series
027 - USGS Topo Map: Year and ASM Number
030 - Location (T, R, Sec. and 1/4 Sec.)
070 - UTM Reference, Specific Site Location
071 - UTM Reference, General Site Location
080 - ASM Site Survey Number
090 - Number of Site Components
100 - Property Type
105 - Site Name(s)
107 - Site Dates
110 - Elevation: Mean Feet above Sea Level
115 - Nearest Named Drainage
120 - Drainage Basin
125 - Permanent Drainage
130 - Bibliographic References
135 - Site Card Date
137 - Reporter(s) and Recorder(s)
140 - Recording Institution(s)
143 - Project Name and Field Number
145 - Photographs
150 - Ownership
160 - Present Use
200 - Major Physiographic Province
210 - Biotic Communities
215 - Natural Vegetation
220 - Contemporary Floral Observations
250 - Topographic Setting
270 - Dominant Substrate Type
280 - Soil Type

Second Level Categories
500 - Component Number and Type
501 - Component Features
505 - Component Identification (Basis for)
510 - Area of Component
515 - Greatest Depth of Component
520 - Depositional Integrity of Component
521 - Historical Integrity
522 - Endangered
525 - Time Control
530 - Component Dates
535 - Cultural Affiliation
537 - Architect/Builder/Original Owner
538 - Architectural Style/Primary Building Material
540 - Period
545 - Phase
550 - National Register Status
551 - National Register Site Entry Date
552 - National Register District Entry Date
553 - National Register Multiple Resource Area Entry Date
554 - National Register Thematic Resource Area Entry Date
557 - National Register-Areas of Significance
558 - Arizona Parks Board Thematic Analysis
        of Significance
560 - State Register Status
565 - State Register Site Entry Date
630 - Ceramic Ware and Type
631 - Ceramic Sampling Method
650 - Lithic Material - Chipped
651 - Lithic Material - Chipped Sampling Method
660 - Lithic Material - Ground
661 - Lithic Material - Ground Sampling Method
670 - Lithic Raw Materials
671 - Lithic Raw Materials Sampling Method
680 - Other Material Items
681 - Other Material Items Sampling Method
690 - Non-artifact Collections
900 - Additional Comments

Fig. 4.3. AZSITE data categories.

tion classification schemes (Brown and Lowe 1974; Mata et al. 1971) for environmental data also helps to maintain objectivity. Data are transferred from site cards, field forms, maps, and other sources of site information onto the AZSITE forms (Appendix 4.A). Students have been employed and specially trained in SELGEM and the AZSITE file structure to do the encoding. When work first began, two approaches to data transcription were attempted. In the first, an individual completed an entire form for each site; in the second, only a block of categories for all sites was transcribed by each student. The latter method provided greater control over the transcription of certain types of information and enabled project personnel to become more familiar with a set of categories, thereby permitting increased efficiency in data transcription.

Data Entry Procedures

Data are keypunched directly from the forms onto magnetic diskettes by a professional keypunching service. Using 80 character records, diskettes can each hold information equivalent to 1898 cards and consequently are easier to work with than computer cards. Data on the diskettes are translated at the University Computer Center into a form usable by the CDC CYBER 175 by an IBM 3747 diskette converter. This information is then stored on a set of magnetic tapes. Tapes are maintained categorically by states. Presently there are separate masterfiles on tape for Arizona, Sonora, and New Mexico. These masterfiles can be merged and treated as a single file or manipulated as separate files as needed.

Two categories of data are verified by the keypunchers: the serial number and the site survey number (category 080). Verification procedures involve the rekeypunching of selected categories that ensure the accuracy of these categories. It is critical that the serial number and site survey number are correct as they are the primary means of site identification. The remaining categories are verified manually by the AZSITE staff using computer generated update reports and a partial listing of the masterfile. Update reports indicate all changes inserted in the file. The corrections for errors in keypunching or transcriptions are coded onto commercial numerical analysis sheets. The formats of these sheets represent IBM computer cards and contain boxes for 80 columns and 40 lines of data. Although this manual editing procedure is time consuming, it is the most effective means of ensuring accuracy in content and format.

The file has undergone a number of changes during use. Categories have been altered for greater clarity and increased objectivity in data entry, the coding form has been modified to facilitate keypunching, and methods of editing and updating have been revised. These changes improved the efficiency of encoding and update procedures.

APPLICATIONS OF THE AZSITE FILE AT THE ARIZONA STATE MUSEUM

The AZSITE file was operational by 1979, although all encoding activities were not completed by that date. File applications have been limited since AZSITE is relatively new, but the most frequent use has been to provide site listings for inventory control. Other types of management indices, as well as some research applications, have been produced and are discussed below.

Inventory

The first AZSITE index produced was a listing of all sites on the State and National Registers of Historic Places. This index has been continually updated, is in masterfile format, and contains all categories of information encoded for these sites. Since most "Register" sites are known by site name rather than site number, a cross-listing of site names in alphabetical order and their corresponding site number was produced to facilitate use of the index. The index was prepared for use by the State Historic Preservation Officer and a reference copy is maintained at the Arizona State Museum where it is continually consulted by ASM archaeologists and students at the University of Arizona.

Additionally, requests for site data have been made by the Papago Indian Tribe, the Navajo Indian Tribe, and the archaeologist for the Navajo-Hopi Joint Use Area. A printout containing information on all sites recorded for these tribal lands was produced by searching on Category 150, Land Ownership.

Management and Research

The Cultural Resource Management Section of the Arizona State Museum has used the AZSITE file in planning and research on several archaeological projects. In 1978 the Arizona Projects Office of the Bureau of Reclamation asked for an evaluation of the known cultural resource base for a 1550 square mile area in Arizona that might be affected by proposed alternatives for the Central Arizona Project (CAP) aqueducts. A chart of the recorded sites in the study area was produced using the AZSITE file, and a selected number of categories were displayed for each record in an easy-to-read format (Fig. 4.4). In addition, to aid project archaeologists in developing a predictive model of cultural resource sensitivity, a series of indices were produced correlating environmental data and site location. Information from these indices were then compared with aerial photographs and other data to determine those biotic zones that were most likely to contain significant cultural resources (Westfall 1979). Alternative aqueduct corridors expected to have the least impact by construction activities were also discerned.

Another Museum management application of the file was production of a printout of site locational data for all recorded sites in Arizona. These data were used to plot archaeological sites on maps with acetate overlays that indicate areas of archaeological survey in the state and archaeological survey project boundaries (Brian Byrd, personal communication). These bound sets of maps and overlays provide another reference for site information at the Museum.

The AZSITE file has also served the management needs of individuals involved in natural resource conservation. The Water Resources Research Center at the University of Arizona was interested in renovating and redeveloping historic and prehistoric water control devices located along drainages in the Tucson Basin. Because there are over 1000 recorded sites in the geographic area under study, a manual search of the site card file would have been a formidable task. For this project the archaeological sites containing water control features were identified by computer and the pertinent records and categories of information were extracted.

Using the AZSITE file has saved many hours of tedious manual searching through the Museum card file and has increased the accessibility to site survey data by providing an inexpensive and efficient way to retrieve information. For example, site survey file information can now be used to provide data for project budget preparation and other activities that require information on the known cultural resource base of an area. Another aid for cultural resource management and project planning is the archaeological project index, which provides a quick reference to the type and number of sites located by past surveys (Fig. 4.5).

The full research value of the file has not yet been tested. The file was also designed to provide information for testing archaeological hypotheses using previously recorded site data. For example, if there is

ARIZONA STATE MUSEUM - UNIVERSITY OF ARIZONA
BUREAU OF RECLAMATION CAP CLASS 1 CULTURAL RESOURCE SURVEY
SITE SUMMARY TABLE - BB09
02/26/79

SITE NO.
---- --

ADDITIONAL INFORMATION
---------- -----------

BB09049

DATE RECORDED: 021465   150

LOCATION:
   COUNTY: PIMA
   USGS TOPO NAME, SERIES: MOUNT LEMMON
   USGS TOPO YR. (ASM NO.):   1957 023311
   TOWNSHIP RANGE: 12.0S 14.0E 04 NW SW
   UTM REFERENCE: 12 507100 3586000
OWNERSHIP: PRI   MCADAMS RANCH
SITE FUNCTION/TYPE: 10F 1 HABITATION
COMPONENT FEATURES: 001 SHERD SCATTER/001 LITHIC SCATTER/MLT STONE ALIGNMENT
CULTURAL AFFILIATION: HOHOKAM
CHRONOLOGICAL PLACEMENT:
   COMPONENT DATES: R A000500 R A001700
   PERIOD: COLONIAL/SEDENTARY
   PHASE: CANADA DEL ORO/RILLITO/RINCON
NATIONAL REGISTER STATUS: STATUS INDETERMIANTE
STATE REGISTER STATUS: STATUS INDETERMIANTE
RECORDER: AYRES/AYRES
DATE RECORDED: 021465

BB09050   075

LOCATION:
   COUNTY: PIMA
   USGS TOPO NAME, SERIES: SABINO CANYON
   USGS TOPO YR. (ASM NO.):   1957 023773
   TOWNSHIP RANGE: 13.0S 15.0E 14 SE SE
   UTM REFERENCE: 12 521400 3573120
SITE FUNCTION/TYPE: 10F 1 HABITATION
COMPONENT FEATURES: 001 VILLAGE/MLT PITHOUSE/001 ARTIFACT SCATTER
CULTURAL AFFILIATION: HOHOKAM
CHRONOLOGICAL PLACEMENT:
   COMPONENT DATES: R A001200 R A001300
   PERIOD: CLASSIC
   PHASE: TANQUE VERDE
NATIONAL REGISTER STATUS: STATUS INDETERMIANTE
STATE REGISTER STATUS: STATUS INDETERMIANTE
RECORDER: MEINEL/AYRES
DATE RECORDED: 030365

BB09051   075

LOCATION:
   COUNTY: PIMA
   USGS TOPO NAME, SERIES: TUCSON NORTH
   USGS TOPO YR. (ASM NO.):   1957 023509
   TOWNSHIP RANGE: 12.0S 14.0E 21   NW
   UTM REFERENCE: 12 507000 3581000
OWNERSHIP: FED USDA FS   CORONADO NATIONAL FOREST

36

Fig. 4.4. Example of a Site Summary Table for a Bureau of Reclamation project.

```
                         ARIZONA STATE MUSEUM
                            PROJECT INDEX
                              09/09/80

ASM ARCHAEOLOGICAL SITE SURVEY
                    AA05004
                              REPORTERS/RECORDERS:  GREENLEAF J C/GREENLEAF J C
                              CARD DATE:            101070
                              REFERENCES:           ABS

CRMS CAP ORME RESERVOIR PHASE I (SALT ARM) F-9
                    AA03013
                              REPORTERS/RECORDERS:  CAP FLORENCE SURVEY CREW/FRITZ G L
                              CARD DATE:            082572
                              REFERENCES:           CANOUTS V 1975 ASASM 92

CRMS CAP ORME RESERVOIR PHASE I SALT ARM F-8
                    AA03012
                              REPORTERS/RECORDERS:  CAP FLORENCE SURVEY CREW/FRITZ G L
                              CARD DATE:            082572
                              REFERENCES:           CANOUTS V 1975 ASASM 92

CRMS SANTA ROSA WASH PROJECT #1
                    AA05005
                              REPORTERS/RECORDERS:  STACY P, PALM W/AYRES J E
                              CARD DATE:            102470
                              REFERENCES:           STACY AND PALM 1970

CRMS SANTA ROSA WASH PROJECT #7
                    AA05007
                              REPORTERS/RECORDERS:  STACY P, PALM W/AYRES J E
                              CARD DATE:            100870
                              REFERENCES:           STACY AND PALM 1970

CRMS SANTA ROSA WASH PROJECT #8
                    AA05008
                              REPORTERS/RECORDERS:  STACY P, PALM W/AYRES J E
                              CARD DATE:            100870
                              REFERENCES:           STACY AND PALM 1970

CRMS SANTA ROSA WASH PROJECT #12
                    AA05006
                              REPORTERS/RECORDERS:  STACY P, PALM W/AYRES J E
                              CARD DATE:            100870
                              REFERENCES:           STACY AND PALM 1970

CRMS SANTA ROSA WASH SURVEY FN-1
                    AA05009
                              REPORTERS/RECORDERS:  LARKIN R, GERMESHAUSEN E/LARKIN R,GERMESHAUSEN E
                              CARD DATE:            090572
                              REFERENCES:           CANOUTS V, GERMESHAUSEN E, LARKIN R 1972 ASASM 18
```

Fig. 4.5. Project index.

a need to determine whether certain pottery types occur together, the computer can count the co-occurrence of the two types as opposed to the number of sites where only one or neither occurs. To determine the percentage of Mogollon sites in Arizona with stone walls as architectural features before A.D. 1200 compared to after A.D. 1200, a cross tabulation of date with architectural features could be made. The file also could be used for eliciting information on changing settlement patterns, changing land use patterns, and similar research concerns involving the comparison of a number of cultural and environmental variables.

PROJECT OVERVIEW

Costs

The transcription of data from the Museum site files into the AZSITE file was accomplished in four phases of work (Rieger 1978) that were funded in part through matching National Historic Preservation Act grants from the Arizona State Parks Board (ASPB). Other sources of financial support for the AZSITE project included the Arizona State Museum, the University of Arizona, and the University of Arizona Foundation. A fixed sum of $10,000 was made available by the ASPB each year. Approximately 2600 sites were entered into the file in Phase I, but the number of sites entered diminished with each successive phase as a result of an increase in the number of data categories encoded, higher wages, increased keypunching costs, and more expensive consulting fees. Also, as the file grew in size so did the amount of computer time needed for data processing. Increased costs were offset by several positive results, however. Increased efficiency in encoding allowed project personnel to transcribe more records per hour, and increased accuracy in keypunching reduced the number of categories of data requiring verification and lowered the error rate. Also, more familiarity with the file format increased the volume of data that was punched per hour. In addition, the use of computer specialists for performing routine data processing functions was eliminated as project personnel were trained in the computer skills necessary for file maintenance, and report production. Computer charges were also reduced by performing fewer updates of the file—the file was updated with three or four batches of data at a time rather than by just one. Finally, costs were minimized by using University work-study students and volunteers in addition to project personnel for encoding and data editing. For these reasons the average $10.00 cost to enter a single site record into the AZSITE file has remained the same since Phase II. This includes all personnel and operational costs.

Problems Encountered

Early production of test indices and experimentation with the file identified several difficulties in data retrieval and encoding. These problems were the result of several factors, including improper encoding of data in content and format, and vague coding instructions in the AZSITE manual. The manual, which is reproduced by Vogler (1980), was altered to provide more specific coding instructions and category definitions. The problems with data retrieval were due to inadequacies in the initial design of the AZSITE file, a result of the file not being thoroughly tested during the AZSITE design phases. An example of a serious error in design was the inability to retrieve multiple lines of data within a category with some SELGEM programs. These difficulties were corrected through costly and time-consuming file-wide editing during Phases II and III of the project. Although not all technical difficulties can be anticipated with a file containing the kinds of data structures present in the AZSITE file, it is our experience that many people must be involved in the design and testing of a computer file. Archaeological input in the developmental stages of the project was more than adequate, but the computer programming expertise was not varied enough to recognize the range of technical problems that might be encountered. After four phases of work more than 12,000 site records have been encoded in the masterfile. In addition to the masterfile, reference indices from the AZSITE file are maintained. These include the project index, index of State and National Register Sites, index sorted on cultural affiliation, and an environmental index. File-wide editing resulted in refinements in file content and changes in the AZSITE manual. Future work includes encoding newly recorded Arizona sites and completing the entry of sites in Sonora, Mexico.

Project Evaluation

AZSITE is the single largest file of its kind operational in Arizona. Because change is inherent in the development and production of a computer file, AZSITE has undergone numerous alterations since it was first developed in 1970. A number of these changes may have been avoided by more review and testing during the design and planning stages of the project, but a number of the limitations were related to the funding that dictated much of the project schedule. During the first three phases of work funds were available for only half-time positions, and half-time employment of the project supervisor limited the type and volume of work that could be performed.

As a regional file AZSITE is an important archaeological research tool, as it currently serves as a central data source for southern Arizona prehistory and history. File-wide computer searches increase access to Museum site survey data for other institutions by enabling the processing of a greater number of information requests. The utility and value of the file has been recognized by a number of institutions in southern Arizona that have indicated a willingness to input their site data in the file and become active users. The Amerind Foundation, Cochise College, and the Eastern Arizona College Museum of Anthropology have expressed interest in computerizing their site data using AZSITE. This would enhance the file by providing a more complete site inventory. Greater dependence on the AZSITE file is predicted for future archaeological site management and research in Arizona.

THE FUTURE OF AZSITE

Once all records in the Museum site survey file are entered into AZSITE, future goals for the file are three-fold: (1) procedures for development and implementation of file maintenance (encoding new site data and updating the masterfile and indices) will be refined to ensure that the file content is always current; (2) data from other institutional site survey files will be entered in AZSITE; and (3) experimentation and testing of expanded file capabilities will be conducted. Each of these future phases of work are described in more detail below.

Development and Implementation of File Maintenance Procedures

Because new sites are recorded in the Museum site survey file on a continuing basis, standardized procedures for entering these sites into AZSITE will be developed to minimize large backlogs of site data. The transfer of data directly from field forms onto AZSITE forms is recommended. Museum field forms contain more complete information than site cards maintained in the Museum card file, and entering data directly from forms completed by archaeologists with first-hand knowledge of the sites ensures greater accuracy and detail. It is not recommended that the field survey personnel complete the AZSITE forms, as persons not trained in SELGEM procedures are unfamiliar with encoding information and could make errors in data entry. All aspects of AZSITE maintenance should be the responsibility of a single individual to ensure consistency.

Data Entry of Other Site Survey Files

The Arizona State Museum acts as custodian of inactive site survey records for a number of other institutions. These data can be entered into the AZSITE file to provide access to information that in its present form is difficult to use. In addition, the Museum could integrate into AZSITE information in functioning site files from other institutions and provide those institutions computer access to the data.

Expansion of File Capabilities

The file has been successfully used with SELGEM programs for sorting, updating, and data queries. The SELGEM package could be interfaced, however, with other program packages to greatly broaden AZSITE data manipulations. For example, the SELGEM program package can interface with CalComp plotting programs available at the University of Arizona Computer Center. With data in the AZSITE file, CalComp can produce distributional maps for several variables based on AZSITE Category 070, the UTM Reference. SELGEM can also be interfaced with the SPSS statistical analysis program package to provide the capability for more sophisticated data analysis than the tabulations possible through SELGEM alone. To increase the usability (and decrease the access costs) of AZSITE, an interactive alternative to the batch-oriented SELGEM data base management system is also being tested. An interactive system providing essentially instantaneous response to complex file queries could greatly enhance the ability to satisfy the growing information needs of cultural resource management in the state.

Centralized computer information is also being considered by other state agencies. For example, the Arizona Outdoor Recreation Committee of the Arizona Natural Heritage Program, has been investigating the feasibility of computerizing environmental and geologic data for Arizona, and the AZSITE file could be coordinated with such activities. The file is gaining recognition through applications by the contract research program at the Museum, by other institutions, and by various state and federal government agencies. The success of this regional file should lead to cooperation with other museums and institutions in Arizona for development of a central cultural resource data bank for the state.

ACKNOWLEDGMENTS

A number of persons contributed to the preparation of this chapter. Dorothy Hall and James Ayres, Arizona State Historic Preservation Officers during the development of AZSITE, not only assisted in acquiring grant funds for computerization of the site files, but also provided valuable information for the discussion of AZSITE. Assistance on early drafts of the chapter was given by Carol Dickens, who served as Data Manager for the Arizona State Museum in 1979. Help was also offered by Susan Ciolek-Torrello, Systems Analyst at the University of Arizona Computer Center, and by Karen Lominac, ASM Data Manager in 1980, who provided the material for Figures 4.1, 4.2, 4.4, and 4.5. R. Gwinn Vivian, Associate Director of the Arizona State Museum, read all drafts and made a number of suggestions for revisions, and Keith Kintigh, Associate Archaeologist, clarified certain sections of the final draft. Sue Ruiz typed several versions of the manuscript. The assistance of all these persons is gratefully acknowledged.

APPENDIX 4.A: ARIZONA STATE MUSEUM
SITE SURVEY FIELD RECORDING FORM

Serial Number _ _ _ _ _ _ _ A

AZSITE

First Level Data

010 _____ —   020 _____ —
16   State   79   16   County   79

025 _____ 75 77 — 79 —
16   USGS Topographic Quad. Name and Series

027 __ __ __ __ __ __ __ __ __ __ __ __ —
16   19   21   26
USGS Topo. Quad. Yr. Pub. & ASM No.

030 __ — ˙__ — __ __ — __ — __ __ __ __ __ __ __ —
16   18   20 22   24   26 28 29 31 32 34 35
Location (T.R. Sec. ¼ Sec.)

070 __ __ __ __ __ __ __ __ __ __ __ __ __ —
16 17 19   24 26   32
Zone   Easting   Northing
      UTM Reference (A) Specific Site Location

071 __ __ __ __ __ __ __ __ __ __ __ __ __ — __ —
16 17 19   24 26   32 33   35
      UTM Reference (B) General Site Location

37 38 39 __ __ __ __ __ 44 46 __ __ __ __ 52 —
      UTM Reference (C)

54 55 56 __ __ __ __ __ 61 63 __ __ __ __ 69 —
      UTM Reference (D)

080 __ — ˙__ __ __ — ˙__ __ __ — __ ˙__ __ __ — __ __
16   18   21   24   27
ASM Site Survey Number

090 __ __ — __ __ —   100 _____ —
16   18   16   24
Number of Site Components   Property Type

105 _____ 79 —
16   Site Name(s)

107 __ __ __ __ __ __ __ __ __ 24 26 __ __ __ __ 34 __ __   110 __ __ __ __ 20 —
16   16   Elevation
              Site Dates

40

AZSITE   Serial Number _ _ _ _ _ _ A

<u>First Level Data</u>

115
  16   Nearest Named Drainage   79   —

120
  16   Drainage Basin   79   —

125
  16   Permanent Drainage   79   —

130
  16   Bibliographic References   79   —

135
  16 Card date 21 —

137
  16   Reporter(s) and Recorder(s)   79   —

140
  16   20 22   79   —
        Recording Institution(s) (Other than ASM)

143
  16   Project Name and Field Number   79   —

145
  16   Photographs   79   —

150
  16 18 20   24 26   30 32   79   —
        Ownership

160
  16   Present Use   79   —

200
  16   25 —
        Physiographic Province

210
  16 18   Biotic Communities   79   —

215
  16   22 24   Natural Vegetation   79   —

220
  16   Contemporary Floral Observations   79   —

250   270
  16   Topographic Setting   79 —   16   Dominant Substrate Type   79 —

280
  16   Soil Type   79 —

AZSITE   Serial Number _ _ _ _ _ _ _

<u>Second Level Data</u>

500 _ _ _ 0 F _ _ _ _____ _
    16   19 20   23 25   Component Number and Type   79

501 __ __ _____ _
    16 18 20   Component Features   79

505 _____ _ 510 _ _ _ _ _ _ _ _ _ 515 __ __ _
    16   Component Identification 79   16   25   16 18
                                            Area of Component   Depth

520 _____ _ 521 _____ _
    16   Depositional Integrity   79   16   Historical Integrity   79

522 _____ _ 525 _____ _
    16   Endangered   79   16   Time Control   79

530 _ __
    16 Component Dates   24 26   34

535 _____ __
    16   Cultural Affiliation   79

537 _____ _
    16   Architect/Builder / Original Owner   79

538 _____ _
    16   Architectural Style/Building Material   79

540 _____ _ 545 _____ _
    16   Period   79   16   Phase   79

550 _____ _
    16   National Register Status   79

551 __ _ __ _ _ 21 _ 552 __ _ __ _ 21 553 __ _ ___ _ 21 554 __ _ ___ _ 21
    16   Site   21   16 District 21   16   MRA   21   16   TRA   21
                National Register Entry Dates

557 _____ _
    16   Areas of Significance   79

558 _____ _
    16   APB Thematic Analysis of Significance   79

560 _____ __
    16   State Register Status   79

565 __ _ _ _ _ 21 __
    16   21
    State Reg. Entry Date

AZSITE   Serial Number _ _ _ _ _ _ _

630 _____
    $\overline{16}$ Ceramic Ware and Type $\overline{79}$ —

631 $\overline{16}$ $\overline{18}$ $\overline{20}$ $\overline{21}$ —
    Ceramic Sampling Method

650 _____
    $\overline{16}$ Lithic Material - Chipped $\overline{79}$ —

651 $\overline{16}$ $\overline{18}$ $\overline{20}$ $\overline{21}$ —
    Lithic Material - Chipped Sampling Method

660 _____
    $\overline{16}$ Lithic Material-Ground $\overline{79}$ —

661 $\overline{16}$ $\overline{18}$ $\overline{20}$ $\overline{21}$ —
    Lithic Material-Ground Sampling Method

670 _____
    $\overline{16}$ Lithic Raw Materials $\overline{79}$ —

671 $\overline{16}$ $\overline{18}$ $\overline{20}$ $\overline{21}$ —
    Lithic Raw Materials Sampling Method

680 _____
    $\overline{16}$ Other Material Items $\overline{79}$ —

681 $\overline{16}$ $\overline{18}$ $\overline{20}$ $\overline{21}$ —
    Other Material Items Sampling Method

690 $\overline{16}$ — — $\overline{19}$ $\overline{21}$ $\overline{22}$ $\overline{24}$ $\overline{72}$ — $\overline{74}$ — — — — $\overline{79}$ —
                      Non-Artifact Collections

900 _____
    $\overline{16}$ Additional Comments $\overline{79}$ —

AZSITE

Additional Line Form

Serial Number __ __ __ __ __ __ __ __

— — —   — — —   ‾16‾   79

Serial Number __ __ __ __ __ __ __ __

— — —   — — —   ‾16‾   79

Serial Number __ __ __ __ __ __ __ __

— — —   — — —   ‾16‾   79

Serial Number __ __ __ __ __ __ __ __

— — —   — — —   ‾16‾   79

Serial Number __ __ __ __ __ __ __ __

— — —   — — —   ‾16‾   79

Serial Number __ __ __ __ __ __ __ __

— — —   — — —   ‾16‾   79

Serial Number __ __ __ __ __ __ __ __

— — —   — — —   ‾16‾   79

Serial Number __ __ __ __ __ __ __ __

— — —   — — —   ‾16‾   79

Serial Number __ __ __ __ __ __ __ __

— — —   — — —   ‾16‾   79

Serial Number __ __ __ __ __ __ __ __

— — —   — — —   ‾16‾   79

Serial Number __ __ __ __ __ __ __ __

— — —   — — —   ‾16‾   79

REFERENCES

Brown, David E., and Charles H. Lowe
    1974   A digitized computer-compatible classification for natural and potential vegetation in the Southwest with particular reference to Arizona. *Journal of the Arizona Academy of Science* 9, Supplement 2.

Chenall, Robert G.
    1975   Museum cataloging in the computer age. *American Association for State and Local History*, Nashville, Tennessee.

Danson, E. B.
    1946   An Archaeological Survey of the Santa Cruz River Valley from the Headwaters to the Town of Tubac in Arizona. M.A. Thesis, University of Arizona, Tucson.

Frick, Paul Sumner
    1954   An Archaeological Survey in the Central Santa Cruz Valley, Southern Arizona. M.A. Thesis, University of Arizona, Tucson.

Lischka, Leslie
    1968   A System for the Storage and Retrieval of Archaeological Site Survey Data. M.A. Thesis, University of Arizona, Tucson.

Lominac, Karen L., and Mike Jacobs
    1979   Integrated Computer File Development at the Arizona State Museum. Paper presented at the 7th Annual Meeting of the Museum Computer Network, Inc., Washington, D.C.

Mata, G. F., J. J. Lopez, X. M. Sanchez, F. M. Ruiz, and F. T. Takaki
    1971   Mapa De Tipos de Vegetacion de la Republica Mexicana. Secretaria de Recursos Hidraulicos, Direccion de Agrologia, Mexico.

Rieger, Anne T.
    1978   The Selgem AZSITE computerization project; activities relating to the computerization of national register and other cultural sites in the Arizona State Museum Site Survey Files, Phase II. *Arizona State Museum Archaeological Series* 122.

Thompson, Raymond H.
    1978   Beyond Significance. *American Society for Conservation Archaeology Newsletter* 5(6): 15–21.

Vogler, Lawrence, Assembler
    1980   The Arizona State Museum Archaeological Site Survey System. *Arizona State Museum Archaeological Series* 128.

Wasley, William W.
    1964   The Arizona State Museum Archaeological Site Survey System. Tucson: Arizona State Museum.

Westfall, Deborah A.
    1979   An archaeological overview of the Middle and Lower Santa Cruz Basin. *Arizona State Museum Archaeological Series* 134.

5. SARG: The Computer in a Cooperative Effort

Fred Plog
Arizona State University

INTRODUCTION

The Southwestern Anthropological Research Group (SARG) is an organization developed to facilitate cooperative research among archaeologists working in the American Southwest. Within this broad perspective the organization has focused primarily on the investigation of locational problems that can be studied using site survey information. From its inception, SARG anticipated heavy reliance on computer hardware and software.

The beginnings of SARG had little to do either with survey data, locational analyses, or computers. The organization emerged from a series of ceramic conferences held annually at the Museum of Northern Arizona. In the fall of 1969 innovations in ceramic analysis were the focus of the conference. Drawing on ideas discussed there, an effort was made to undertake cooperative research based on a shared approach to investigating design variation in painted ceramics. At the subsequent meeting in 1970, it became obvious that: (a) the research in question entailed levels of detail in both analysis and recording that most participants were not in a position to undertake, and (b) pursuing cooperative research would take the ceramic conference in directions other than those for which it had traditionally been used.

Because the interest in cooperative research remained strong, a meeting to explore potential questions on which research might focus was held at Arizona State University in 1971. Guided by research goals of interest to those expected to participate in SARG, a decision was made to concentrate on site distributional questions. A second meeting was held at Prescott College in April at which the original SARG research design evolved (Gumerman 1971). A summary list of variables to be recorded by each participant was identified (Plog and Hill 1971), as were the general questions to be addressed using the data in question. A major focus of discussions at the SARG meeting in the spring of 1972 was the actual computer format to be used. The computer format generated at this meeting, while it has been refined considerably, structured the basic directions in which SARG has moved (see Appendix 5.A).

By the spring of 1973, participants had some field experience in attempting to employ the data recording format. There was substantial agreement that the 1972 format was unworkable. Attention focused on the need for a numeric format that would facilitate the solution of interface problems when packaged statistical and mathematical programs were used for data analysis, and on keeping the number of cards used to create the data record as low as possible. As a result of the 1973 conference a new format was developed by Gaines. At this same meeting an agreement was reached by SARG members to maintain a single computerized file using the UNIVAC 1110 computer at Arizona State University in Tempe. Procedures for data entry and analysis were established and have been summarized by Gaines (1978: 121):

1. Individual participants obtain blocks of SARG Site Numbers from the Data Bank Coordinator at ASU. Investigators working jointly on the same project are encouraged to use a single block of numbers for the project and not to request individual blocks of numbers unless they are involved in investigations in diverse areas. SARG Site Numbers are issued in blocks of 999 for an individual or for a single project. If a project requires additional site numbers, additional blocks will be issued.

2. Individual participants keypunch the site information and mail the punched cards to the data bank along with the listing. Participants are encouraged to submit data cards in sequential order since this provides an easy

check for lost data. If any sequential numbers within a block remain unused, these should be specifically noted.

3. Information from the data bank may be requested to be in the form of computer hardcopy printouts, punched cards or magnetic tape. Magnetic tape must be supplied by the requester. Requests may pertain to any combination of the following: (a) specific variables, (b) individual data sets, (c) complete data base of all data sets, or (d) execution of specified statistical, mapping or plotting programs on any of the above.

The task of managing the rapidly accumulating data was addressed next. Existing data management systems were reviewed but found to have weaknesses when research and analysis functions were also needed. While these could have been modified, the time and expense involved appeared excessive. Similar problems would have been created had SARG members attempted to develop their own system. For these reasons a canned computer program package, SPSS (Nie et al. 1975) was selected. While archaeologists are familiar with SPSS primarily as an analytical program, there are substantial data management capabilities embedded in it, and the package has proven satisfactory as a management, as well as an analytical, tool. SPSS is a flexible system that permits the structuring and restructuring of files, data and file transformation, and the generation of new variables from existing ones. The program permits analysis of the entire data set as well as of subfiles within it. Available statistics range from simple descriptive to complex multivariate ones. (See Fig. 5.1 for Summary of the File Structure.)

By 1975 our data base incorporated seven individual projects, totaling 2500 sites. Additional refinements in variable definition, coding, and format resulting from the 1975 SARG workshop (Gaines 1978) illustrate not simply a growing proficiency in working with a computerized data base but fundamental discoveries concerning the subject of our research and the research process itself that developed from the effort. These discoveries are perhaps best illustrated by considering the structural and compositional differences between the original 1972 format and the revised format.

STRUCTURAL DIFFERENCES

The coding structure generated in 1972 (Plog and Hill 1972; Green 1972) consisted of three elements: a dictionary, a "tag system," and a discussion of how the two were to be combined. This structure directly reflected compromises between SARG participants on two issues. First, some participants advocated a coding system that used numeric symbols to record specific attribute states, while others preferred a free-text system that permitted both greater flexibility and

greater detail in generating site records. In a microcosm, this debate itself reflected some conflict over whether SARG participants were attempting to collect relatively standardized information on relatively few sites and contextual phenomena, or whether they were attempting to generate a data base from which such standardization might be derived at a later point. Second, and the issue is clearly related to the first, was a discussion as to whether the purpose of SARG was data recovery or data analysis. Clearly, the structure selected embodies elements satisfying the various opponents on all of these issues. For example, the tag system allows free text while the dictionary attempts to standardize somewhat the text that will be used. It is probably more of a comment on compromises in general than on this specific format that only one SARG participant actually managed to code data using it.

These difficulties led to discussions at subsequent SARG meetings resulting in the computer format described by Gaines (1978; see Appendix 5.B). This structure involves a series of five to seven discrete cards, each containing information concerning a particular domain of variation. For each variable, numeric codes are used to define alternative attribute states

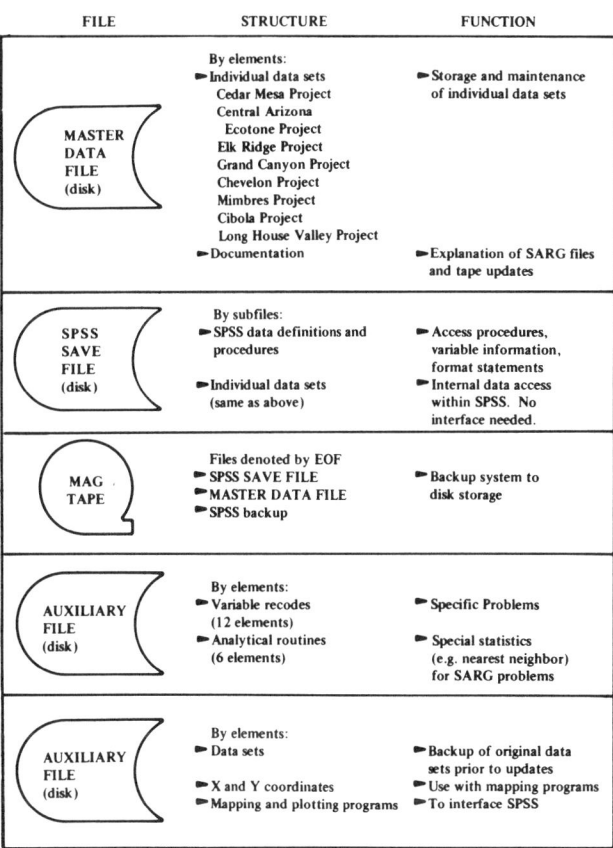

Fig. 5.1. Summary of the file structures.

or specific quantified information is recorded. While this structure more closely approximates what one side of the 1972 debate advocated, it in no sense represents the victory of one position over the other. A comparison of the attribute states with the "dictionary of terms" from the 1972 format indicates clearly that, had the 1972 states been adopted, far less information than is now deemed necessary would have been recorded. This is particularly noteworthy in the relatively casual treatment of site type in 1972 compared with the much more detailed information on site characteristics required from completing cards 2 and 3 in the 1978 format. I suggest, then, that the format shown in Appendix 5.B is a compromise between the different perspectives as to how the computer is best used, an experience in which few of the participants had expertise in 1972.

There are two pertinent issues. First, those who had advocated a numeric recording system had generally attempted to keep the number of attribute states simple. In so doing, they greatly truncated the descriptive detail required to assure some comparability of observation and inference. Second, those who advocated a free-text system underestimated the difficulty of ever achieving comparability if each investigator were allowed to pursue description in whatever conceptual direction seemed warranted. The issue in question is by no means resolved (Sullivan and Schiffer 1978), but in the context of SARG it has at least been identified. Specifically, in the process of attempting to develop and implement a usable computer format, it has become obvious that one can insure comparability neither through standardization of data recording procedures and format nor through "trusting" one's colleagues to observe, infer, and record in a directly parallel fashion. If the use of the computer has highlighted this problem in SARG, it has also revealed its intrinsic and highly problematical role in all efforts at comparing and synthesizing archaeological data.

COMPOSITIONAL DIFFERENCES

The differences between the two computer formats also reflect changes in the nature of the information that is recorded. These modifications reflect changes in archaeology, changes in other disciplines, and experience in attempting to apply or operationalize particular variables.

Changes in archaeology are perhaps best reflected in a dramatic shift in concern with site location. The original dictionary left open the question of whether the locational record was to be kept using longitude and latitude or Universal Transverse Mercator Coordinates (UTM), while UTM was specified in the sub-

sequent format. While participants in early SARG conferences were certainly aware of locational analysis, awareness of computer routines for investigating spatial patterns was minimal, as it was generally within the discipline. As familiarity with computer graphic routines such as SYMAP and GYPSY increased, the potential that might be realized from comparisons based on them was obvious (Effland 1978). For this reason, agreement on common use of the UTM system became more widely accepted.

The fact that this process is continuing is perhaps best reflected in the drainage rank variable. Our initial intention was to use Strahler's approach (1964). We were unaware that a new method based on a logarithmic procedure was replacing the Strahler approach (Woldenberg 1967). It is our intention to shift to this new system in recording drainage rank from now on.

The most basic changes that have been or will be implemented, however, reflect experience in attempting to use particular variable definitions. Perhaps the major illustration is the effort to characterize the landform on which a site is located. Every SARG participant came equipped with a readymade set of intuitive landform categories: hills, ridges, knolls, buttes, mountains, mesas, and so on. Developing some standardized approach to recording this information quickly proved impossible. In the course of preparing the 1972 dictionary, it became apparent that geologists and geographers no longer assumed the adequacy of such terms. For that reason, a slope-relief system was adopted and subsequently experienced limited use; it simply took too much time to record the information for any large number of locations. Therefore, a completely new way of approaching landform has been developed. First, vertical relief within 100 m and 1 km of each site will be recorded, providing a measure of the magnitude of elevation variability around a site. Second, local relief will be characterized by indicating whether a site is situated in a valley, on an upland surface, or in a position between the two. This variable will record the relative position of the site in the context of local variation. Finally, the "landform profile" will be used to record the shape of both the local and regional landform on which a site occurs. Landform profiles are defined on the basis of variation in the four most relevant directions from the site. Figure 5.2 shows the general format of this evaluation (in each direction, slope may be up, down, or nonexistent), and illustrates what we regard as some interpretable combinations. The system was devised by identifying all possible combinations of + (up), − (down), and zero (flat) and then asking which could exist in the real world. While the potential of this approach remains unproven, it has received favorable reaction from geologists and geographers.

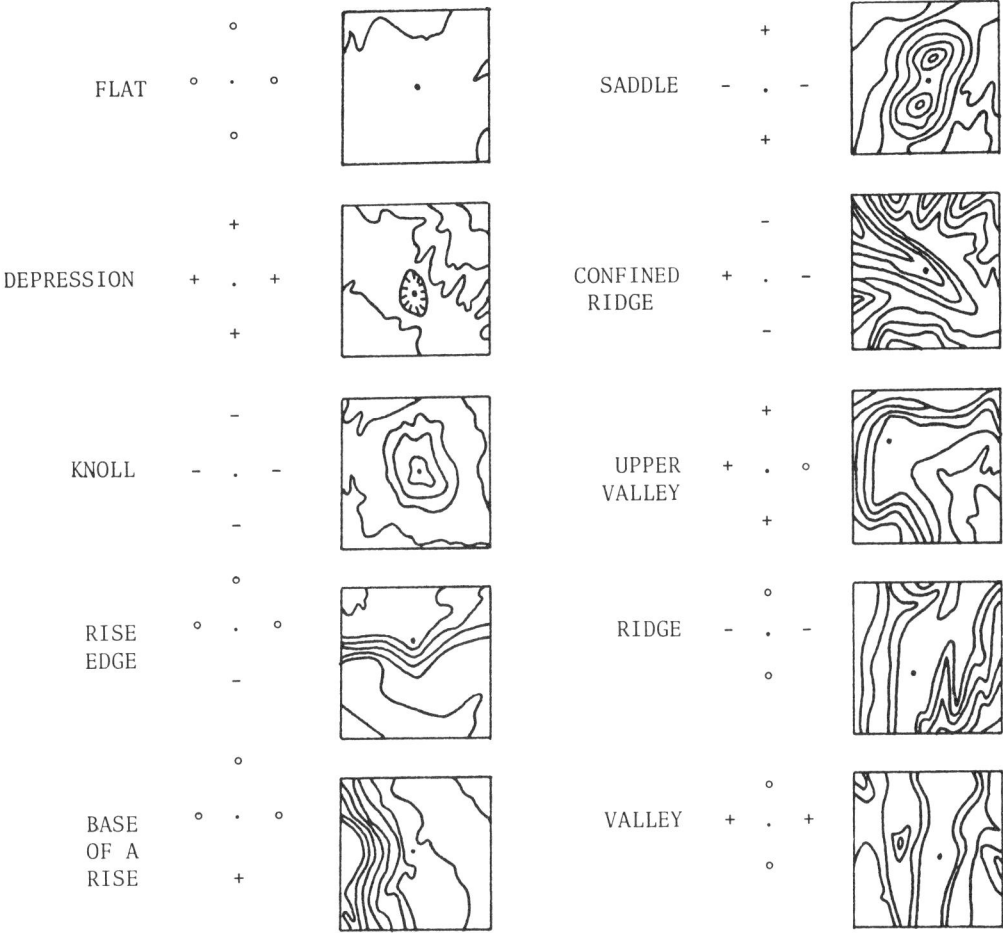

Fig. 5.2. Landform profiles, designed to provide a three-dimensional portrayal of the landform associated with a site. This is only a partial depiction of possible combinations. (Reproduced by permission of the Museum of Northern Arizona.)

FUTURE DIRECTIONS

It would surely be myopic if the only changes in the SARG approach to date involved modifications of the variables that we initially set out to study. In fact, changes that go beyond the approach and organization originally envisioned have occurred. The best example of change in approach concerns the articulation of different environmental variables.

The 1972 research design anticipated a relatively partitive approach to data analysis: the examination of site frequencies in different environmental settings. Yet, as we began to manipulate the various data sets, the need for a more holistic or systemic approach was obvious for two reasons. First, some of our more interesting results are derived from synthethic treatments of drastically different variables such as relief-vegetation relationships. Second, differences in scale, the territory surveyed in particular projects, necessitated means for translating between the results of surveys of small localities of a few dozen square kilo-

meters as opposed to regions of a thousand or more square kilometers.

These problems led to the development of a technique of conceptualizing overall environmental variation in terms of four categories: (a) homogenous, overlapping—zones defined over discrete environmental variables overlap to a substantial degree; (b) homogenous, cross-cutting—zones defined over discrete variables cross-cut each other in so complex a fashion that microzones with all combinations of characteristics exist in close proximity to one another; (c) heterogeneous, fine-grained—discrete variables coincide to form proximate but discrete zones; and (d) heterogeneous, coarse-grained—discrete variables coincide to form discrete but nonproximate zones. These patterns are illustrated in Figure 5.3.

Such zones should be definable for any environmental variable, although in most instances they will be more complex and their definition at least somewhat more problematical than the illustrations suggest. The pattern can be defined for either or both local and

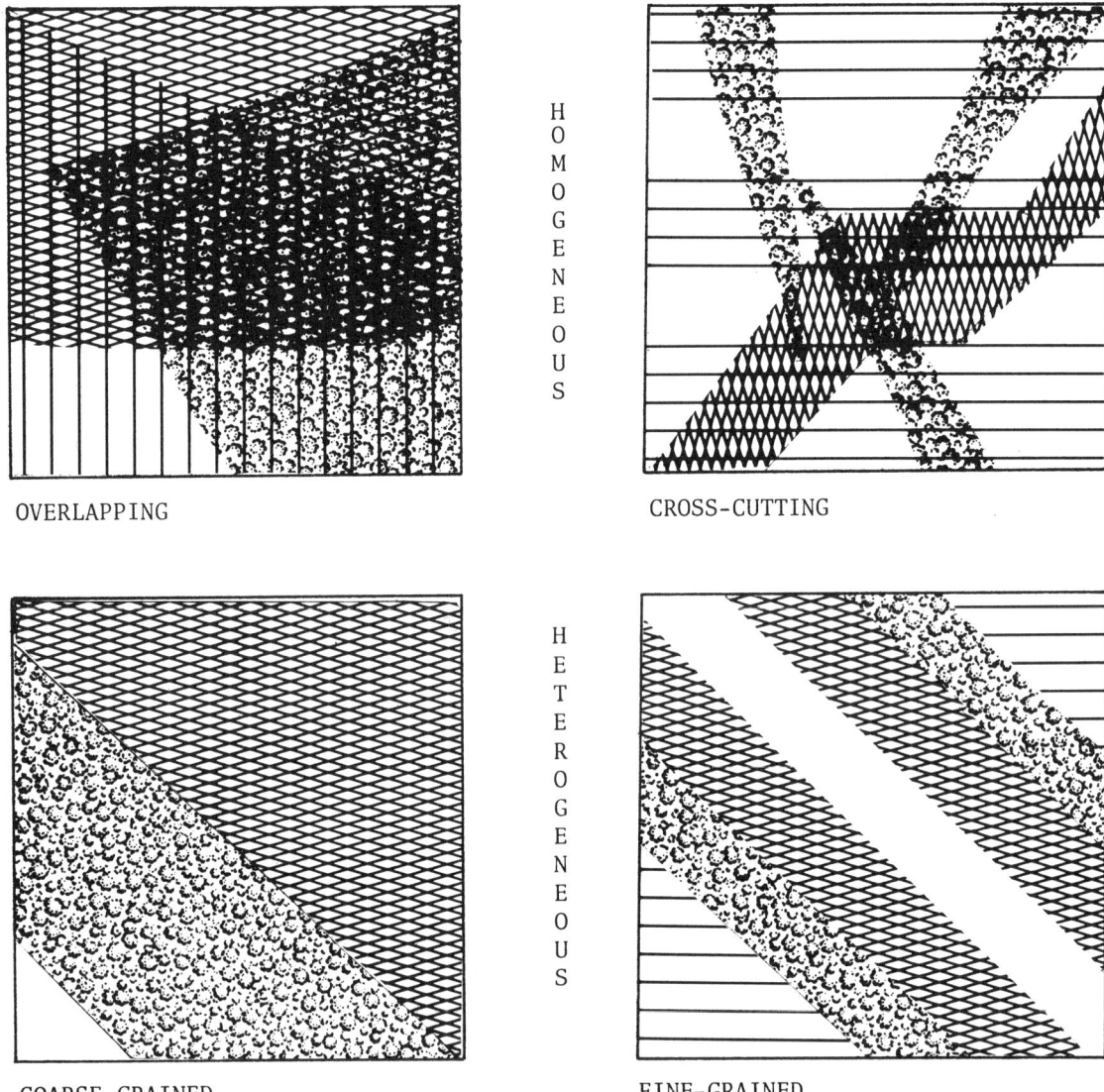

OVERLAPPING

H
O
M
O
G
E
N
E
O
U
S

CROSS-CUTTING

COARSE-GRAINED

H
E
T
E
R
O
G
E
N
E
O
U
S

FINE-GRAINED

Fig. 5.3. Environmental patterning. (Reproduced by permission of the Museum of Northern Arizona.)

regional patterns. That is, one could have a homogenous, overlapping local environment within a heterogeneous, coarse-grained regional context. The patterns can be defined for any number of variables. However, it is unlikely that such an effort will prove profitable until a relatively small number of critical resources (variables) have been identified. Thus, while immediate research will be undertaken with these ideas in mind, their actual implementation will come somewhat later in the research process. At least in part, this involves overcoming the allure of the relative ease with which partitive analyses can be done on the computer and finding ways to achieve more difficult, holistic approaches in computer-assisted research. At the same time, our experience does suggest that not only can such approaches be defined, implemented, and coded, but that both the necessity of developing them and the paths that such developments may take result from partitive analyses done on the computer.

Two examples of organizational changes are occurring for quite different reasons. First, the drainage rank variable generated from maps will be recorded for all sites by a single individual and entered into the data bank. The problem necessitating such a step is evidence of observer error in defining this variable. Both because the quality and detail of maps available to different investigators varied and because quite different decisions concerning map-definition of the first rank drainage were made, a means of instituting a higher degree of standardization was needed. Otherwise, we risked a situation in which the major sources of variation in the relationship between sites and drainage were map quality and recording decisions. In this case, a means of standardizing the variable was relatively simple. As discussed earlier, simplicity is not always possible.

Second, we are investigating means of employing individuals at a single location who will be responsible for transcribing field records or coding forms, and converting them into machine-readable formats. Although in early discussions we worried over the amount of field-recording time that would be necessary to implement SARG, it became obvious that the cost of spending time at sites was a minor component; getting to the site was a major factor. At the same time, our greatest problem in creating the data base was in generating the machine-readable record itself. By centralizing this operation, we will realize not only the economies of scale that result when a few individuals specifically trained for a particular task are doing it, but also the possibilities of identifying means of achieving standardization and comparability of variable definitions in ways that we are not currently envisioning.

EVALUATION

SARG represents a unique effort to assemble a large data base collected by different investigators as a part of research projects undertaken for a diversity of reasons in culturally and naturally disparate settings. Eight years into the effort, only preliminary results have been obtained. Has it been worth it? I suggest that such a question must be evaluated not simply in terms of what has been learned of the questions central to the research design, but what has been learned about undertaking such research and broader empirical and methodological issues associated with it.

Certainly if no progress has been made in understanding the manner in which the natural environment affects the location of sites, the contribution of the effort would be dubious. The results obtained to date more than adequately demonstrate success in this regard, not only in the case of specific projects but panregionally (Euler and Gumerman 1978). For specific project areas, there is now understanding of which variables are more important than others. Moreover, the refinement of variables and the research design discussed throughout this chapter indicate far better understanding of the approach that must be taken if the questions are ever to be answered. None of these results would be evident without the careful attention that has been given to computer formats and the eventual use of the computer in analyzing data.

There have also been side benefits in a number of areas. First, the SARG data demonstrate that the "rancheria" pattern postulated for the Kayenta area by Jennings (1966) is, in fact, typical of the prehistoric Southwest at most times and in most places: the average habitation site has 6.5 rooms. Equally clear, there is variation from area to area and time period to time period that must be understood in the context of this overall homestead-farmstead pattern if we are to successfully interpret Southwestern prehistory. There have been other benefits in regard to our refinement of the broad patterns of Southwestern prehistory.

Second, the effort has led to a better understanding of the relationship between standardization and comparability. While the use of the computer may guarantee standardization of data recording, it does not guarantee comparability. At the same time, the exploration of how one may use standardization to attain comparability is surely preferable to assuming comparability without undertaking appropriate testing.

Third, we now have a better sense of the cost of different components of the research process. Initially, our fear was that SARG would require too great an investment in field recording time. It is now evident that getting to sites is more costly than recording data while there, and that our concern should have been over processing the information prior to computer storage.

Finally, we have learned something of the difficulties that still exist with respect to evaluating the results of investigators who use particular techniques to test hypotheses concerning prehistory. This problem became evident when two separate investigators examined the statistical results generated by SPSS. In both instances, completely different interpretations of data could be generated depending on whether the investigator (1) used the *same statistical test* for evaluating every pair of environmental and locational variables or (2) used different tests for different variable pairs, evaluating each pair using *whatever test showed the strongest relationship* between the two variables. In other words, the strength of the statistical association between any two variables varied considerably depending on which test was employed, and the magnitude and direction of variation in test results was inconsistent from one pair of variables to another. Precisely how major this problem is remains to be seen. However, the use of a standardized data format and standardized statistical analyses indicates that it may be potentially immense: tests of an hypothesis or a model by different investigators using different procedures may apear to be the same when in reality they are not, and may appear to be different when actually they are not. Through the standardization characteristic of the SARG approach this problem has become obvious.

APPENDIX 5.A: 1972 CODING FORMAT

Maximum Spaces	Attribute Names	Data for keypunching	Maximum Spaces	Attribute Names	Data for keypunching
5	SARG site number	100 _ _ _ _ _	20	Vertical distance low-site w/n 100 m	310 _____
20	Researcher's site number	110 _____	20	Vertical distance low-site w/n 1 km	320 _____
20	Researcher's name	120 _____	20	Percentage of arable land	330 _____
20	Site Type	130 _____	20	Regional plant community	340 _____
160	Structures	140 _____	20	Plant map used	350 _____
160	Features	150 _____	80	Other plant communities w/n 1 km	360 _____
160	Artifacts	160 _____	80	Other plant communities w/n 5 km	370 _____
20	Site size in square meters	170 _____	20	Average annual rainfall	380 _____
20	Date of site	180 _____	20	Drainage rank	390 _____
20	Date range of site	190 _____	20	Average drainage rank	400 _____
20	Date basis	200 _____	20	Stream classification	410 _____
50	Site location	210 _____	20	Water sources w/n 100 m	420 _____
20	Number sites w/n 1 km	220 _____	20	Water sources w/n .5 km	430 _____
20	Number habitation sites w/n 1 km	230 _____	20	Water sources w/n 1 km	440 _____
20	Number sites w/n 5 km	240 _____	20	Distance to water w/n 1 km	450 _____
20	Number habitation sites w/n 5 km	250 _____	20	Distance to water w/n 500 m	460 _____
50	Regional landform	260 _____	20	Distance to water w/n 100 m	470 _____
20	Percentage composition of slope w/n 100 m	270 _____	20	Size of project area	480 _____
20	Percentage composition of surface w/n 1 km	280 _____	320	Free text on local vegetation	900 _____
20	Vertical distance high-low w/n 100 m	290 _____	480	General free text	950 _____
20	Vertical distance high-low w/n 1 km	300 _____			

APPENDIX 5.B: REVISED COMPUTER FORMAT

Card No. 1 HEADER CARD

Col. 1-6 = SARG SITE NUMBER

In cases of multiple component sites, investigators may assign a separate SARG number and prepare a separate card set for each occupation if the individual components are judged to have substantially different SARG attributes. For example, a site consisting of a pithouse village overlain by a pueblo should be assigned two SARG numbers.

Col. 7 = 1 (Abbreviation for HEADER CARD)

Col. 8-10 = Reserved for investigator's initials. If only 2 initials, right justify. A listing of investigators' names will be published periodically along with their SARG SITE NUMBERS.

Col. 11-17 = DATE (Submission of data deck)
FORMAT:
DAYMONTHYEAR
XXYYYZZ
e.g. 20JAN74
07MAY75

Col. 18-19 = LEAVE BLANK

Col. 20-36 = UTM site location or Latitude/Longitude site location

Column	UTM	Column	Latitude/Longitude
20-21	ZONE format: XX e.g. 11 12 13	20-27 20-21 22-23 24-27	LATITUDE Degrees format: XX Minutes format: XX Seconds format: XX.X
22	Blank		
23-29	METERS NORTH format: XXXXXXX e.g. 3500155	28-36	LONGITUDE
30	Blank	28-30	Degrees format: XXX
31-36	METERS EAST format: XXXXX e.g. 500055	31-32 33-36	Minutes format: XX Seconds format: XX.X

Col. 37-48 = DATE OF SITE (BP = BEFORE 1950 A.D.)
FORMAT: (right justify if less than 1000 B.P.)
Col. 37-40 = INITIAL DATE
Col. 41-44 = TERMINAL DATE

Col. 45-48 = PROBABLE MEDIAN DATE OF
MAIN OCCUPATION
(This is intended to reflect the investigator's
best estimate of peak of main occupation.)

Col. 49 = SOURCE OF DATE
1 = Radiocarbon
2 = Dendrochronology
3 = Archaeological Basis
4 = Other

Col. 50-54 = SIZE OF PROJECT AREA IN SQ. KM

Col. 55-80 = INVESTIGATOR'S SITE DESIGNATION

Card No. 2 *SITE DESCRIPTION CARD*

Col. 1-6 = SARG SITE NUMBER

Col. 7 = 2 (Abbreviation for SITE DESCRIPTION CARD)

Col. 8 = SITE TYPE
1 = Habitation
2 = Special use
3 = Other
4 = Unknown

Col. 9-14 = SIZE OF SITE (in sq. meters)

Col. 15 = DEGREE OF NATURAL SHELTERING
1 = Site open, not naturally sheltered
2 = Site partially open, partially sheltered
3 = Site naturally sheltered, as in a rock shelter or cave

Col. 16 = SUMMARY DESCRIPTION OF SITE (use the one code that best describes site)
1 = Surface rooms (including kivas)
2 = Surface rooms (including kivas) and pithouses (not kivas)
3 = Pithouses
4 = Structures other than surface rooms (including kivas) and pithouses
5 = Midden only
6 = Surficial artifact scatter only
7 = Water control
8 = Other

Col. 17-19 = COUNT OF ROOMS AND/OR PITHOUSES
(Use estimate if precise figures are not available)

For our purposes we are defining "artifact" as broadly as possible to include debitage and sherds as well as more finished items. In Cols. 20 and 21, use a 0 if artifacts are absent from the surface of the site; use a 1 if artifacts are present but less than 50 are estimated to be present on the surface of the site; use a 2 if between 50 and 500 artifacts are estimated to be present on the surface of the site; use a 3 if more than 500 artifacts are estimated to be present on the surface of the site; use a 4 if such artifacts are present but it is impossible to estimate even roughly from the information at hand whether their frequency falls in one of the three frequency classes just described. Leave blank only if no information is available.

Col. 20 = Ceramics

Col. 21 = Chipped stone

In Col. 22-32, use a 0 if such artifacts are absent from the surface of the site, and a 1 if they are present on the surface of the site. If no information on presence or absence, leave blank.

Col. 22 = Ground stone

Col. 23 = Bone artifacts

Col. 24 = Non-artifactual bone

Col. 25 = Shell

Col. 26 = Unworked shell

Col. 27 = Textiles

Col. 28 = Basketry

Col. 29 = Wooden artifacts

Col. 30 = Metal

Col. 31 = Glass

Col. 32 = Other

In Col. 33-80, use 00 if feature/structure does not occur at the site. If feature/stucture is present, but counts cannot be estimated, use *99*. If counts can be estimated, enter count in space provided, using numbers 1-98. The number 98 shall mean both 98 and more than 98. Leave blank only if no information is available.

Col. 33-34 = Pithouse, ordinary sized kiva

Col. 35-36 = Pithouse, great kiva

Col. 37-38 = Pithouse, habitation

Col. 39-40 = Pithouse, other function

Col. 41-42 = Pithouse, indeterminate function

Col. 43-44 = Surface room, masonry, habitation (a room is a space thought to have been roofed and more or less fully enclosed by walls)

Col. 45-46 = Surface room, masonry, storage

Col. 47-48 = Surface room, masonry, other function

Col. 49-50 = Surface room, masonry, indeterminate function

Col. 51-52 = Surface room, perishable wall material (includes adobe, jacal, slab-based walls, etc.), habitation

Col. 53-54 = Surface room, perishable wall material, storage

Col. 55-56 = Surface room, perishable wall material, other function

Col. 57-58 = Surface room, perishable wall material, indeterminate function

Col. 59-60 = Surface room, wall construction indeterminate, habitation

Col. 61-62 = Surface room, wall construction indeterminate, storage

Col. 63-64 = Surface room, wall construction indeterminate, function indeterminate or other

Col. 65-66 = Wall, any construction, not part of a room

Col. 67-68 = Ramada, windbreak, or other partial shelter

Col. 69-70 = Midden

Col. 71-72 = Surficial artifact scatter (this will probably be a characteristic of most sites)

Col. 73-74 = Outdoor hearth or firepit

Col. 75-76 = Outdoor storage cist or pit

Col. 77-78 = Outdoor roasting pit

Col. 79-80 = Courtyard

Card No. 3 *CONTINUATION OF
SITE DESCRIPTION CARD*

Col. 1-6 = SARG SITE NUMBER

Col. 7 = 3 (abbreviation for CONTINUATION OF SITE
DESCRIPTION CARD)

In Col. 8-80, use 00 if feature/structure does not occur
at the site. If feature/structure is present, but counts cannot be estimated, use 99. If counts can be estimated, enter
count in space provided, using numbers 1-98. The number
98 shall mean both 98 and more than 98. If no information,
leave blank.

Col. 8-9 = Plaza

Col. 10-11 = Ball court

Col. 12-13 = Platform mound

Col. 14-15 = Tower

Col. 16-17 = Defensive structure

Col. 18-19 = Water/soil control structure, check dam

Col. 20-21 = Water/soil control structure, terrace

Col. 22-23 = Water/soil control structure, stone alignment
transverse to slope

Col. 24-25 = Water/soil control structure, ditch or canal

Col. 26-27 = Water/soil control structure, waffle garden

Col. 28-29 = Water/soil control structure, reservoir

Col. 30-31 = Water/soil control structure, other

Col 32-33 = Water/soil control structure, character indeterminate

Col. 34-35 = Petroglyph

Col. 36-37 = Pictograph

Col. 38-39 = Bedrock mortar

Col. 40-41 = Bedrock abrading grooves

Col. 42-43 = Pecked steps in bedrock

Col. 44-45 = Water/soil control structure, stone alignment
parallel to slope

Col. 46-47 = Shrine

Col. 48-49 = Quarry

Col. 50-51 = Road/trail

Col. 52-53 = Gathering area

Col. 54-55 = Kill/butchering area

Col. 56-78 = Space for possible future additions to fea-
ture/structure list

Col. 79-80 = Other

Card No. 4 *SOCIAL ENVIRONMENT, PLANT
COMMUNITIES, AND LAND FORMS CARD*

Col. 1-6 = SARG SITE NUMBER

Col. 7 = 4 (Abbreviation for SOCIAL ENVIRONMENT, PLANT
COMMUNITIES, AND LAND FORMS CARD)

In columns 8-9 and 14-15, use 0's if values are zero; leave
blank if no information. 99 shall mean both 99% and 100%.

Col. 8-9 = PERCENT OF 1 KM RADIUS CIRCLE AROUND
SITE THAT HAS BEEN SURVEYED

Col. 10-13 = LEAVE BLANK

Col. 14-15 = PERCENT OF 5 KM RADIUS CIRCLE AROUND
SITE THAT HAS BEEN SURVEYED

Col. 16-19 = LEAVE BLANK

Col. 20-21 = PLANT COMMUNITY FOUND ON SITE (Use
one of the following codes)

    01 = Western Spruce-Fir Forest
    02 = Pine-Douglas Fir Forest
    03 = Arizona-Pine Forest
    04 = Spruce-Fir, Douglas-Fir Forest
    05 = Southwestern Spruce-Fir Forest
    06 = Juniper-Pinyon Woodland
    07 = Oak-Juniper Woodland
    08 = Great Basin Sagebrush
    09 = Blackbrush
    10 = Saltbush-Greasewood
    11 = Alpine Meadows and Barren
    12 = Grama-Galleta Steppe
    13 = Galleta-Three-Awn Shrubsteppe
    14 = Grama-Tobosa Shrubsteppe
    15 = Other
    Leave Blank if no information

Col. 22-37 = REGIONAL PLANT ENVIRONMENT (Use the
following codes)

    0 = Community does not occur within 5 km
    1 = Plant community of site (even though already
        given above)
    2 = Plant community within 1 km, but not at site
    3 = Plant community within 5 km, but not within 1 km
    Leave Blank if no information

Col. 22 = Western Spruce-Fir Forest

Col. 23 = Pine-Douglas Fir Forest

Col. 24 = Arizona-Pine Forest

Col. 25 = Spruce-Fir, Douglas-Fir Forest

Col. 26 = Southwestern Spruce-Fir Forest

Col. 27 = Juniper-Pinyon Woodland

Col. 28 = Oak-Juniper Woodland

Col. 29 = Great Basin Sagebrush

Col. 30 = Blackbrush

Col. 31 = Saltbush-Greasewood

Col. 32 = Alpine Meadows and Barren

Col. 33 = Grama-Galleta Steppe

Col. 34 = Galleta-Three-Awn Shrubsteppe

Col. 35 = Grama-Tobosa Shrubsteppe

Col. 36 = Other

Col. 37 = Unknown

Col. 38-39 = REGIONAL LAND FORM (Use one of the
codes below; leave blank if no information)

    01 = Plains (Use only if subcategory was not
        determined)
    02 = Flat plains
    03 = Smooth plains
    04 = Irregular plains, slight relief

05 = Irregular plains

06 = *Plains with hills and mountains* (Use only if subcategory was not determined)

07 = Plains with hills

08 = Plains with high hills

09 = Plains with low mountains

10 = Plains with high mountains

11 = *Open hills and mountains* (Use only if subcategory was not determined)

12 = Open low hills

13 = Open hills

14 = Open high hills

15 = Open low mountains

16 = Open high mountains

17 = *Hills and mountains* (Use only if subcategory was not determined)

18 = Hills

19 = High hills

20 = Low mountains

21 = High mountains

22 = *Tablelands* (Use only if subcategory was not determined)

23 = Tablelands with moderate relief

24 = Tablelands with considerable relief

25 = Tablelands with high relief

26 = Other

In columns 40–77, use 0's if values are zero; leave blank if no information. In columns 40–63, and 76–77, the number 99 shall mean both 99% and 100%. In columns 64–75, the number 999 shall mean both 999 meters and more than 999 meters. (Columns 40–63 may prove difficult to determine. These may be left blank at the discretion of the individual.)

Col. 40–41 = PERCENT OF LAND SURFACE WITHIN 100 M WITH SLOPE OF 1–4%

Col. 42–43 = PERCENT OF LAND SURFACE WITHIN 100 M WITH SLOPE OF 5–8%

Col. 44–45 = PERCENT OF LAND SURFACE WITHIN 100 M WITH SLOPE OF 9–12%

Col. 46–47 = PERCENT OF LAND SURFACE WITHIN 100 M WITH SLOPE OF 13–25%

Col. 48–49 = PERCENT OF LAND SURFACE WITHIN 100 M WITH SLOPE OF 26–50%

Col. 50–51 = PERCENT OF LAND SURFACE WITHIN 100 M WITH SLOPE OF MORE THAN 50%

Col. 52–53 = PERCENT OF LAND SURFACE WITHIN 1 KM WITH SLOPE OF 1–4%

Col. 54–55 = PERCENT OF LAND SURFACE WITHIN 1 KM WITH SLOPE OF 5–8%

Col. 56–57 = PERCENT OF LAND SURFACE WITHIN 1 KM WITH SLOPE OF 9–12%

Col. 58–59 = PERCENT OF LAND SURFACE WITHIN 1 KM WITH SLOPE OF 13–25%

Col. 60–61 = PERCENT OF LAND SURFACE WITHIN 1 KM WITH SLOPE OF 26–50%

Col. 62–63 = PERCENT OF LAND SURFACE WITHIN 1 KM WITH SLOPE OF MORE THAN 50%

Col. 64–66 = VERTICAL DISTANCE OF HIGHEST TO LOWEST POINT WITHIN 100 M (in meters)

Col. 67–69 = VERTICAL DISTANCE OF HIGHEST TO LOWEST POINT WITHIN 1 KM (in meters)

Col. 70–72 = VERTICAL DISTANCE OF LOWEST POINT WITHIN 100 M TO SITE ELEVATION (in meters)

Col. 73–75 = VERTICAL DISTANCE OF LOWEST POINT WITHIN 1 KM TO SITE ELEVATION (in meters)

Col. 76–77 = PERCENT OF ARABLE LAND WITHIN 1 KM RADIUS TO THE NEAREST %

Col. 78–80 = DISTANCE TO THE NEAREST EDGE OF WHERE YOU THINK THEY DID THEIR FARMING

Card No. 5 *WATER RESOURCES CARD*

Col. 1–6 = SARG SITE NUMBER

Col. 7 = 5 (Abbreviation for WATER RESOURCES CARD)

Col. 8–10 = AVERAGE ANNUAL RAINFALL (in mm)

Col. 11–12 = DRAINAGE RANK OF CLOSEST STREAM (from 1:250,000 map)

Col. 13–14 = AVERAGE DRAINAGE RANK (within 5 km radius of site)

Col. 15 = PERMANENCE OF NEAREST STREAM (Use following code)

1 = Impermanent

2 = Semi-permanent

3 = Permanent

4 = No information

Col. 16 = NEAREST PROBABLE MAIN DOMESTIC WATER SOURCE TYPE

1 = Stream or river

2 = Spring

3 = Seep

4 = Lake or pond

5 = Reservoir

6 = Ditch or canal

7 = Pothole

8 = Other

9 = Unknown

Col. 17 = PERMANENCE OF NEAREST MAIN DOMESTIC WATER SOURCE

1 = Impermanent

2 = Semi-permanent

3 = Permanent

4 = No information

Col. 18–21 = DISTANCE TO NEAREST MAIN DOMESTIC WATER SOURCE (in meters)

For Col. 22, 26, 30, 34, 38, 42, 46, and 50, use the following code:

0 = Source is not present within 1 km

1 = Source exists within 1 km and is impermanent

2 = Source exists within 1 km and is semi-permanent

3 = Source exists within 1 km and is permanent

Col. 22 = Stream or river

Col. 23–25 = Distance to stream or river (if within 1 km) in meters

Col. 26 = Spring

Col. 27-29 = Distance to spring (if within 1 km) in meters

Col. 30 = Seep

Col. 31-33 = Distance to seep (if within 1 km) in meters

Col. 34 = Lake or pond

Col. 35-37 = Distance to lake or pond (if within 1 km) in meters

Col. 38 = Reservoir

Col. 39-41 = Distance to reservoir (if within 1 km) in meters

Col. 42 = Ditch or canal

Col. 43-45 = Distance to ditch or canal (if within 1 km) in meters

Col. 46 = Pothole

Col. 47-49 = Distance to pothole (if within 1 km) in meters

Col. 50 = Other

Col. 51-53 = Distance to other sources (if within 1 km) in meters

Col. 54-56 = Nearest probable water source type for agricultural purposes
  1 = Rainfall
  2 = Wash, stream, or river
  3 = Spring
  4 = Seep
  5 = Lake or pond
  6 = Reservoir
  7 = Ditch or canal
  8 = Pothole
  9 = Other

Format:

Col. 54 = Primary source

Col. 55 = Secondary source

Col. 56 = Tertiary source

REFERENCES

Effland, R.
  1978   Applications of computer graphic techniques to SARG data. In *Investigations of the Southwestern Anthropological Research Group,* edited by R. Euler and G. Gumerman, pp. 149-167. Flagstaff: Museum of Northern Arizona.

Euler, R., and G. Gumerman, editors
  1978   *Investigations of the Southwestern Anthropological Research Group.* Flagstaff: Museum of Northern Arizona.

Gaines, S.
  1978   Computer applications of SARG data: An evaluation. In *Investigations of the Southwestern Anthropological Research Group,* edited by R. Euler and G. Gumerman, pp. 119-138. Flagstaff: Museum of Northern Arizona.

Green, D.
  1972   The computer code format. In Proceedings of the Second Annual Meeting of the Southwestern Anthropological Research Group, edited by G. Gumerman, pp. 21-24. *Prescott College Anthropological Reports* 3.

Gumerman, G., editor
  1971   The distribution of prehistoric population aggregates. *Prescott College Anthropological Reports* 1.

Jennings, J.
  1966   Glen Canyon: A summary. *University of Utah Anthropological Papers* 81.

Nie, N. H., C. H. Hull, J. G. Jenkins, K. Steinbrenner, and D. H. Bent
  1975   *Statistical Package for the Social Sciences,* 2nd edition. New York: McGraw-Hill.

Plog, F., and J. Hill
  1971   Explaining variability in the distribution of sites. In The distribution of prehistoric population aggregates, edited by G. Gumerman, pp. 7-36. *Prescott College Anthropological Reports* 1.
  1972   The Southwestern Anthropological Research Group: Revision of the research design. In Proceedings of the Second Annual Meeting of the Southwestern Anthropological Research Group, edited by G. Gumerman, pp. 7-20. *Prescott College Anthropological Reports* 3.

Strahler, A.
  1964   Quantitative geomorphology of drainage basins and channel networks. In *Handbook of Applied Hydrology,* edited by V. Chow, pp. 4.39-4.76. New York: McGraw-Hill.

Sullivan, A., and M. Schiffer
  1978   A critical examination of SARG. In *Investigations of the Southwestern Anthropological Research Group,* edited by R. Euler and G. Gumerman, pp. 168-178. Flagstaff: Museum of Northern Arizona.

Woldenberg, M. J.
  1967   Concepts and applications—spatial order. Geography and the properties of surfaces series. *Harvard Papers in Theoretical Geography* 1: 95-189. Cambridge: Harvard University Press.

6. The ORACLE Computerized Information Retrieval System

W. Fredrick Limp
Arkansas Archeological Survey

Thomas Genn Cook
Indiana University and Northwestern University

ARCHAEOLOGICAL BACKGROUND

In the mid 1970s two divergent pressures have appeared requiring both rapid and extensive analysis of archaeological site survey records. One pressure involves the increasing emphasis on research questions dealing with sites in relationship to various biophysical features. The second pressure results from cultural resource management and its concern with site presence or absence and site "significance."

The first pressure is generated by simultaneous interest in intensive regional-oriented studies and an increasing re-emphasis on the fundamental importance of space-time systematics. Concern with prehistoric regional trade, for example, makes knowledge of the spatial distribution of "exotic" raw materials of great interest (Struever and Houart 1972, Seeman 1977). Concern with the differential utilization of major resource zones necessitates rapid and intensive access to the distribution of site and activity locations.

The second area of pressure is generated by the increasing demands of cultural resource management. Extensive construction activities in many areas and the concomitant, often overwhelming, need to both rapidly and accurately assess the significance of a great number of impacted archaeological sites have also increased the need for methods to process these large and ever-expanding data sets. Response to these pressures by many institutions has been the adoption of computerized information retrieval systems for archaeological survey data.

In 1975 it was determined that the survey records of the Glenn Black Laboratory of Archaeology at Indi-

ana University should be computerized. After examining available systems in use, it became clear that, although they were all excellent systems, they were not specifically designed to deal with the unique data set and interrelationships within the data set that characterize an archaeological survey. Because they were general systems, they could serve all masters, but none truly well. In our view, a system designed from the ground up for archaeological data and archaeological questions was the most desirable. With this in mind the ORACLE project was initiated.

The naiveté of this decision became clear only after many years of intensive effort. Though not without its grim moments, the ORACLE system was successfully designed, programmed, and brought on-line in 1977. The implementation has been a joint effort of the Department of Computer Science and the Glenn Black Laboratory of Archaeology. By 1979 the ORACLE system contained a 4000 site data base and served both research and cultural resource management applications.

This chapter describes the basic structure of the system, illustrates its general use, and considers its impact on a number of research and cultural resource management projects. Finally, a number of potential improvements to the system are proposed.

SYSTEM DESIGN AND IMPLEMENTATION

It was clear from the beginning that the development of an effective computerized information retrieval system was *not* a computer problem; rather it was, essentially, a human problem. As Scholtz and

Chenhall (1976) so cogently pointed out, effective design of a computerized information retrieval system must follow a thorough consideration of the nature of the data to be encoded, the types of questions to be addressed, and the requirements of the potential user. In the design of the ORACLE system, therefore, primary importance was given to the nature of the archaeological data, to the archaeological questions which would be directed to the data, and, perhaps most important, to the archaeologists who would use the system.

It was determined that: (1) the full range of biophysical variables that could be used to characterize a site should be encoded; (2) detailed artifactual data should be entered in a flexible but comprehensive data entry and classification structure; and, (3) no computer programming knowledge should be required to use the system.

Data Selection

There are 46 different kinds of basic information encoded for each site. Table 6.1 lists the site data. The selection of the data to be encoded was based on an evaluation of the research goals that archaeological surveys might be expected to meet in the absence of a computerized retrieval system (cf. Ruppé 1966, Hole and Heizer 1973, Redman 1973, Binford 1964, Judge 1973). In other words, utilization of a computer-based system *per se* should not impact the type of

TABLE 6.1
ORACLE Site Data and Retrieval Keywords

Site Data	Description	ORACLE Retrieval Keyword	Site Data	Description	ORACLE Retrieval Keyword
Site	County code and site number (e.g., D 19)	SITE	Dis	The distance, in meters, from the site to the nearby water source	DIST
Other Nos.	Other site numbers	OTHN			
Site Name	Site Name	SNAM	Size	Site size, in units of 100 square feet	SIZE
Date Rept.	Date site first reported	DATR			
Owner	Site owner's name	ONAM	Elev	Elevation of site in feet ASL	ELEV
R. R. Street	Owner's street address	OADD	Soil 1	The soil directly underlying the site, based on USDA Soil Map codes AY-50	SIL1
City State	Owner's city and state address	OCTY			
Tenant	Tenant's name	TNAM			
R. R. Street (tenant)	Tenant's street address	TADD	Soil 2	The major soil, by area, within a 2000 m radius around the site	SIL2
City State (tenant)	Tenant's city and state address	TCTY	Soil 3	The second soil, by area, within a 2000 m radius around the site	SIL3
County	County where site is located	CNTY			
Cong. Loc.	Congressional location: township, range, and section	LOCA	Physio. Zone	The topographic feature and physiographic zone	ZONE
UTMN	Universal Transverse Mercator North Value	UTMN	Cultural Affil.	Cultural affiliation(s) of the site	CULT
			Habit. Type	Character of site (i.e., village, rock shelter, etc.)	HABT
UTME	Universal Transverse Mercator East Value	UTME			
Major Watershed	One of 25 defined watershed rivers in the state	BASN	Surface Materials	Overview of artifact classes recovered from site	SURF
			Map Quadrangle	U.S.G.S. quad map title	QMAP
Nearby water	The name, if any, of the nearest water source	WNAM	Recomd	Excavation, National Register, etc., recommendations	RECM
Body code	The code indicating the nature of the nearby water (i.e., stream, lake, spring, etc.)	BODY	Fut 3	For future use	FUT3
			Veg 1	Presettlement vegetation in the immediate area of the site	VEG1
Class code	The code indicating the size of the nearby water source	CLAS	Veg 2	Major presettlement vegetation, by area, in a 2000 m radius around site	VEG2
Intr. code	The code indicating the presence (or absence) of an intersecting stream and its size	INTR			
			Veg 3	Secondary presettlement vegetation, by area, in a 2000 m radius around site	VEG3
Dirc	The direction from the site to the nearby water source	DIRC			

data encoded. Conceptually it is our view that a computer based system should be considered as a device to increase the speed of access to information, not to alter its character.

Binford (1964) stressed the interrelationships between the results of an archaeological survey and the either implicit or explicit theoretical orientation of the investigator. When considering the development of a computerized retrieval system, however, the designers must be aware that the system may serve many researchers with differing theoretical concerns. An intentional "tilt" toward one paradigm would reduce the usefulness of the system. The ORACLE system approach, insofar as possible, has been to organize both the data base and the retrieval structures so as not to exclude research orientations based on alternative theoretical frameworks.

One of the primary concerns in the design of the ORACLE system was the need for data encoding structures that would allow the entry and manipulation of detailed information about the biophysical characteristics of each site. It was clear that an encoding system could be designed to either encompass only broad characteristics or to include extensive detail about each individual biophysical variable. Excessive subdivisions create considerable encoding effort and add to the system's cost while insufficient detail causes important factors to be obscured. The approach used in the ORACLE structure is based on Cowgill's (1975: 262) conclusion that effective, but not unlimited, variable stratification can be developed by "intelligent use of prior information or hypotheses." As an example of the level of detail used in the ORACLE system, Table 6.2 provides a partial list of the topographic features recognized by the system. Along with the variable stratification, biophysical data was hierarchically structured with broad classifications subdivided into units containing increasing detail. This structure allows, for example, a search for all sites on "terrace features," regardless of the specific terrace or whether the area is a terrace margin or terrace flat. Detailed definitions of the topographic variables, along with maps and cross-sectional views allowing the encoder to determine which feature is involved, are found in Limp (1978a). Other encoded biophysical variables also have comparable structures and encoding details.

For each site there can be from 0 to 99 survey records. These surveys can be considered separately, survey by survey, or grouped. In this way some of the problems of differing survey qualities can be controlled. For each survey the date, surveyor's name, affiliation, accession numbers, photo record, nature of pick-up, surface conditions, and the artifacts recovered are encoded.

A substantial portion of the data is entered in numerically coded formats. For example, a site on a second terrace margin would have the code "102" entered in the topographic zone data entry field. This approach contrasts with systems oriented to the entry of character strings or literal terms such as the word TERRACE. The decision to use codes was a difficult one, made only after a detailed consideration of the implication of the alternatives. Entry of a character string often makes data entry straight-forward and allows entries to be sight proofed, while a numeric code necessitates use of a code book to check the proper entry. However, character string entry has the potential for substantial variation in the term entered with "projectile point," "points," and "proj pts" all referring to the same object. A search of a data base in which all these variants might be present would be a costly

TABLE 6.2
Topographic Codes Currently Used in the ORACLE System

Feature	Numeric Input Code	Output Code
Natural Levee	010	LEVEE
Floodplain Ridge	040	FLDPLAIN RIDGE
Floodplain Flats	060	FLOODPLAIN
Riverbank/Buried	061	BURIED BANK
Terrace Remnant on Floodplain	045	TERRACE REMNT
T–1 Margin	101	T-1 MARGIN
T–1 Flats	111	T-1 FLATS
T–2 Margin	102	T-2 MARGIN
T–2 Flats	112	T-2 FLATS
T–3 Margins	103	T-3 MARGINS
T–3 Flats	113	T-3 FLATS
Ohio Lacustrine Plain	620	LACUSTRINE
Dune on Terrace	170	TERRACE DUNE
Talus	210	TALUS
Hillside	230	HILLSIDE
Bluff Base	200	BLUFF BASE
Low Terminal Ridge Spur	220	LOW SPUR
Top of Bluff "Linear"	510	BLUFF TOP
Bluff Top, Head of Gully	530	GULLY TOP
Bluff Top, Ridge Spur	500	SPUR BLUFF
Upland Flats	300	UPLAND FLATS
Watershed Knob	320	KNOB
Watershed Ridge Crest	340	CREST
Watershed Saddle	330	SADDLE
Esker	440	ESKER-KAME
Kame (same code)	440	ESKER-KAME
Moraine Slope	420	MORAINE SLOPE
Moraine Crest	430	MORAINE CREST
Intermorainal Swale	400	MORAINE SWALE
Upland Remnant "on" Terrace	150	UPPER REMNT
Upland Remnant "on" T–1	151	REMNT ON 1
Upland Remnant "on" T–2	152	REMNT ON 2
Upland Remnant "on" T–3	153	REMNT ON 3

procedure. Reliance on numeric codes, in contrast, makes data screening and searching more efficient since the acceptable codes are known prior to the data entry and can be checked against a computer-based dictionary. It is reasonable (but onerous), therefore, to require the "one time" entry of data via numeric codes. Future searches and analyses of the data base, however, should not be based on these same numeric codes since they are not easily remembered. A search of the data base is initiated by entry of a string such as TERRACE; the system then refers to a series of input dictionaries to determine first, if TERRACE is acceptable. If acceptable, the entry is translated into the appropriate numeric code for the internal search process.

Structure of Artifactual Data

Artifact classification and encoding are two of the most difficult areas to deal with in a computerized retrieval system, in part due to the conflicting views of the nature, intent, and effect of artifact typologies and classifications (Spaulding 1960, Ford 1954, Dunnell 1971). Whatever approach is used must be explicit and not a "cryptoclassification" (Spaulding 1974: 515). The ORACLE artifact encoding uses a data structure that can be described as a cross-linked hierarchy. Figure 6.1 illustrates this structure schematically.

There are three modes of accession into this structure: (1) vertical accession, (2) lateral accession, and (3) toggeled accession. In vertical accession the user might ask for all ground stone celts that are polled, or all chipped stone end scrapers made from Harrison County chert. In lateral accession the user might ask for all celts *regardless* of whether they are chipped or ground stone. Alternatively, all items manufactured from Harrison County chert might be accessed. Toggeled access links vertical and lateral with a search for all chipped stone objects made from Harrison County chert regardless of whether they are celts, knives, or scrapers. For projectile points this structure allows both "splitters" and "lumpers" to access the data at whatever level of definition they desire.

As an illustration we can consider the following group of commonly occurring late paleo-Indian projectile points: Dalton (Chapman 1948), Meserve (Bell and Hall 1953), Greenbrier and Hardaway (Cambron and Hulse 1964). These points are morphologically similar and appear to come from contemporaneous deposits. Alternatively, there are often notable differences in their specific appearance, such as degree of resharpening.

Within the ORACLE system's hierarchical structure, a series of point clusters are defined. In our example these points are all within the Dalton cluster. A lumper may search for sites with Dalton cluster points. Sites with *either* a Dalton *or* a Meserve *or* a Greenbrier, *or* a

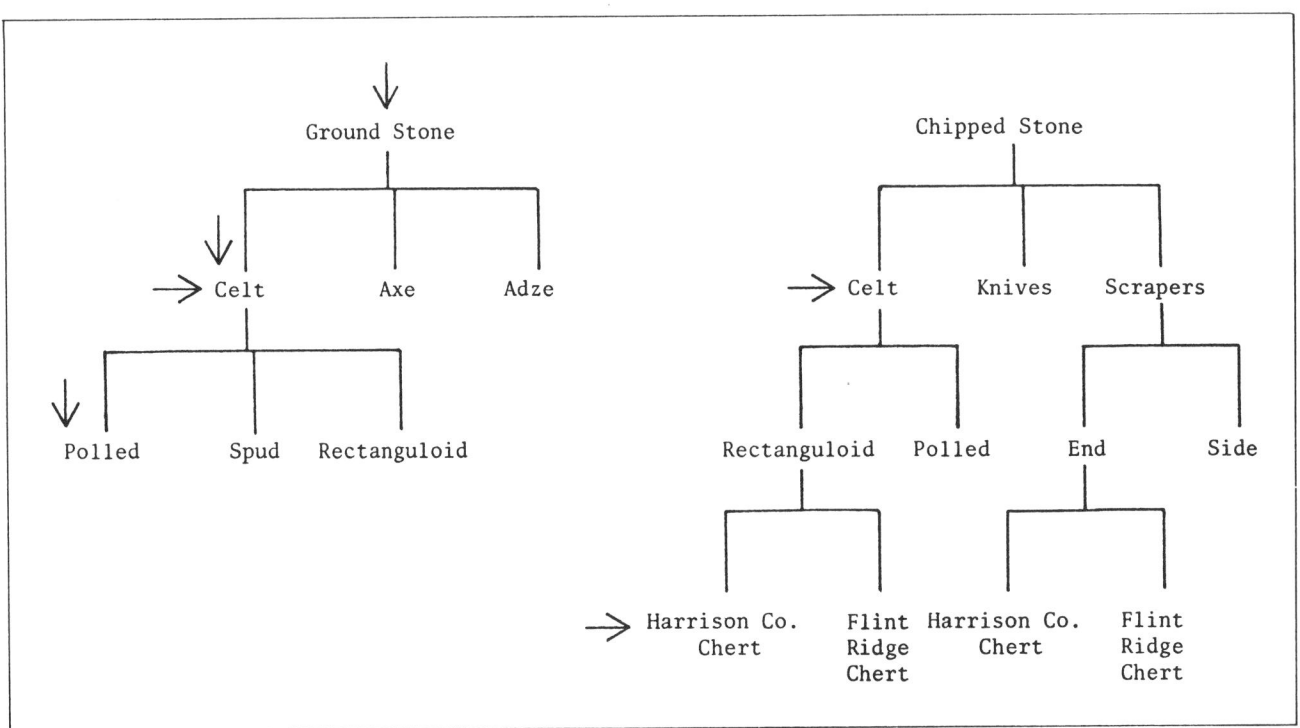

Fig. 6.1. ORACLE cross-linked hierarchy for artifact classifications.

Hardaway named type will be found. A splitter may, in contrast, search for only Meserve named type points. The classification structure is flexible and allows new artifact types to be entered and old ones changed. A comparative collection of the ORACLE artifact and raw material classes has been developed to standardize the identification and encoding process.

While the development of programs to implement the features discussed here has created an effective and useful data processing framework, the final evaluation of a retrieval system is based on whether it helps the *user*. From the beginning, the ORACLE procedure was designed as a user-oriented system.

User Access

Current developments in computer programming are rapidly moving toward natural language structures. In this framework the potential computer user is required to learn only a limited number of commands in order to use the system. The ORACLE system follows this lead and uses a limited series of easy-to-learn commands. Only a few of these ORACLE language features are presented here (see Limp 1978b for details).

After the user has obtained access to the system, dialogue is initiated to determine which (if any) of a number of various system operating modes are desired. These modes include master/private file structures, interactive query-interactive data processing, interactive query-batch processing, mini file creation, an SPSS interface, and other options. Selection of these optional states is effected by a series of yes/no answers or brief answers to a series of system questions. The answer to the first question causes specific alternatives to be presented in the second and so on.

After the optional basic system modes are selected the next stage of processing is the QUERY SYSTEM. In this stage the data report format, survey integration, and data base search criteria are determined. Figure 6.2 illustrates one ORACLE session. In this session the user selected the DEFAULT option for the operation mode that is structured interactively, using the master data file, with results outputted to a terminal. After the operating mode has been selected, the system moves to QUERY processing.

Figure 6.2 illustrates one QUERY BLOCK. Up to 30 QUERY BLOCKS are possible with each block producing an independent search through the data base. In each QUERY BLOCK the user indicates whether or not the 0-99 surveys for each site are to be searched as independent units or grouped prior to the search. The response to the system inquiry: TYPE REPORT MODE (ALL, SITE, SURVEY, NUMBER, VLIST) indicates the format in which the data are to be printed. Report Mode ALL, causes all variable data about sites meeting the search criteria to be printed; in SITE

mode, only the site data fields are reported while in SURVEY mode, only the survey data fields are listed. In NUMBER mode, only the trinomial number, (e.g., 12-Sp-137) for the selected site is printed. In VLIST mode, only selected variables are listed. Figure 6.2 displays a portion of the site and survey information as printed by the ORACLE system under the Report Mode ALL.

After entry of the Report Mode the actual search criteria are entered. The six logical operators used to develop search criteria are: MORE, LESS, SPAN, ANY, ALL, and NONE. These six operators are used with a FIELD KEYWORD and one or more TARGET(S). The FIELD KEYWORDS are the four letter field identifiers shown in the far right column of Table 6.1. The keyword DIST, for example, is the keyword for "distance to nearest water source, in meters." The criteria LESS DIST 100 would be used to search for sites located less than 100 meters from the nearest water source. SPAN DIST 100, 1000 would be used to search for sites between 100 and 1000 meters from the nearest water supply.

The operators ANY, ALL, and NONE use non-numeric matching targets. The system compares the target value of a character string to the values recorded for each site. The FIELD KEYWORD, WNAM, for example, is used for the name (if any) of the nearby water source. The search criteria ANY WNAM BLUE R, GREEN R, WHITE R would be used to search for site records with either "Blue" or "Green" or "White" rivers as the water name data field; any of these possibilities would be satisfactory. The FIELD KEYWORD CULT is the identifier for the cultural affiliation field. In this complex field up to 120 different affiliations, in 20 major classes, can be entered. The criteria ANY CULT (P, EA, MA) would locate sites with *either* paleo-Indian (P) or Early Archaic (EA) or Middle Archaic (MA) affiliations present. Use of the keyword ALL as in ALL CULT (P, EA, MA) would be used to search for sites with paleo-Indian (P) *and* Early Archaic (EA) *and* Middle Archaic (MA) affiliations. In other words, *all* of these targets must be satisfied. The operator NONE is just the logical negation of ANY.

The criteria block shown in Figure 6.2 was used to search for sites located on Wildcat Creek, North Fork, more than 100 units in surface area (a unit equals 100 square feet), below 575 feet ASL in elevation, and within a one square km area with limits at the UTM (Universal Transverse Mercator) coordinates of North 4,476,000 m to 4,477,000 m and East 517,000 m to 518,000 m.

Typing the word HALT indicates that the entire query session is completed. If END is typed, a second query block, BLOCK 2, would be created. When HALT is entered the data base is searched.

For comparison with the Figure 6.2 DEFAULT session, a nondefault session is shown in Figure 6.3. Instead of the standard DEFAULT options, the user wished to process a previously created private mini file identical in structure to the MASTER data file but comprising only a subset of the data. The mini file is created from the MASTER and allows a substantial improvement in processing time when repeated queries are submitted to a definable subset of the large MASTER file.

Statistical analysis of the data base is made possible in the ORACLE ARCSTAT-SPSS operating mode. In ARCSTAT-SPSS the ORACLE system produces an SPSS data file and an SPSS data definition file (Nie, Bent, and Hull 1970). In the first QUERY of the session the user indicates the variables desired in the SPSS

```
/-oracle

ENTER THE ORACLE SYSTEM PASSWORD (3 ATTEMPTS)
?


            GLENN BLACK LABORATORY OF ARCHAEOLOGY
                    INDIANA UNIVERSITY
        THE ORACLE INFORMATION RETRIEVAL DATA BASE SYSTEM


FOR JOB DEFAULT HIT CARRIAGE-RETURN, ELSE TYPE: STEP


        #### THE QUERY SYSTEM ####


QUERY BLOCK  1
TYPE SEARCH MODE (ALLSURV,SINGSURV)
?allsurv
TYPE REPORT MODE (ALL,SITE,SURVEY,NUMBER,VLIST)
? all
ENTER CRITERIA OF QUERY BLOCK, USE + FOR CONTINUATION
? any wnam wildcat cn
? less elev 575
? more size 100
? span utmn 4476000, 4477000
? span utme 517000, 518000
? halt


YOUR OUTPUT IS APPROXIMATELY   7 PAGE(S) LONG
IF WANT OUTPUT TO TERMINAL, HIT CARRIAGE-RETURN, ELSE TYPE: SAVE
?



----------------NEW QUERY BLOCK-----------------------------


1QUERY FILE    SITE
  ANY WNAM WILDCAT CN
  LESS ELEV 575
  MORE SIZE 100
  SPAN UTMN 4476000, 4477000
  SPAN UTME 517000, 518000
                -------------------


                        SITE   T  0076

    OTHER NUMS:                SITE NAME :
    DATE REPRT: 1976/03/26     DATE L SUR:  1976/03/26
    NUM SURVYS:           1    OWNER NAME:  BROWN DALE
    OWNER ADDR: 5901 E200N           CITY STATE:  LAFAYETTE IN
```

Fig. 6.2. ORACLE session using DEFAULT mode. The user entries are in lower case, computer responses in upper case.

run by entering their FIELD KEYWORDS. In the session shown in Figure 6.3, variables such as the name of the nearest water source (WNAM), the topographic zone (ZONE), and the cultural affiliations (CULT) are used. In addition, the total number of various artifact classes is also requested. Each entry of the keyword TYPE creates an independent accumulator, so that the entry TYPE (HC) gives the total number of items at the site made from Harrison County chert. The entry TYPE (PP) causes the printing of the total number of projectile points at sites meeting the search criteria, while TYPE (CS) yields the total number of chipped stone items. The accumulators are independent, so a projec-

tile point made from Harrison County chert increments both the TYPE (PP) and TYPE (HC) accumulators.

In addition to the SPSS data file, the system automatically produces an SPSS data definition file. The user then needs to enter only the statistical TASK DEFINITION cards in the data definition file and, via a system utility, the SPSS analysis is initiated.

The major features of the ORACLE system as described above illustrate the design philosophy of the ORACLE project; the system *must* be by and for *archaeologists,* not computer scientists. As a result, the analytical framework, logical operations, data encoding, and search methods have exact and meaningful

```
              GLENN BLACK LABORATORY OF ARCHAEOLOGY
                      INDIANA UNIVERSITY
            THE ORACLE INFORMATION RETRIEVAL DATA BASE SYSTEM

     FOR JOB DEFAULT HIT CARRIAGE-RETURN, ELSE TYPE: STEP
   ? step
     USING MASTER DATA FILE: (YES,-CR-(=NO))
   ?
     ENTER YOUR PRIVATE FILE NAME
   ? new2
     USING ARCSTAT-SPSS: (YES,-CR-(=NO))
   ? yes
     ENTER A 1 DIGIT JOB SEQUENCE NUMBER (1-9)
   ? 2
     TYPE YOUR INITIALS,ACCNT-NUM,PASSWORD
     EXAMPLE:   XXX,9999,EXAMP
   ? abc,1234,password
     TYPE FILE NAME FOR SPSS DATA FILE (MAX 7 CHAR)
   ? spdata
     TYPE FILE NAME FOR SPSS DATA-DEFINITION CARDS
    ? spdef


          #### THE QUERY SYSTEM ####
          ( THIS IS A SPSS-QUERY JOB)


     QUERY BLOCK  1
     TYPE SEARCH MODE (ALLSURV,SINGSURV)
   ? allsurv
     ENTER VARIABLES IN VLIST EX: SVOR,WNAM,TYPE(/CLO,DEB),CULT,HALT
   ? wnam,clas,intr,dist,zone,cult,surf,type(pp),type(ds),
   ? type(cs),type(pp,/clo,clo,hc),type(cs,scr,end),type(hc),halt
     ENTER CRITERIA OF QUERY BLOCK, USE + FOR CONTINUATION
   ? any zone 04*, 06*
   ? end


     QUERY BLOCK  2
     TYPE SEARCH MODE (ALLSURV,SINGSURV)
   ? allsurv
     ENTER CRITERIA OF QUERY BLOCK, USE + FOR CONTINUATION
   ? any zone 111,112,200
   ? halt
     TYPE: SUBMIT,SPSSGO,B   TO COMPLETE SETUP
   /submit,spssdo,b
    16.09.38.WFLSCNP
   /1j
   WFLSCNP INPUT (2402)
```

Fig. 6.3. ORACLE session illustrating PRIVATE FILES and ARCSTAT-SPSS operating modes.

archaeological correlates. The system, in short, is designed to fit the data and the needs of its users.

ORACLE AND ARCHAEOLOGY

Any assessment of a computer information retrieval system must be made by the users of the system as they address significant problems. Assessments cannot be based on measures of computational efficiency or other comparable program or hardware factors. This is not to say that such factors are unimportant, far from it; rather it is to focus again on the user as the final judge.

The ORACLE system has been utilized in a number of recent and ongoing research and cultural resource management efforts. Four of these are reviewed briefly, and they illustrate the flexibility, ease of use, and extensive data base that are provided by the ORACLE system.

The Little Indian Creek Intensive Survey

The Little Indian Creek intensive survey is an investigation of 27 square km in the heavily dissected watershed of Little Indian Creek located in Monroe County, Indiana. The survey began in 1973 and is directed by Patrick and Cheryl Munson, in conjunction with the Glenn A. Black Laboratory of Archaeology, Indiana University. Because upland areas of the midwest are often forested or in heavy ground cover such as pasture, conventional archaeological surveys can present a severely biased sample of the prehistoric record because only a small fraction of the area is exposed in plowed fields. While extensive shovel testing can be conducted in such areas, high cost and small exposures are major limiting factors. Throughout the course of a multi-year survey, however, many normally unplowed areas will be subjected to plowing. By 1979, ten percent of the total area (2.7 square km) had been examined and 100 archaeological sites had been documented. Paralleling our concern with documenting the cultural history of this area, emphasis has been placed on assessing the methodological questions dealing with the character of an effective archaeological survey. The cultural affiliation assigned to each site as well as the overall settlement pattern undergo substantial alteration as increased information is gathered about each occupational locus. During the survey, sites have been repeatedly resurveyed, some up to ten times.

The ongoing work involves the ORACLE system at a number of levels. At the most fundamental level the system allows rapid access to the basic site information. More significant, however, are evaluations of correlations between locational variables and differential utilization of the area by different cultural groups. The capability of ORACLE to isolate artifactual data by survey will be utilized to conduct measurements of survey intensity necessary to develop an accurate picture of the sites and culture history in the area, addressing questions such as: (1) are single surveys appropriate in some locations but not in others, and (2) can the results of the surveys be utilized to estimate the survey intensity necessary in any given environment?

To investigate the character of the bias inherent in a typical six week survey, the ORACLE files will be screened by survey date and an evaluation will be made of the culture history and settlement pattern that would result from an investigation of this limited duration.

Resource Utilization and Location Choice

Another use of the ORACLE system involved a project concerned with prehistoric site selection. In the Grandview-Rockport locality of the Ohio River Valley in Indiana, Limp intensively investigated the characteristics of resource distribution and location choice. The area encompassed some 220 square km and was gridded into more than 21,000 alternative locales, each a hexagonal unit with a radius of 100 m. Every unit was scored for 13 location properties such as distance to water, slope, and soil permeability. Using a location choice model derived from axiomatic choice theory, Limp developed computer programs that processed the resulting 330,000 observations and generated "predictions" of specific locales that would be occupied under alternative location choice strategies. The ORACLE system was utilized to determine if any of the 136 sites in the area were found at the predicted locales.

The investigation demonstrated that predicted resource distribution varied with the spatial extent of the resource. If, for example, a significant resource or set of resources were located at a large number of locales, then any particular location had a low unit predictability. In the study area important nut resources such as hickory and acorn were very common and, as a result, prediction of nutting activity locations was diffuse. In contrast, some resource sets were spatially restricted and sites/activity locations involving these resource sets had a high predictability.

This example of the use of the system illustrates the benefits of the ORACLE structured data and formatting options. Since input and output characteristics of the system were defined, it was possible to develop interface software that integrated user programs with ORACLE.

Ohio River Valley Cultural Resource Inventory

As part of a developing master plan for cultural resources in the Ohio River Valley, the Army Corps of Engineers contracted with the Glenn A. Black Laboratory of Archaeology to inventory the known cultural resources of the Ohio River floodplain in Indiana. As a result, more than 1000 prehistoric archaeological sites were entered into the ORACLE data files and inventoried (Munson, Limp, and Barton, 1977). The ORACLE system was utilized to develop listings of the sites by various search criteria such as cultural affiliation, river mile, and distance to the river. A graphics package, ARCMAPPER, prepared detailed site distribution maps for the entire river course using the ORACLE UTM data as input. The ORACLE data files created during this project are now available for more intensive query when future construction activities are proposed in any portion of the valley.

Archaic Settlement Patterns in the Central Indiana Uplands

The ORACLE data base and processing capabilities are being used increasingly for academic research. One example is a settlement pattern study by John Richardson, a graduate student at Indiana University. The data base for the study area comprised 1000 prehistoric sites in four counties near Bloomington, Indiana. A number of ORACLE applications were used in the course of the investigation.

1. Analysis of topographic data stored in the ORACLE system demonstrated the comparability of two drainages in the study area.

2. Distance from sites to seasonally abundant resources were analyzed and evaluated within a framework of economic geography models.

3. Artifact information in the ORACLE data base provided the means for evaluating site distributions in terms of tool clusters and resource seasonality.

4. An evaluation of spatial relationships between tools and debitage was performed.

5. Richardson developed a graphics package to interface with ORACLE.

EVALUATION AND RECOMMENDATIONS FOR FUTURE ENHANCEMENTS

As archaeologists become more familiar with computer based studies, the earlier ready acceptance of conclusions drawn from computerized analysis, *simply* because they were computerized, is being replaced by a more selective appreciation of the multi-faceted nature of such analysis. Concurrently, the proclivity by some, to totally reject such studies, also is being re-placed by a more sophisticated understanding of what can and cannot be expected.

If we recognize the strengths and weaknesses of a computer assisted analysis, then easily and rapidly formulated propositions, illustrated in the above examples, can serve as important intermediate steps to more firmly based conclusions that follow one another in a series of successive approximations. Weaknesses in the initial proposition can be identified, rectified, and a new level of analysis performed.

We have not considered a number of problems that can beset such a system—problems generally of quality control. How does one insure the reliability of the cultural affiliation assignments or the artifact identifications? Such questions are critically important. For the ORACLE system considerable effort was expended to carefully define and delimit the nature of the encoded information (Limp 1978a, 1978b, 1978c).

The integrity of the data base must be assured by explicit, detailed, updated options. Access to permanent data transformations in the master data base must be strictly limited. Data base reliability, reproducibility of the encoding procedures, and a wide range of other factors must be anticipated and structures developed to regularize their operation.

Although there have been three versions of the ORACLE system, there remain areas where substantial improvement is possible. In general, enhancements would include: (1) development of a random or virtual access data structure to augment the current sequential search structures, (2) addition of between-criteria logical operators, (3) improvement in the entry of curation information, and (4) expanded data fields for survey condition information.

Of more practical interest would be the development of a machine-independent version of ORACLE. The current version includes a number of elements that are Control Data Corporation (CDC) machine dependent. In particular the structure of the CDC 60 bit word is utilized extensively.

SUMMARY

This chapter has described the ORACLE computerized information retrieval system developed at the Glenn A. Black Laboratory of Archaeology. Particular attention has been given to the characteristics of the artifacts and biophysical variable encoding and the natural language structure of the query system. In 1979 the ORACLE system had approximately 4000 archaeological sites in the master data base.

Applications involving the ORACLE system have included a cultural resource management inventory of all prehistoric archaeological sites in the Ohio River floodplain in Indiana; a study of Archaic settlement patterning in a heavily dissected upland area; an investigation of prehistoric area location choice and resource distribution in the Grandview-Rockport locality; and an assessment of the impact of an intensive six year survey of a limited small stream drainage basin.

Rapid access to these large data sets makes it feasible to evaluate archaeological questions on a broad scale in ways totally impossible in the absence of an effective retrieval system. The specific projects discussed in this chapter indicate the important role access can have on the formulation and testing of multi-stage investigations. The ORACLE system provides a means for eliminating nonviable alternatives, for synthesizing massive data sets, and for producing general patterns that lead the archaeologist to further research. In the final analysis, however, the test of any system is how well it serves its designed purpose. Although this can only be evaluated in time, the ORACLE system has effectively served a number of research and cultural resource management projects.

REFERENCES

Bell, R., and R. Hall
1953   Selected projectile point types of the United States. *Bulletin of the Oklahoma Anthropological Society* 1: 1–16.

Binford, Lewis
1964   A consideration of archaeological research design. *American Antiquity* 29: 425–441.

Cambron, James, and David Hulse
1964   *Handbook of Alabama Archaeology, Part I: Point Types.* Birmingham: University of Alabama Press.

Chapman, Carl
1948   A preliminary survey of Missouri archaeology, Part IV. *The Missouri Archaeologist* 10(4): 135–164.

Cowgill, George
1975   A selection of samplers: comments on archaeostatistics. In *Sampling in Archaeology,* edited by J. Mueller. Tucson: University of Arizona Press.

Dunnell, R. C.
1971   *Systematics in Prehistory.* New York: Free Press.

Ford, James
1954   On the concept of types. *American Antiquity* 56: 42–54.

Hole, Frank, and R. F. Heizer
1973   *An Introduction to Prehistoric Archaeology,* 3rd ed. New York: Holt, Reinhart, and Winston.

Judge, James
1973   *Paleoindian Occupation of the Central Rio Grande Valley in New Mexico.* Albuquerque: University of New Mexico Press.

Limp, W. Fredrick
1978a   The ORACLE System Survey Manual. *Research Report* 3, Glenn Black Laboratory of Archaeology.
1978b   The ORACLE System User's Manual. *Research Report* 2, Glenn Black Laboratory of Archaeology.
1978c   The ORACLE System Preliminary Artifact Encoding Guide. *Research Report* 4, Glenn Black Laboratory of Archaeology.

Munson, Cheryl, W. F. Limp, and D. Barton
1977   *Cultural Resources of the Ohio River in Indiana.* Huntington: U.S. Army Corps of Engineers.

Nie, Norman, D. Bent, and C. H. Hull
1970   *Statistical Package for the Social Sciences.* New York: McGraw Hill.

Redman, Charles
1973   Multistage fieldwork and analytical techniques. *American Antiquity* 38: 61–79.

Ruppé, Reynold
1966   The archaeological survey: a defense. *American Antiquity* 31: 313–333.

Scholtz, Sandra, and R. Chenhall
1976   Archaeological data banks in theory and practice. *American Antiquity* 41: 89–96.

Seeman, Mark
1977   The Hopewell Interaction Sphere: The Evidence for Inter-regional Trade and Structural Complexity. Ph.D. Dissertation, Indiana University. Ann Arbor: University Microfilm.

Spaulding, Albert
1960   Statistical description and comparison of artifact types. *Viking Fund Publications in Anthropology* 28: 60–92.
1974   Review of Systematics in Prehistory, by R. C. Dunnell. *American Antiquity* 39: 513–515.

Struever, Stuart, and Gail Houart
1972   An analysis of the Hopewell interaction sphere. In *Museum of Anthropology, Anthropological Paper 46,* edited by E. Wilmsen. Ann Arbor: University of Michigan.

7. The Koster Project Information Retrieval Application

James A. Brown, Stanley Clayton, Timothy Wendt, and Bernard Werner
Northwestern University

INTRODUCTION

Between 1972 and 1976 a computerized data processing and information retrieval system was developed to facilitate the archaeological investigation of the Koster site. This system provided basic support to a complex, multidisciplinary research project by processing information from a large-scale excavation of a deeply stratified site. The Koster Project application of computer technology began with a need to speed up field and lab processes, and grew from a simple expediting role in the project into a combined data management and field research instrument. In the course of this development the application was modified to meet the changing field research needs and to accommodate changes in computer hardware. From the start, specific concrete expectations were held of this application that guided subsequent development. At no point was this application conceived as a universal data processor, since many categories of field observations and collections were not incorporated in the system. Two basic uses of the information contained in the files were expected: (1) to refine stratigraphy, and (2) to isolate gross activity areas in each component. But, despite the limitations placed on the scope of the system as a by product of excavation strategy, there exist features in the system of potential utility for other applications, notwithstanding the enormous advances achieved by modern computer technology.

The Koster Project was unusual at the time of its inception for it included the collaboration of several disciplines in the investigation of Archaic Period cultural and ecological change (Brown and Struever 1973). A multidisciplinary approach was employed from the project's inception after the importance of the site was determined by the 1969 testing, and it is one that has continued to the conclusion of the project, albeit with changes in personnel and particular disciplines. Full-scale excavations were conducted from 1970 to 1978. The computerization of archaeological information in the field was not part of the original research organization. Only in 1971, after an appreciable lag developed between excavation and analysis, did the necessity for rapid and reliable data management become apparent. Hence the computer system arose to bridge a specific data management and analytical gap in the overall research project. Accordingly, in 1972 a system was designed and implemented to fulfill data processing needs. This system, with modifications, served important functions until the close of the excavations.

THE KOSTER SITE

Located 70 miles north of St. Louis in a rural area of Illinois, the site occupies the eastern edge of the broad floodplain of the Illinois River valley where the accumulation of colluvial loess has created an unusual record of discrete stratification for 8000 years (Butzer 1977). Koster is an open-air site that was repeatedly occupied as the ground surface gradually rose. As a result, 24 separate components (called horizons) can be identified in the upper 25 feet of colluvium (Brown, Bebrich, and Struever 1980). Below this unit lie Pleistocene alluvial silts and clays (Butzer 1977).

Occupation began around 9000 B.P. in the Early Archaic period. Following two distinct Early Archaic phases are four Middle Archaic, one Late Archaic, and at least five ceramic phases, the latest dating around A.D. 1200. The site has a particularly detailed sequence of 16 Middle Archaic components that have been the center of most of our research (Brown and Vierra 1979).

THE KOSTER PROJECT

The Koster site archaeological project was aimed toward the systematic study of change in Archaic period subsistence and settlement. This focus has become important to research in the Lower Illinois valley in order to establish the origins of late Woodland period subsistence-settlement patterns (Struever 1968, Brown and Struever 1973).

After the first season of tests we discovered the site had extraordinary potential for research into Archaic subsistence and settlement (Houart 1971). The excellently preserved fauna, flora, and features promised a full record for the period. To complete this promise, distinct episodes of occupation were separated by sterile lenses, thereby significantly lessening the stratigraphic confusion that has hampered interpretation of other deeply stratified sites in the Midwest (Griffin 1968). Hence, each Archaic component can be regarded as a separate record of subsistence and site utilization uncontaminated by later occupations. In the Midwest, this aspect of the site constituted a crucial asset toward establishing fine chronological control over changes in technology, subsistence, and settlement.

Unlike technology and subsistence, which, in many respects, can withstand the sampling limitations of excavations in deeply stratified sites, settlement pattern research is greatly limited both by the confined area and predetermined location of deep excavations (Brown 1975) and by the narrow perspective that a single site example contributes to comprehending a multipart settlement pattern. No matter how long a particular location may have been used over time, certain site types seem to correspond with particular settings. In the case of the Koster site, this limitation was balanced by other factors that worked in favor of the project's objectives. The open setting of the Koster site is particularly critical since it created a discovery potential denied to rock shelters. Whereas deeply stratified sites in rock shelters are invariably limited to a narrow range of settlement types, open unbounded sites are not, since they lack the constraints that rear walls and dripline have on the location of features and activity areas in shelters. Without the limitations of shelters, Koster offered the prospect of yielding a larger variety of settlement types in a single excavation sample. An important settlement type found in an open site is a multiseasonal base camp, the mark of relatively permanent occupation. It is poorly documented before the Late Archaic period, but this uncertainty may be due to the bias toward shelter excavation. Thus the Koster excavations held the opportunity to provide documentation of the early shift to permanent residence signaled by the appearance of base camps in the Archaic period.

Although the site's research assets determined the nature of the information sought, the excavation strategy exercised a more immediate effect on the role of computer data processing systems in the project. First, all finds were collected in 6-by-6 foot squares by arbitrary levels that were separated into natural layers and features when they could be recognized. The standard level was 3 inches thick, resulting in a standard level volume of 9 cubic feet. Basic collecting was by screen-recovery of shoveled earth backed up by flotation of a half-bushel (0.6 cubic foot) sample of screened dirt. This methodological procedure was altered completely in 1976 when excavation concentrated only on Horizon 11, which was dug in 2 inch levels by trowel. This change in collecting strategy reduced the immediate feedback role of the data processing system.

The screen and flotation sampling ensured recovery of remains that were not limited by minimum size. Hitherto, fish bone and most plant remains were seriously underrepresented because they were too small and fragile for screen recovery (Asch, Ford, and Asch 1972). But problems of a different type emerged from the objective of settlement analyses. It is desirable to excavate over broad, continuous areas (block excavations) to recover the structure of activities. Excavation in blocks entailed little problem in the upper layers, but as depth increased the problems of maintaining a block became acute. It was most critical in Horizon 11 at an average of 22 feet below surface. A certain minimum size excavation was necessary to enable recovery of variation in activity indicators and to ensure duplication of activities among different components. Large excavations also ensured recovery of adequate artifact numbers from components with a scarcity of diagnostic tools.

Consequently, a large excavation evolved with setbacks at the top to provide a safe operation at the bottom. An inevitable by-product of excavation at this scale was the collection of massive quantities of artifacts, ecofacts, and flotation samples. In the case of the last item, however, the sheer bulk of the samples dictated that a sampling design had to be established early to economically select a representative sample for comparative analysis (Fig. 7.1).

COMPUTER APPLICATION

From the foregoing, it is plain that a computerized data processing system was needed for two reasons: (1) to store and organize key information recovered from the field according to archaeological components, and (2) to provide an inventory of flotation units for rational sampling among each of the components.

In order to fulfill these simple research requirements, it was necessary first to exhaustively cross-check field stratigraphy. The problem was to resolve ambiguities in field assignments of components and to separate the thicker occupational horizons into discrete components, ideally conceived as "living floors." Statistical methods employed to separate thick horizons are described elsewhere (Brown, Bebrich, and Struever 1980). Secondly, it was necessary to aid the sampling program with provisional maps of "activity areas." As a by-product of this function, it was possible to provide feedback to the field on the trends and changes taking place in the units the excavations had completed. At the inception of this system, it was thought that timely feedback to the field would help guide the direction of excavation. However, the inflexibility in altering the area of excavation became too great with depth to allow significant utilization of feedback knowledge.

In short, the basic role of computerized data management was to provide the necessary inventory, information management, and data sorting support for a large-scale and complex excavation. This role was particularly important since the massive data collection required by the activity area research had to be intelligently sampled to economically study the small scale food remains.

The system devised in 1971 and completed in 1973 was created around the idea that timely processing of key bits of information would quickly prepare field data for lab analysis and contribute to the solution of interpretative problems in the field. Thus the system was really an information processor that organized information usefully before the ordinary detailed analyses were initiated by field specialists. Although this processor had research analytical capabilities, it was designed primarily as a logical precursor for research.

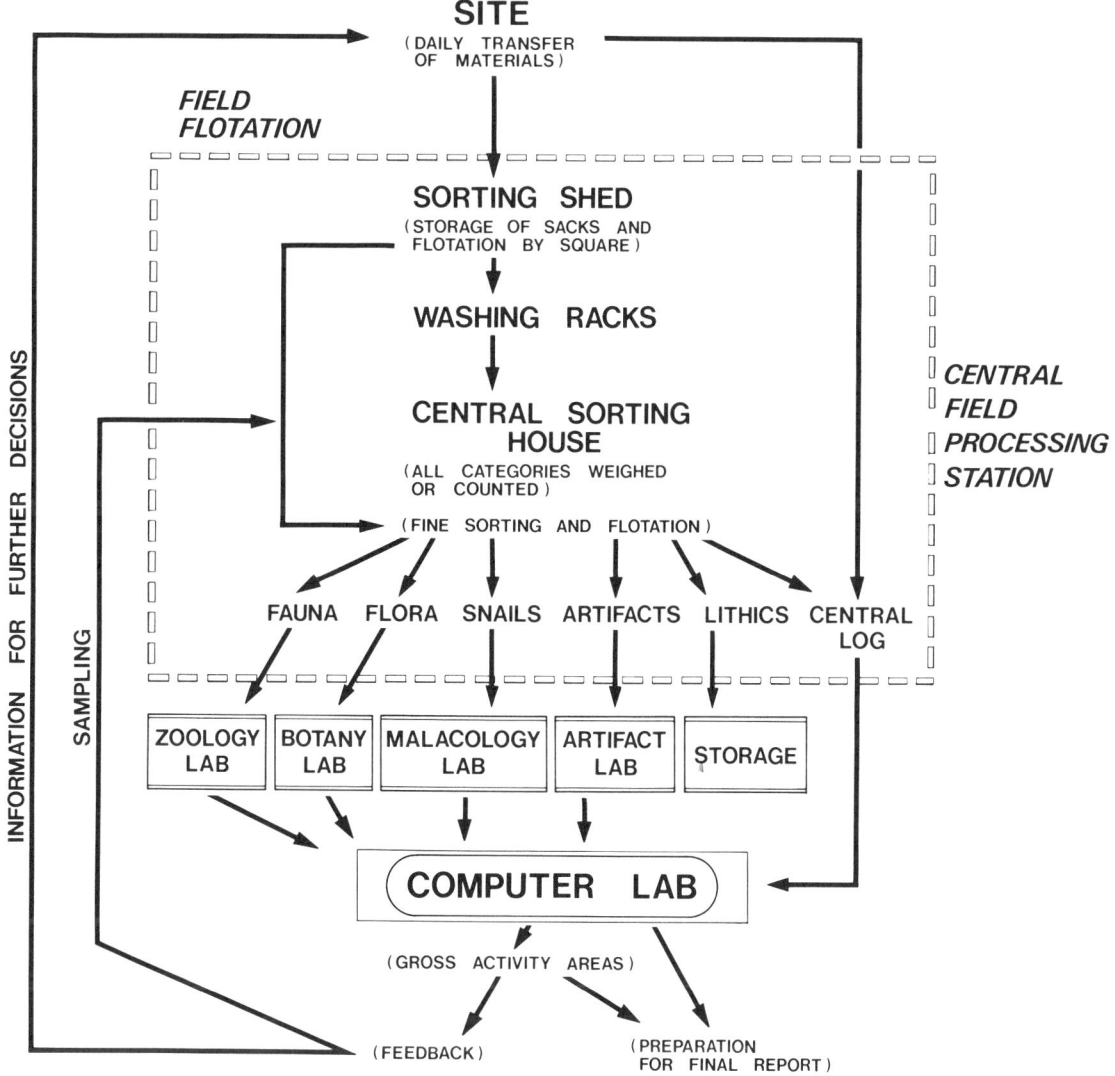

Fig. 7.1. Information flowchart for the Koster research project. (After Brown and Struever 1973, with modifications.)

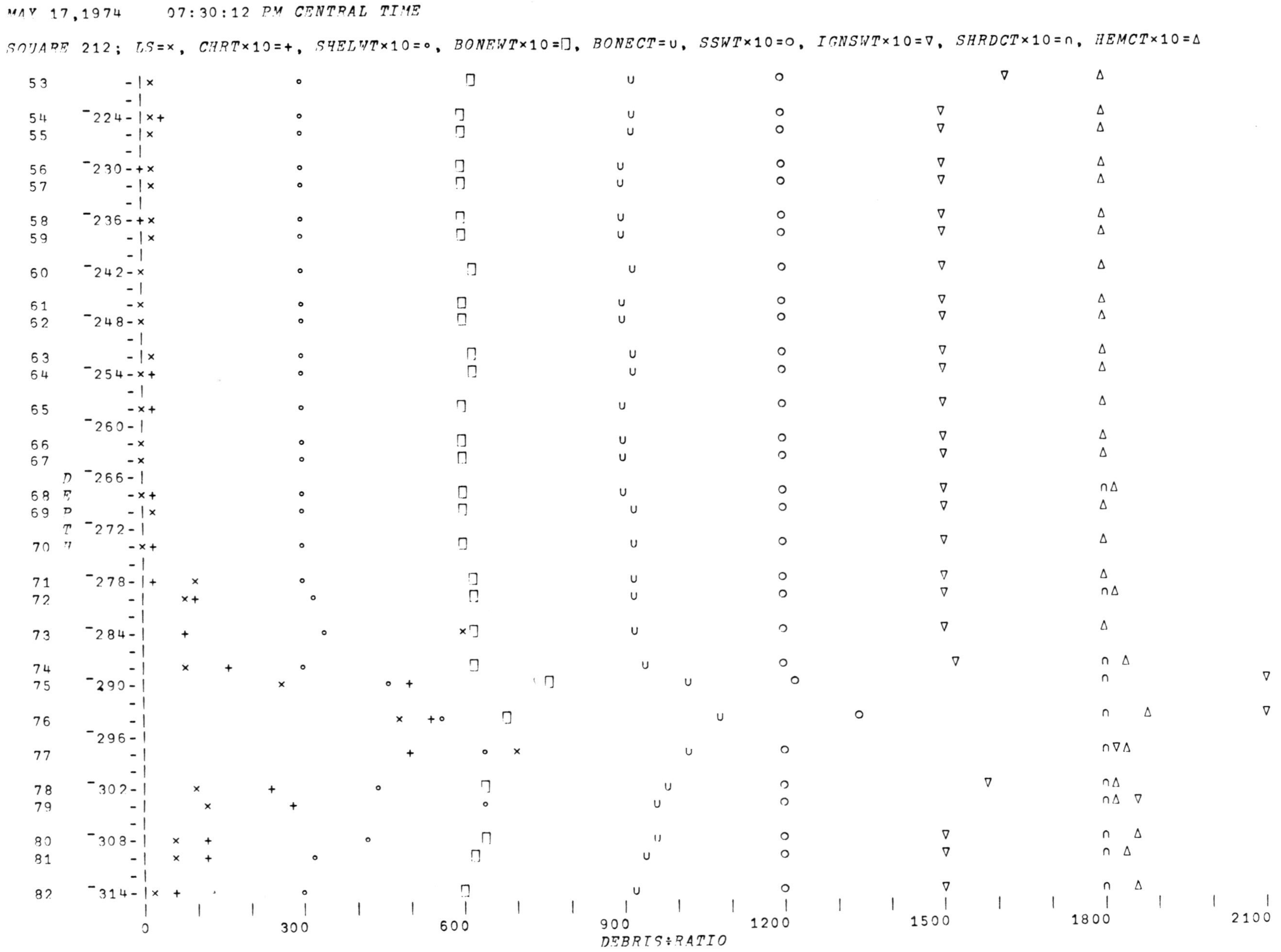

Fig. 7.2. Computer output for stratigraphic review (PLOT). Standardized information from the master file is ordered by depth for levels 53-82 in square 212. Each category of debris occupies a separate column on the same scale.

The system was designed around a highly structured file (hereafter called the master file) composed of key information from all arbitrary levels and features. The task of the computerized application was to make possible both rapid and accurate compilation of this master file as well as flexible retrieval of lists and diagrams through the help of square, location, elevation, and cultural component indices. Two common outputs utilized variation in the density of human occupation to produce histograms through the depth of a square for stratigraphic work (Fig. 7.2) and to make maps of variations in debris density by component for activity pattern research (Figs. 7.3, 7.4). It had already been established by the 1969 work that histograms of common materials (e.g., the category chert) were an indispensable aid to stratigraphic research (Houart 1971). Beyond these timely outputs, the master file is a basic resource describing the occupational history of the site. Feature analyses by Wolynec (1977) and settlement variation studies by Carlson (1979) are based on the information in this file.

COMPUTER SYSTEM

The Koster computer system was designed around a quickly compiled and easily accessed master file. For this purpose the large storage capacity of a major computer installation was desired. This capacity had to be accessible in the field through remote terminal hookup. Although large computers were readily accessible by telephone, our concern over the reliability of country telephone lines impelled us to select a rapid interactive system that operated in a simple, yet powerful language in order to reduce the time spent on line. Our solution was to adopt APL and to use tape cassettes for off-line data compilation. APL allowed us to minimize the impact of telephone line fatigue that was a recurrent problem in hot weather. In addition, the simplicity of APL allowed the imputing of data directly from lab tally sheets.

In the beginning a commercial time-sharing system was used. Scientific Time Sharing sold time on a system operating on an IBM 370/158 accessed by telephone from Bethesda, Maryland. This system utilized an extended version of APL (APL PLUS) that added file building and manipulating capabilities to the language's matrix manipulation strengths; it also allowed us to communicate at 30 CPS and use tape cassettes and other off-line devices that were unavailable then in the computing system at Northwestern University.

Considerable changes were made in the system over time in the interest of economy that eventually resulted in switching to the Northwestern University CDC 6400 computer system. At the start of the project, when emphasis was on system building, the terminal used was an IBM communicating Selectric typewriter. In 1973 when timely data input was initiated, an IBM communicating Mag card Selectric was used. This was replaced in the following two years by a Texas Instruments 733 ASP terminal with magnetic tape cassettes. In 1976, when the demand for off-line data compilation declined, an Anderson-Jacobson 630A was used that made possible a practical switch to operating with the CDC 6400 hardware. The AJ 630A could communicate in either IBM correspondence code or ASCII.

The creation of files, the entry of records, and the correction and retrieval of records are accomplished completely through remote terminal. The entry programs collate all inputs into the file and efficiently minimize storage. All entries in the update are checked and edited at the time of transmission and after the daily summary of entries is available.

The master file in the Koster System is organized as a serial list of numeric matrices, one for each 6-by-6 foot square or for each feature. Each row of these matrices is a record (or level of an excavation) and each column is a variable. It is possible to retrieve any single column or row or any combination of columns

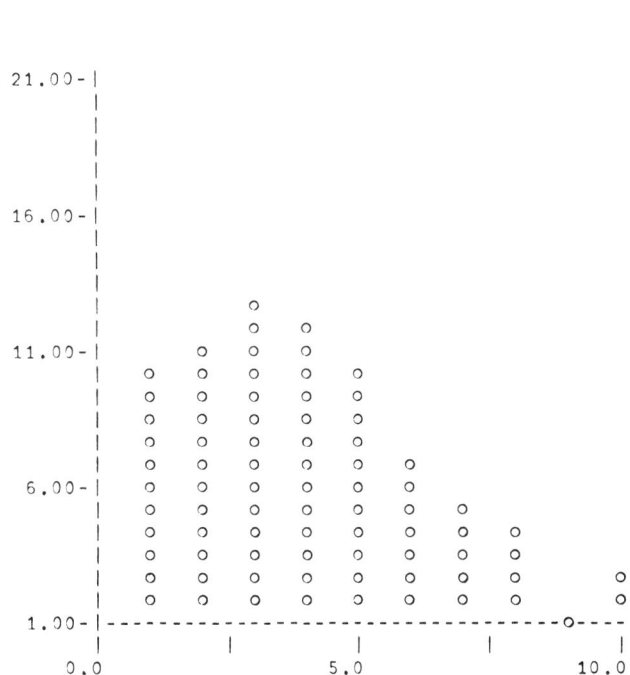

Fig. 7.3. Computer output for spatial analysis. This histogram represents limestone weight divided by chert weight (in decile scale) of units assigned to Horizon 6Low.

ENTER COLUMN NAMES
L.S.WT CHRTWT
ENTER HORIZON NUMBER

6LOW

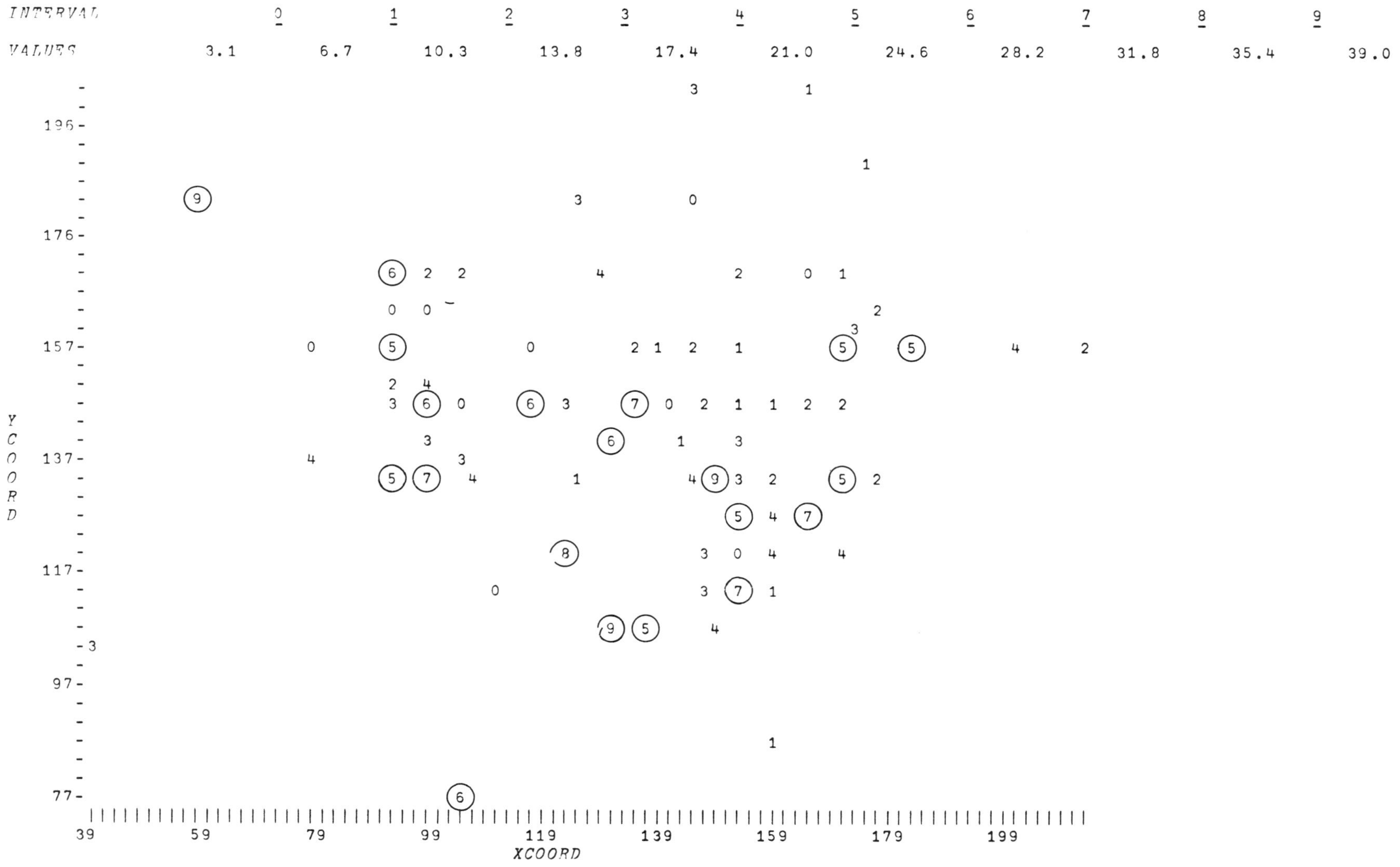

Fig. 7.4. Computer output for spatial analysis (VIEW2). Values for all levels of 6Low in Figure 7.3 are combined for each square and are plotted in their approximate site location. The denser half of each square has been circled to clarify the spatial behavior on the output.

and rows over a specific subset of matrices. These matrices are actually preceded by a directory, stored in the first component of the file, so that indirect addressing is used. The directory allows the archaeologist to refer to squares or features by the numbers assigned rather than by the arbitrary sequential numbers used in the File Subsystem (for further details see Brown and Werner 1974).

Since the data are entered in two modes—one for counts and weights, the other for square/level dimensions and locational information—program instructions and provenience data take a relatively high proportion (15 percent) of the keyboard input. The level dimensions themselves are 36 percent of the input, the counts and weights are 21 percent.

DATA PROCESSING ROUTINE

The materials recovered from the Koster excavations flow through two routes, depending on whether their recovery is from screening or flotation. The screened materials are brought daily to the Central Data Processing station where they are promptly washed, sorted, and recorded. Records of these materials are compiled according to information priorities. Typically, records are compiled in order of completion, with gross attributes of number and weight by material category taken first for the master file, followed by compilation of an artifact catalog and more detailed study by category. The master file contains the counts and weights of 14 common material categories, including chipped stone, various other mineral categories (limestone, sandstone, and igneous rock), animal bone, and mussel shell. The route through which the flotation fraction flowed involved delayed processing until sufficient information was available from analysis of the master file to adequately sample the flotation.

Information concerning the location and size of the collecting units was calculated from the field notes and drawings. With the addition of this information, weights and counts could be standardized to allow comparison of a sequence of levels or the compilation of maps of a component. Counts and weights were recorded separately from provenience information, since the two types of data arrived on different schedules.

The data sheets were gathered each morning for recording into the data processing system. Each day the master file was updated by remote terminal. The normal lag between excavation and data input was three days. The relationship of the Central Data Processing station, the Computer Lab, and other labs is summarized in Figure 7.1.

DATA PROCESSING SEQUENCE

The implementation of APL at the Northwestern University computing center includes features that encourage flexibility in the design of systems involving data and file organization. Programs can be grouped into packages, and large data matrices can be easily handled. There are several other important features in the Northwestern system such as (1) the structure of the storage space allotted to a user, called a Workspace in APL; (2) the relative efficiency of data structure; and (3) the degree of accessibility to data files.

Programs, called functions in APL, are written in a single WS (workspace) that currently comprises 64K bytes of storage. When the WS has been loaded into core, all functions are equally accessible by simply entering their name, and supplying any necessary arguments. The same conditions hold true for data variables and the calling of functions and variables by other functions. The 64K bytes of storage is adequate space for many complex functions and variables, and so enables quite complicated data processing systems to be written.

As the primary storage unit for functions is the WS, so the file is the primary storage unit for data. The file subsystem for APL, as implemented at Northwestern, is designed to be easily accessible to functions and programmers, with effective security measures to prevent accidental abuse or unauthorized use, and is compatible with the space limitation imposed by the WS.

There are two file types maintained as the master file for the Koster excavation data: data files, and indices to those files. The data files themselves are divided into square level files and feature level files. Both the data and index files themselves are in turn indexed by a directory indicating in which component data from a major excavation unit (square or feature level) may be found. The directory to each file is easily accessed under program or keyboard control, and is itself a part of the file.

There are, at any one time, four main usable data files, two for squares and two for features. These are subdivided on the basis of their currency to minimize searching during data entry. Files holding data from a still incomplete digging season are identified by the suffix -PART, for PARTials. Thus the files that held the 1975 data at the end of the season were SQPART (square partials) and FTPART (feature partials). The older main data files, not subject to constant updating, and much larger, are identified by the prefix KOS-, thus KOSSQ (Koster squares), and KOSFT (Koster features).

The format of the KOSSQ file is basic. Column one contains the provenience number, followed by nine classes of nonartifactual debris; sherd, bone, and hematite counts, plus weights of limestone, sandstone, igneous rock, chert, bone, and shell in columns 2–10 and coordinate data in columns 11–15. KOSFT is modified by the addition of a 16th column containing the square level from which the particular feature level was taken. The partials files reflect this organization, though their creation and updating is somewhat different.

The first step in entering any data is the coding of the data onto a terminal with off-line storage capability, a process that may take several hours. Data types are segregated on the storage medium so that one tape may have only counts and measurements on it, and another only measurements of squares. There are five types of data to be routinely entered and all of them go through the same initial steps to be entered into the data storage devices at Northwestern's computing center. These data types fall into three general classes of debris data and measurement, consisting of square and feature debris data, square and feature measurement data, and feature volumetrics (including assignments to square levels). When all of the data types have been entered, each tape is rewound and its contents are printed out and checked against the master data forms for errors and omissions; if any are found they are corrected before going on-line. When this process is completed, the user logs onto the computer.

The first step (Figure 7.5) is to read the data from a tape to its respective buffer file (for example, the

SQMES tape to the SMBUF file). When five tapes have been entered in this manner, a check is again made for errors, and any found are corrected before proceeding.

When this step is complete the user attaches the relevant partials files and actual updating begins. At this point, the user is in APL, has compiled the buffer files, attached the partials files, and is in the ENTRY WS.

Debris data from both squares and features are processed by a sort and merge function that takes input data from the prepared buffer file and appends them to the SQPART or FTPART files. The appropriate file is searched and the line of input data is appended to a component, summed with the data from an existing line, or appended as the first line of a new component, depending on the data already in the file. Data are grouped in the file by assigning all levels of an excavation unit to a single component, and summing the debris from all bags in a single level.

The sort/merge function then calls a system subroutine called EDIT that writes a new directory of the now updated partials file. The determination as to whether a file processed by EDIT is an addition (new component) or a replacement is made on the basis of the original file. If a component does not appear in the old directory, it is placed in the new directory and is added to the file. If a component is being updated, a replacement is performed (the old version, however, is saved and is accessible).

After all EDITs are completed in the job, an EX-

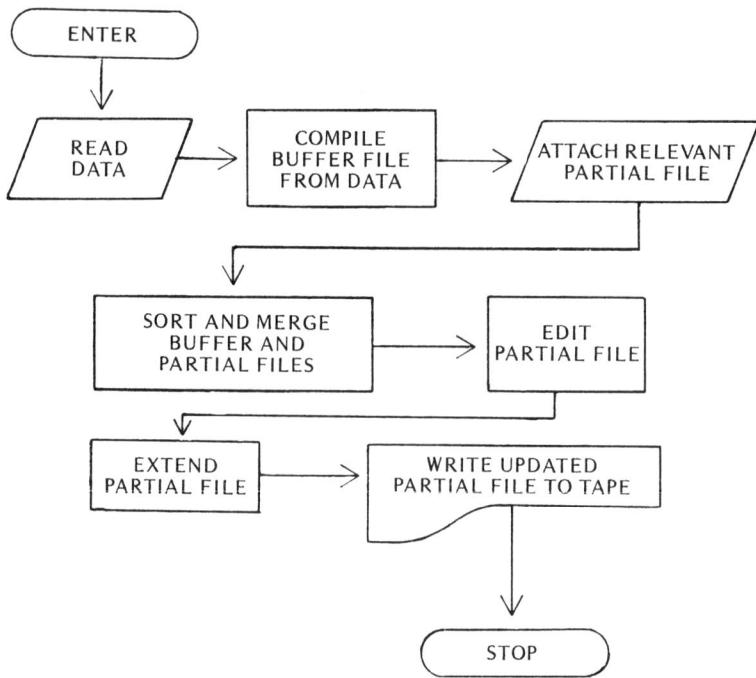

Fig. 7.5. Flowchart of the Entry phase of the Koster computer system.

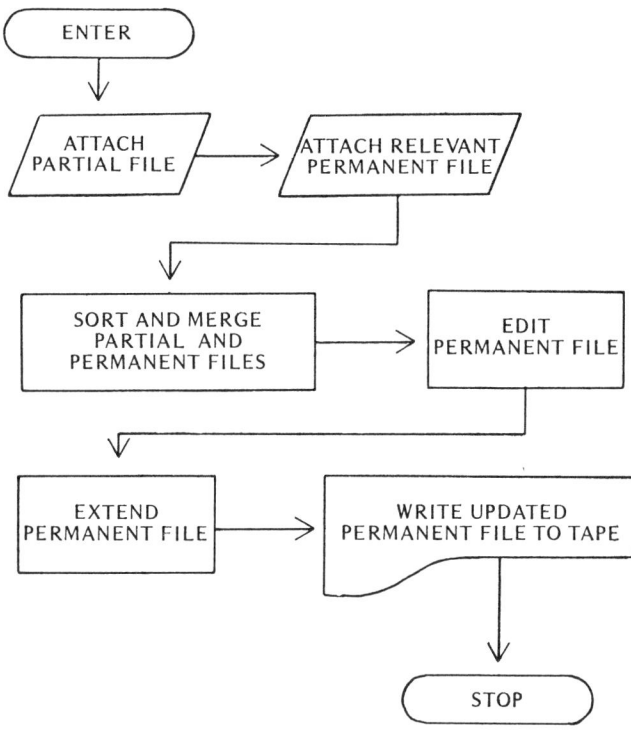

Fig. 7.6. Flowchart of the Sort / Merge phase of the Koster computer system.

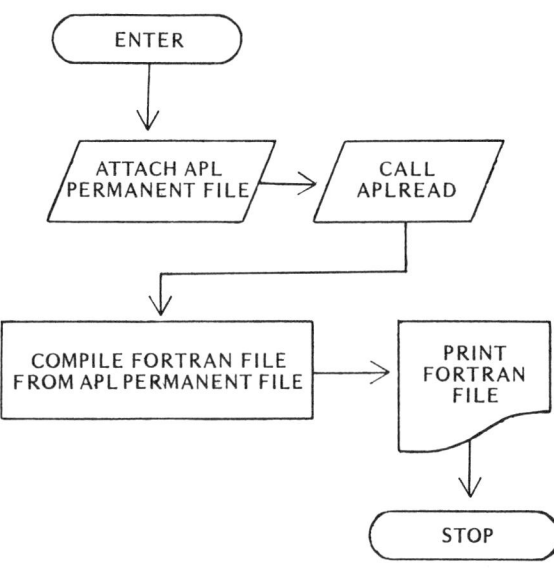

Fig. 7.7. Flowchart of the Copy phase of the Koster computer system.

PAND is executed on the now updated and EDITed partials files, making the changes permanent. The final process of partials updating is to write them out to a mass-storage tape for keeping until the next updating. The Koster Project maintains two tapes for this purpose. The tapes are used alternately, so that the current version and the previous version are always available. This system is further needed in case a tape should be damaged or erased by the failure of a system, faulty tape drive, or other cause.

At the end of the field season, when all of the data have been incorporated into the partials files, one last function takes the partials files and appends them to the main data files. The process here is quite simple and rapid. The user attaches the partials file and its relevant main data file (for example, the SQPART and the KOSSQ) and merges them with the same sort/merge function used with the buffer and partials files (Fig. 7.6). The updated permanent main file is then EDITed and EXTENDed to make the changes permanent and is written back onto tape. Here we use three tapes—the same two used for partials data, plus a third kept in the computer lab of the Koster Project as an added security measure.

The APL as implemented at Northwestern University has some limitations. Its main shortcoming experienced by the Koster Project is its inability to produce on-line printer output directly from APL files. Poten-

tially, this can have severe implications for the archaeologist. Why computerize the data if in the end you may still be forced to search through X-number of file cabinets to find out how many pieces of chert occurred at a certain level throughout the site? Fortunately, there is a way to get around this problem. The systems personnel at Northwestern have implemented a series of FORTRAN callable subroutines that will open, read, and write APL files.

Each spring the Koster Computer Laboratory compiles output of the main data files for the other Koster labs (see Fig. 7.1). After logging in and copying the data files from tape to disc, the user attaches the desired APL file, either the KOSSQ or the KOSFT file, or both. At this point a FORTRAN function is called, and the randomly indexed APL file is then compiled into a sequentially indexed FORTRAN file to which headers can then be written and any desired number of copies may be printed on the on-line printer (Fig. 7.7).

Although extensive checking measures are employed during the creation and updating of data files, it is entirely possible for errors and omissions to occur in the process. Therefore, a number of function groups have been written in the UT (UTility) WS to make small scale corrections and additions to the files. In the left column of Figure 7.8 is the function group for editing the main data files (this is not to be confused with the system function EDIT). In left-center are functions for small-scale editing of the partials files. Except for the files that they operate on, these two function groups are virtually identical. At right-center is a group for making horizon assignments to square and feature levels, while at far right are functions for displaying small portions of either a partials or a main data file.

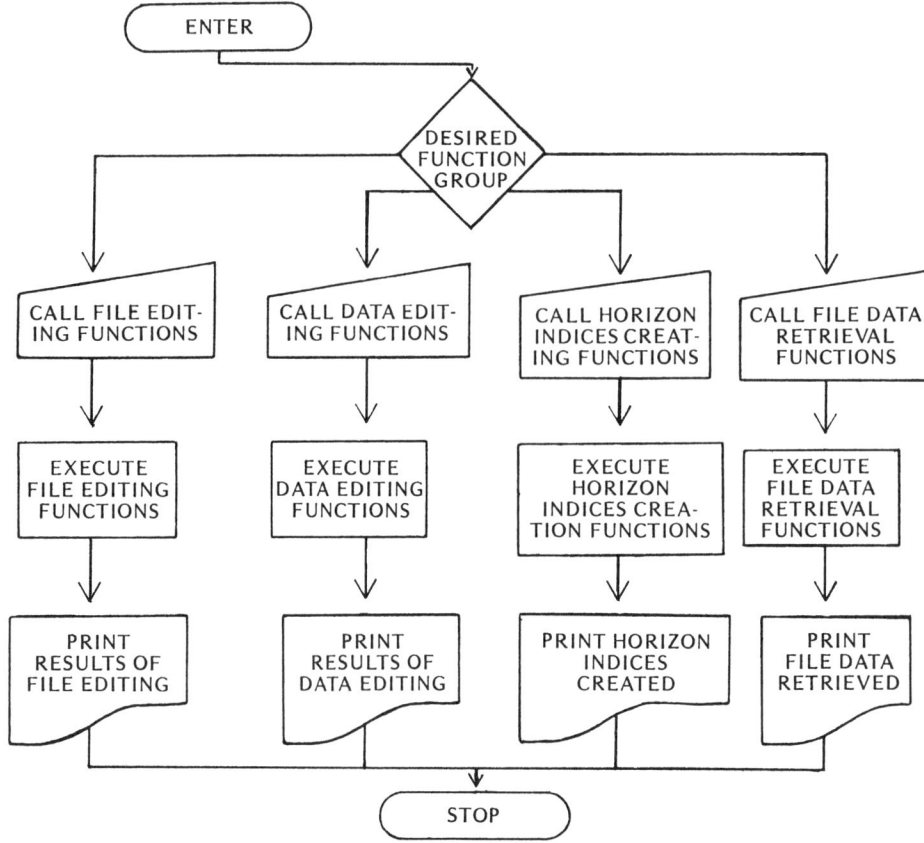

Fig. 7.8. Flowchart of the Revise phase of the Koster computer system.

OUTPUT REPORTS

So far we have concentrated on the creation and updating of the Koster data files. However, we also maintain three workspaces that are totally concerned with analysis of those data.

The first of these to be examined is the PLOT WS (Fig. 7.9). This function group is designed to display vertically the identification of occupational zones and their correlation between squares. The user enters the desired square numbers, and the debris density is calculated versus a vertical depth scale. The user then chooses the type of graph desired and it is plotted on the terminal. When finished, the user has the choice of replotting the same data with a different graphing option, or entering entirely new data to be graphed. The vertical display may not only be used to correlate the stratigraphy among already excavated squares, but also to anticipate the stratigraphy in squares not yet excavated.

The second analytical function group to be examined is in the VIEW2 WS (Fig. 7.10). Whereas PLOT displays data vertically through the site, in VIEW2 the horizontal variation among squares within a particular defined stratigraphic zone is displayed (see Fig. 7.4). The user enters the desired square numbers and horizon to be examined, whereupon a function calculates point plots showing scaled average debris density or a ratio of two debris types. The user then chooses from three types of scaling: Regular, Mean, or Decile.

In Regular scaling the range of values produced is divided into ten equal segments and a value is assigned a number from 0 through 9 on the basis of the interval to which it belongs, with 0 the lowest and 9 the highest.

In Mean scaling the values are arranged in an ascending order, and the mean is found. The class interval is then defined as the mean value of the square minus the lowest value of the square divided by five.

In Decile scaling the values are assigned intervals on the basis of percentile rank; 0 is assigned to the lowest 10 percent, 1 to the next lowest 10 percent, and so on (see Fig. 7.3). Again, the user then has the choice of replotting the data or plotting new data.

The purpose of the horizontal display in VIEW2 is twofold: analysis and prediction. These plots not only allow easy identification of patterns of spatial variation within horizons, but also extrapolation from the

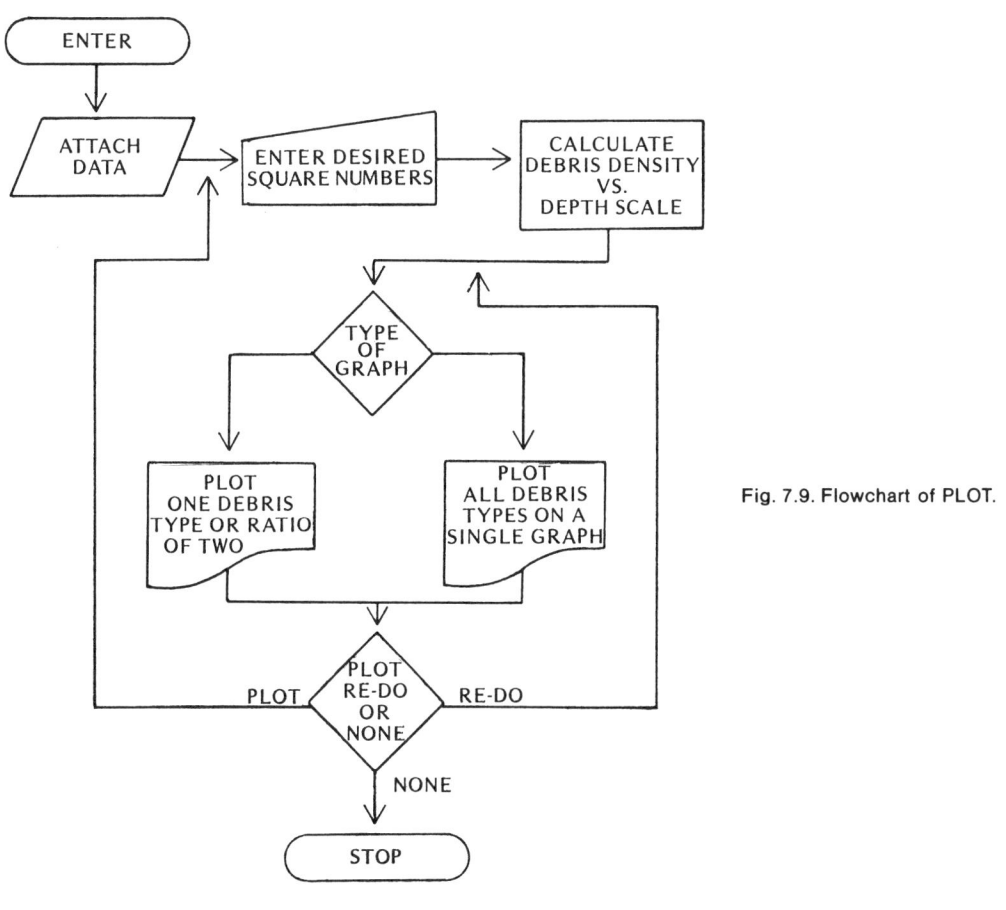

Fig. 7.9. Flowchart of PLOT.

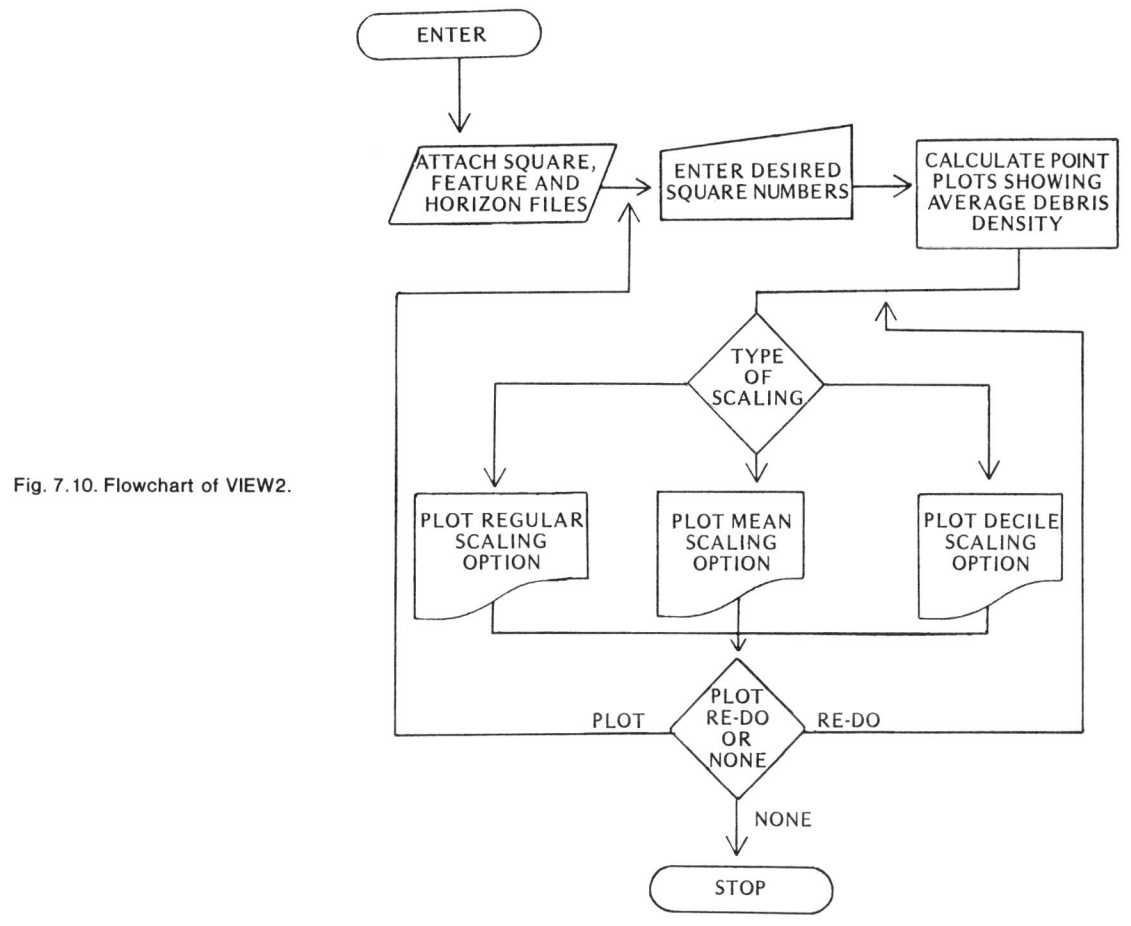

Fig. 7.10. Flowchart of VIEW2.

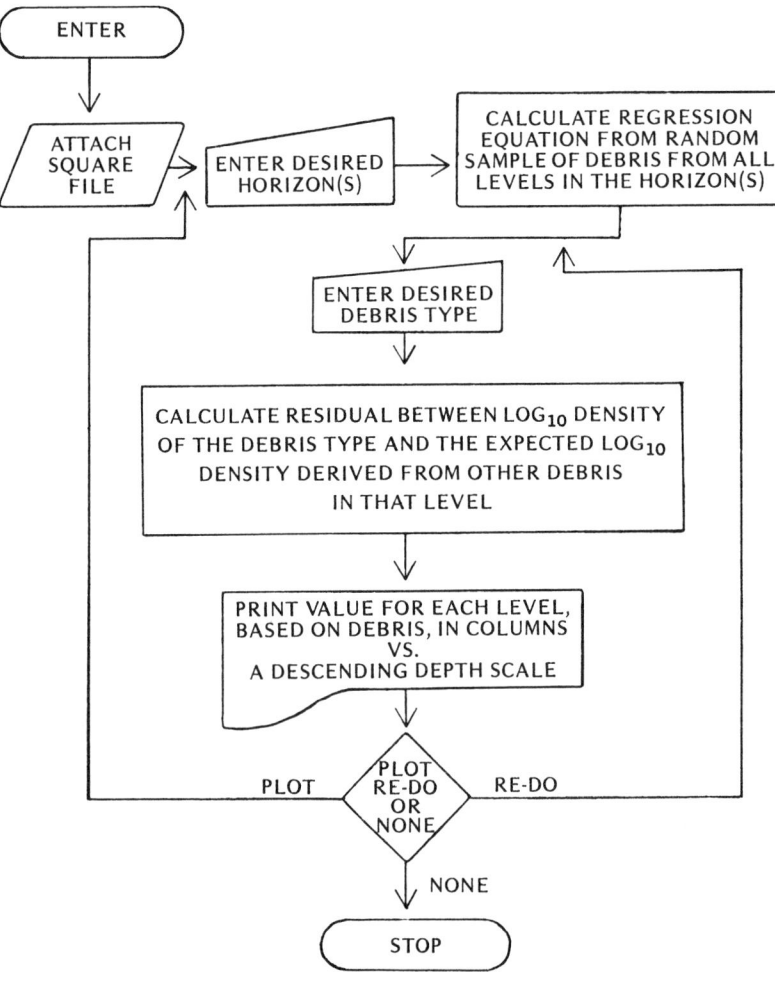

Fig. 7.11. Flowchart of RES.

known excavation into as yet unexcavated areas, and help make predictions about the nature of the deposit that may in turn help form our digging strategy.

The last function group that we examine here is the RES (RESiduals) WS; it is designed to help clarify the structure of the deposit within user defined stratigraphic zones, using relationships between data (debris) types to separate substrata (Fig. 7.11). Residuals from a regression are used to identify those values that conform to a general statistical description of the stratigraphic zone and those that do not. The process can show distinct layering of deposits, and subsequently is of value as a refinement to the analysis calculated in the VIEW2 WS (Brown 1974; Brown, Bebrich, and Struever 1980).

SYSTEM PERFORMANCE

The computerized file processing and data retrieval system described here worked successfully in the summers of 1972–1975. This file was kept up-to-date all summer, and was complete the day following the close of excavation.

A few words about the cost efficiency of commercial versus university installations may be useful. During the month of July, 1974, we spent a little over $1000 for file updating alone in the commercial system. In July, 1978, at a university computing center we spent only $300 for a comparable amount of work. Although the change from an IBM to a CDC (Control Data Corporation) computer presented a number of problems in conversion, our savings more than offset them.

SUMMARY

The overall operation of the Koster computer system has been described to show the close interrelationship between this data management system and the field-research strategy of the Koster Project. The system was developed to accomplish high priority data processing tasks in order to resolve field stratigraphic problems, to organize materials for specialized lab analysis, and to enable efficient sampling of flotation samples for each horizon. The field environment in which data compilation and information retrieval took place made special demands on system design. These demands were met by dial-up service to a large computing system that permitted rapid communication with a remote terminal in the APL language.

ACKNOWLEDGMENTS

This is an expansion of a paper by Brown and Clayton delivered at the 41st annual meeting of the Society for American Archaeology, St. Louis, May 1976, partly drawn from Brown and Werner (1974) and Brown, Bebrich, and Struever (1980). The authors wish to acknowledge the assistance that Gail L. Houart, Michael Schwartz, and Owen McGlaughlin provided to the success of the system in the first year. Funding was provided by NSF Grants GS-33865 and GS-41242, and general support came from the Foundation for Illinois Archaeology, Inc.

REFERENCES

Asch, Nancy B., Richard I. Ford, and David L. Asch
  1972   Paleoethnobotany of the Koster site: the Archaic horizons. *Illinois State Museum, Reports of Investigations* 24.

Brown, James A.
  1974   A statistical method for discovering microstratigraphy. Paper delivered at the 41st International Congress of Americanists, Mexico City.
  1975   Deep-site excavation strategy as a sampling problem. In *Sampling in Archaeology,* edited by James W. Mueller, pp. 155-169. Tucson: University of Arizona Press.

Brown, James A., Carl A. Bebrich, and Stuart Struever
  1980   Koster Site research: the initial investigations, 1970-75. *Northwestern Archaeological Program, Prehistoric Records.*

Brown, James A., and Stuart Struever
  1973   The organization of archaeological research: an Illinois example. In *Research and Theory in Current Archaeology,* edited by Charles L. Redman, pp. 261-280. New York: Wiley.

Brown, James A., and Robert K. Vierra
  1979   Koster Site research: an overview. Paper read at the 44th annual meeting, Society for American Archaeology, Vancouver.

Brown, James A., and Bernard Werner
  1974   An on-site data management system application in field archaeology. *Communications of the ACM* 17: 644-646.

Butzer, Karl W.
  1977   Geomorphology of the lower Illinois Valley as a spatial-temporal context for the Koster Archaic Site. *Illinois State Museum, Report of Investigations* 34.

Carlson, David L.
  1979   Hunter-gatherer Mobility Strategies: An Example from the Koster Site. Unpublished Ph.D. dissertation, Northwestern University.

Griffin, James B.
  1968   Observations on Illinois prehistory in Late Pleistocene and early Recent times. In The Quaternary of Illinois, edited by Robert E. Bergstrom, pp. 123-137. *University of Illinois College of Agriculture, Special Publication* 14.

Houart, Gail L.
  1971   Koster: a stratified Archaic site in the Illinois Valley. *Illinois State Museum, Report of Investigations* 22.

Struever, Stuart
  1968   Woodland subsistence-settlement system in the lower Illinois Valley. In *New Perspectives in Archaeology,* edited by Sally R. Binford and Lewis R. Binford, pp. 285-312. Chicago: Aldine.

Wolynec, Renata B.
  1977   The Systematic Analysis of Features from the Koster Site, a Stratified Archaic Site. Unpublished Ph.D. dissertation, Northwestern University.

8. Computer Data Bank Application at a Remote Site Location

Sylvia W. Gaines
Arizona State University

INTRODUCTION

During the early 1970s a number of data bank applications made their appearance in archaeology. Some seemed to be project oriented and constrained by the parameters of a research design; others were considerably more flexible and broad in scope. Regardless of the particular goals, the majority had one aspect in common—data processing was accomplished at the computer facility location. The data bank application described in this chapter is unique in that all computer interface was performed in a field location, remote from the computer facility.

The objective of this application was to develop data bank management techniques to assist in field excavation and survey, and to test their feasibility. In the early 1970s, a direct link between a field location and a computer was a new application in archaeology and the problems and benefits were speculative. The purpose of this chapter is to review what was learned from this early field experience with on-line computers and to indicate the directions this technique may take in the future (Gaines 1971, 1973, 1974, 1977).

The techniques utilized involved a remote terminal connected by telephone service to a computer at Arizona State University in Tempe, some 300 miles distant from the research area. By having immediate access to the computer and the data bank of current information recovered from the field, the project sought to demonstrate the utility of a computer to aid in decision-making procedures in a remote archaeological field situation.

The research was conducted under the auspices of the Arizona State University Archaeological Field School in the summer of 1971. Field personnel surveyed, mapped, excavated, and processed artifacts in the field laboratory, and analyzed and classified material during the course of the session.

The project linked the area of investigation on the Navajo Indian Reservation in northeastern Arizona with the computer on the campus of Arizona State University. Hunters Point Bureau of Indian Affairs School provided laboratory space for the computer-associated equipment in one of the classrooms. Fieldwork was conducted at White Goat Rincon, 3.7 km southeast of the school. The data from excavation and survey underwent daily laboratory processing and analysis at the school. Data were then entered into the computer on a daily basis, via the remote terminal, and stored in an on-line data bank for further analysis. Various computer analyses were requested from the terminal and the results were transmitted to Hunters Point within seconds (Fig. 8.1). The Honeywell GE255 computer providing the time-sharing service required for the methodology was housed at the Computer Center on the Arizona State University campus in Tempe, Arizona.

RESEARCH GOALS

Although the expanded capabilities for data handling provided by electronic computer technology offer tremendous potential for resolving problems of the description, analysis, and interpretation of masses of data, archaeologists are only beginning to appreciate and exploit computers as field research tools. We sought to evaluate the ability to use a computer to aid in making the tactical decisions during an archaeological excavation and survey. In a field situation, decisions range from initial selection of a site through the daily choices affecting the excavation in progress. By analyzing information from the excavation with a battery of simple statistical tests, the process of making decisions was more precise and less biased than it would have been had we used only the normal subjective procedures. An additional aim of the project was to identify modifications in laboratory techniques, excavation, and survey procedures to gain maximum benefits from computer use.

There are general problems in the use of a remote terminal, and other problems that archaeologists, in particular, must face. Among these are the following.

1. Although remote terminals are often used in laboratories, providing on-line computer capability at a remote field location is not as simple. There are problems of poor telephone service, the need for interaction with the field laboratory to provide daily evaluation of excavation or survey data, and lack of support facilities for either equipment repair or consultation.

2. The feasibility of storage and continual update of massive quantities of data necessary to this application had to be demonstrated. In typical batch processing systems the majority of the information usually is stored off-line and only rarely is the full file capability exploited. However, in this field situation, using time-sharing service, each recorded bit of data had to be stored in a data bank accessible to search at all times.

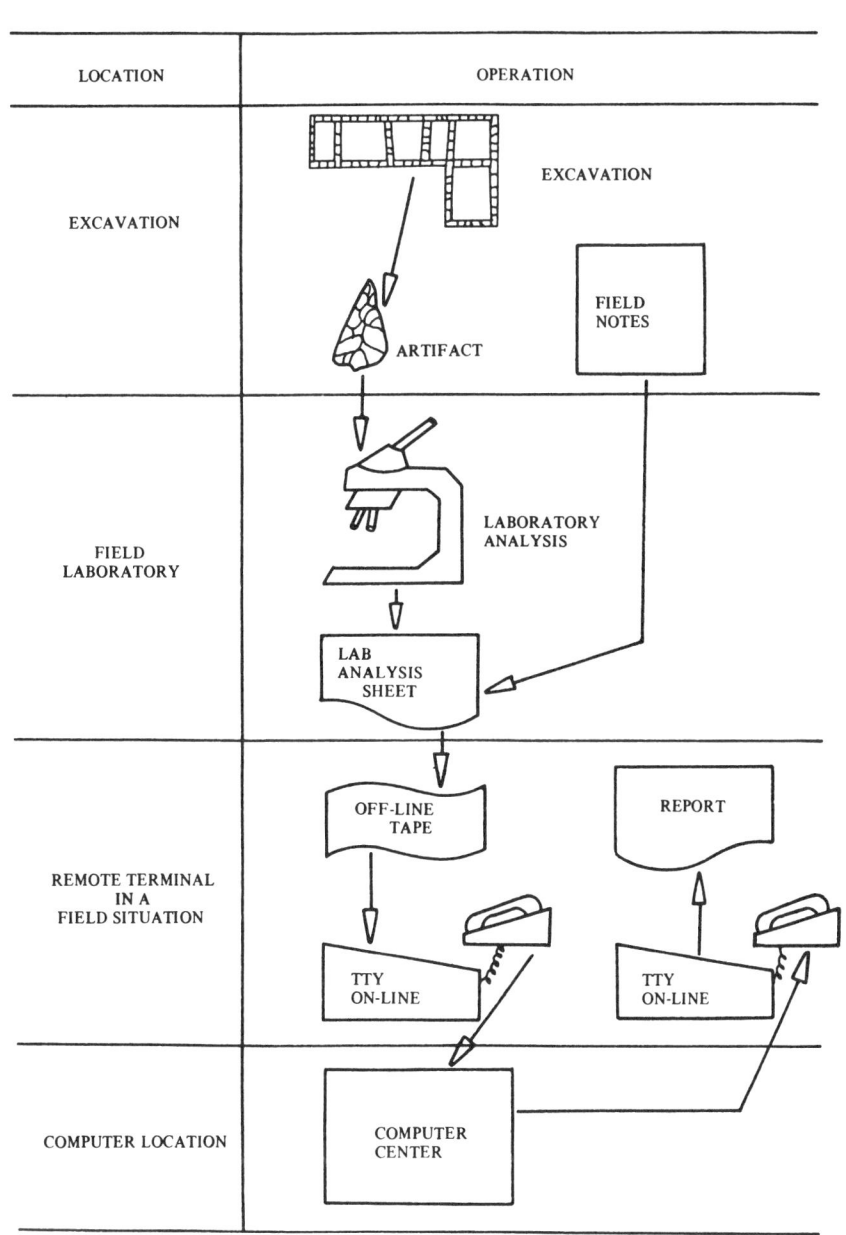

Fig. 8.1. Flowchart of computer application.
(Reproduced by permission of the Society for American Archaeology from *American Antiquity* 39: 455.)

3. A "user-tolerant" system had to be developed so that field personnel (nonprofessional programmers) could prepare and enter input information and isolate the errors that are inevitable in such situations without destroying or losing information.

4. The usefulness of this type of application depends on the ease with which personnel can gain access to the information in the data bank and retrieve meaningful results. For this purpose, a specialized language was needed that would allow archaeologists to generate sophisticated reports in various formats, to recall selective information from the data bank, and to apply specific statistical tests and calculations without the aid of professional consultation or assistance.

RESEARCH PLANNING AND DEVELOPMENT

The particular functions that data base applications perform will be a reflection of the research design employed. Unless specifically designed for a single, unique application, a data base management system will generally be flexible enough to handle a variety of data management and manipulatory aspects. At the inception of this project no data base management system existed that offered the capabilities required for remote field data processing. As a consequence,

considerable effort went into the design and development of a programming system which would provide the necessary functions. The four phases of pre-fieldwork are outlined in Figure 8.2.

Data Organization

Data were organized to allow retrieval based on several criteria. Each data item was identified by provenience, class, and type, providing a general descriptive system that permitted a search of the stored information by provenience (site, feature, level), or conversely, by category (class or type names). These traditional data categories were utilized because field laboratories are not usually equipped to handle in-depth artifact analysis. Finer levels of analyses, performed in a post-field environment, can be readily accommodated into the data base.

For the excavated materials we decided to limit the class of stored information to ceramics because of the short field session and personnel limitations, particularly in the laboratory. Twenty-five ceramic types were identified prior to the beginning of fieldwork, although the list was expanded to 55 by the end of the field session to encompass the numerous unanticipated tradewares. As work at the field school progressed,

PRE FIELD PLANNING AND DEVELOPMENT

PHASES	DECISIONS
I. Development of a Research Design	How the computer will be utilized
II. Facilities/Staff Planning	Budget (staff, services, computer time) Computer facility to be used Communication facilities Field location facilities Staff Training Consultation/programming aid
III. Data Organization	Data base management system Data categories and how to characterize Organization of data and file structures

IV. Development of Computer Program	Choice of library or unique programs
	Type of data processing
	Programming language
	Analytical routines
	Selection or development of programs to:
	    Input and verify data
	    Data base building
	    Data analysis

Fig. 8.2. Prefield planning and development.
(Reproduced by permission of the Society for American Archaeology from *American Antiquity* 39: 457.)

we expanded the computer application to the field survey and included such data as vegetation, site situation, site type, site condition, architecture, and site size.

The storage of large amounts of archaeological data required the establishment of an indexing scheme of unique data names to assure unambiguous searches and retrieval of information. This index information was compiled in open-ended "dictionaries" or directories of allowed names, and they were expanded in the field as new proveniences or data categories were identified. From a logical standpoint, the order in which data categories appear in the dictionaries is unimportant. However, to accelerate computer searches it is advantageous to list more frequently encountered data names at the beginning of the dictionaries. At the completion of the field school the computer system dictionaries contained 87 distinct loci from the excavation, 19 multi-component sites from the survey, and 129 descriptive data categories for the survey, as well as the 55 ceramic type names mentioned above.

Development of the Data Base Management System

Rationale

The philosophy behind the development of the computer programs was to provide a simple and easily understood interface for the archaeologist. We recognized that the users of the program would not be professional programmers, and that when large amounts of data are entered, there always will be clerical, procedural, syntactical, and semantic errors. Therefore, the approach emphasized a user-tolerant system. The input format was simple and patterned closely after the field recording forms to minimize transcription errors. No encoding of the data was required by the user. Alphanumerical data were entered literally in the same form in which they appear in laboratory or field forms. However, it was necessary to enforce discipline on spelling and abbreviations so that terms were always the same. All items entered were checked automatically by the computer against dictionary names and if spellings were not exact, the terms were rejected and the operator notified by the computer of where the errors were located in the input data. The errors could then be corrected on-line.

To implement our philosophy a series of decisions had to be made. The most important decisions to this application involved: (1) choice of programming languages; (2) selection of methods of storing data and on-line updating, including backup files for the protection of stored data; (3) establishment of procedures for data preparation and entry from the remote terminal; and (4) development of a set of statistical and mathematical programs for use in an on-line environment characteristic of a field situation.

Computer Programming System

The result of these decisions was a set of computer programs, a file system, and a specialized archaeological language for use in both logical searches and statistical tests. The acronym given the system is ADAM, standing for *Archaeological DAta Management* system. The programs are written in Extended BASIC. ADAM has three major divisions: (1) programs to input and verify data and to generate daily reports of data entry; (2) programs to sort, merge, index, and store the data into a master file (data bank); and (3) inquiry programs to search and analyze the stored data, and to prepare reports of the search and analysis.

Functions of the first division are (1) to check the input data for format, spelling, and syntactical consistency, and (2) to provide a report format that allows the user to scan for semantic errors that are not detectable by the computer.

The second major division of programs provides file building routines that update the data bank.

The function of the third major division of ADAM is interrogation of the files and generation of results, accomplished by two basic types of programs: (1) analysis, and (2) search. The analysis program extracts from the data bank specifically requested information and applies specified calculations or statistical tests. To initiate an interrogation, the archaeologist simply specifies the information he wants in terms of provenience and classificatory unit and the statistical tests or calculations to be used. Keywords (macro-instructions) are used to control the search for the requested information; however, the user is not required to learn a special terminology. Rather, the objective is to provide the archaeologist with a computer language in a parlance familiar to him, and with a syntax simple enough to permit him to learn the procedure quickly and to apply it with a minimum of error. Calculations and statistical tests ranged from simple percentages, sums, and ratios, to chi square contingency tables and correlation coefficients.

The program for the second type of file inquiry permits the user to ask logical questions of the data bank such as "list all north-facing sites containing Tusayan Corrugated ceramics, dating A.D. 950–1050 and not containing Little Colorado Corrugated ceramics." In actual practice the format of the question is shortened and the user initiates the search with a simple input statement specifying a series of terms or names that are connected logically, requiring either their presence or absence. The computer program translates the statement into the proper internal code, selects those records that satisfy the criteria, and prints the results.

FIELD METHODOLOGY

The multiple phases of the field methodology consisted of: (1) field and laboratory procedures, (2) preparation of computer data, (3) data entry, (4) computer file building and updating, and (5) file inquiry and analysis (Fig. 8.3). Each step was a link in a chain of complex manipulations necessary for the successful demonstration of the validity and utility of a computer to aid in data bank development and decision-making procedures in an archaeological field situation.

Several research projects were conducted simultaneously. One program, an intensive survey of the area, recorded cultural and environmental information. The second project was the excavation of a small pueblo site. White Goat House, AZ K:8:2 (ASU), was selected for excavation, in part because of the time depth (A.D. 900–1325) suggested by surface collection. In addition, it was anticipated that excavation would produce sufficient data to: (1) test computer storage and retrieval capabilities, (2) analyze intrasite relationships,

and (3) permit comparisons with data from sites identified only from survey.

The site has two parallel rows of rooms and a trash mound. During excavation, 11 rooms, 1 kiva, 1 storage cist, 1 pit house, and 4 extramural use surfaces were identified. The total area of the site approximated 126 square meters, but because of erosion it was estimated that little more than half of the original site remained.

Materials from both excavation and survey were processed daily in the field laboratory in an attempt to keep processing current with data recovery from the field. The objective was a daily turn-around. After analysis and classification the provenience and data category dictionaries were updated if new sites or data names had been identified. The data were punched onto paper tape and entered into the computer which then automatically verified the data, entered the new data in the master data file, and generated a daily report (Fig. 8.4).

The daily reports often provided insights into the data which then could be explicated by means of the file inquiry analysis and search programs. Significant advantages in this type of data inquiry occurred in the rapid interaction between the computer and the archaeologist. Although the computer cannot accom-

FIELD IMPLEMENTATION

PHASES	DECISIONS

I. Data Preparation	Lab processing - identification
	                       - quantification
	                       - classification
	
	Preparation of format for computer entry
	              - keyboard
	              - tapes
	              - cards

II. Data Input and Verification	Batch or on - line Verification - manual or automatic Types of verification - syntax, semantic Report generation format - hardcopy or display
III. Data Base Building	Back-up tapes Hardcopy Security procedures - passwords, private discs, control numbers
IV. Data Base Queries	Searches Mathematical and statistical tests Report format - hardcopy, display

Fig. 8.3. Field implementation.
(Reproduced by permission of the Society for American Archaeology from *American Antiquity* 39: 460.)

```
RPTGN2        18:22      WED       08-04-71

DATE      STATE       SITE      INSTIT    FEATURE
JUL 26     AZ        K:8:2      ASU         FA
```

CLASS	TYPE	SPEC NO	LOCUS	NO OF ITEMS
TIME	T6	1	LO	1
CERAMIC	LIT-COLO-CORR	3	LO	121
CERAMIC	PUERCO-B/W	3	LO	39
CERAMIC	TUSAYAN-CORR	3	LO	9
CERAMIC	ST-JOHNS-POLY	3	LO	4
CERAMIC	WINGATE-B/R	3	LO	1
CERAMIC	LINO-GRAY	3	LO	1
CERAMIC	HOLBROOK-B/W	3	LO	1
CERAMIC	PUERCO-B/R	3	LO	1
CERAMIC	KLAGETO-B/W	3	LO	3
CERAMIC	KLAGETO-B/Y	3	LO	4
CERAMIC	TULAROSA-B/W	3	LO	3
CERAMIC	TUSAYAN-B/R	3	LO	2
SITUATION	N-CLIFF-TAL	1	LO	1
VEGETATION	SALT BUSH	1	LO	1
VEGETATION	S-FACE	1	LO	1
SITE-TYPE	PUEBLO	1	LO	1
SITE-TYPE	KIVA	1	LO	1
SITE-TYPE	RECT	1	LO	1
SITE-TYPE	S-ORIENT	1	LO	1
ARCHIT	SEL-BLOCKS	1	LO	1
SIZE	NO-ROOMS	1	LO	25
SIZE	SIZE-6	1	LO	1
CONDITION	REFUSE-CONCEN	1	LO	1
CONDITION	HI-MOUND	1	LO	1
CONDITION	MASONRY	1	LO	1
CONDITION	WALLS	1	LO	1

END OF DAYS FILE

Fig. 8.4. Computer generated daily report.
(Reproduced by permission of the Society for American Archaeology from *American Antiquity* 39: 458.)

plish tasks impossible by more conventional means, it did allow analysis of large amounts of data rapidly enough so that decisions could be made while work was in process. With the daily turn-around, the computer results aided in tactical decisions affecting field procedures for the following day. The results of the search and analysis programs also assisted in constructing a frame of reference for selecting subsequent excavation and survey areas. A good example of this interaction was the case of an archaeologist using the search programs and modifying his search criteria as he observed the results of the search.

The immediate computer feedback also made it possible to explore emerging distributional relationships among features and among artifact types during the excavation. With traditional approaches, the majority of analyses would have been conducted in a post-fieldwork environment, and consequently, would not have affected field tactics.

The methodology outlined above was tested in three major ways: (1) explication of the inter-relationships of features at White Goat House, (2) increased knowledge of the surrounding area by use of a search program to determine cultural patterning of survey data, and (3) appraisal of the modus operandi of the excavation and possible new approaches resulting from computer utilization.

Intrasite Study

A number of interesting questions arose during the course of excavation dealing with the problems of (a) inter-feature relationships, (b) the use of features, (c) chronological occupation of the site, and (d) ceramic varieties and their distribution. The mathematical/statistical capabilities of the programming system provided an additional source of information on which the archaeologist could base his interpretations.

a. Inter-feature relationships. Ceramic frequencies from various floor levels of four features were subjected to chi square and correlation coefficient tests which demonstrated, in all cases, that no relationship existed between ceramic types and loci. Additionally, ceramic percentages from floors, fill, and over-burden in six additional features were utilized to express general trends in feature relationships.

b. Use of features. Although statistical tests were not applied in defining possible feature use, computer generated comparison of ceramic percentages and ratios did provide some general trends. For time control, the earlier occupied area of the site was distinguished from the later occupation. Comparison was based on work areas, living areas, and storage areas. The negative results obtained from this approach was due to a number of reasons. Much destruction had occurred to many of the features resulting in an insufficient amount of data. Only the living areas of the earlier occupation remained intact and seemed to demonstrate a reasonable degree of relationship. Although it was recognized that "use" could not be determined on the basis of ceramics alone, since this was the only data category being entered into the excavation computer files, it did provide a basis for exploring this type of computer approach.

c. Site chronology. Many of the ideas generated during the excavation were based on the occurrence of Little Colorado Corrugated and Tusayan Corrugated ceramic types. Although these two types are generally considered contemporary, earlier features produced a preponderance of Tusayan Corrugated in relation to Little Colorado Corrugated. The relative frequency of Tusayan Corrugated appeared to diminish later in time. A computer generated ratio table was produced that ranked features from the highest to lowest occurrence of Tusayan Corrugated in relation to Little Colorado Corrugated, indicating a general chronological sequence from early to late. This trend seemed to substantiate the use of these ceramic types as a time indicator for this site. More sites in the same area would have to be tested for any conclusive results; however, this approach did demonstrate the usefulness of such a procedure for an on-going investigation.

d. Intrasite distribution of ceramic varieties. The question of the distributional patterning of Pureco Black-on-white ceramic varieties also arose during the course of excavation. Since three varieties, Escavada, Gallup, and Puerco, occurred in varying frequencies in the features of White Goat House, we sought to determine if these varieties exhibited modalities with respect to variation through time. Some initial trends were established: Escavada does appear to be the earliest variety and it persists through the sequence;

the Gallup variety also appears fairly early although not in as high proportions as the Escavada or Puerco; Puerco appears to be the latest in time with frequencies similar to those of the Escavada variety.

As well planned as research may be prior to field work, there will always be ad hoc questions and problems the archaeologist would like to resolve "on the spot." If the data have been structured and recorded at a level of specificity appropriate to a problem, then computer retrieval and analysis is a rapid means of deriving answers. Many questions arising during an excavation can be dealt with in this manner. It is usually the case that one question generates another. Computer capabilities provide a way of discovering such relationships in an on-going excavation. Although these approaches may seem relatively unsophisticated in light of computer-oriented research designs of the late 1970s, they did demonstrate the possible approaches offering the archaeologist on-the-spot information from the use of computer processing.

Survey Data Study

The second test of the methodology concerned the use of the logical search programs to place the surveyed sites of the area into a chronological framework with reference to the stratigraphic excavation. The archaeologist is often faced with a series of sites and a limited time in which to select particular sites for further investigation. By use of a computer search of the data bank, the user may select specified parameters and generate a list of sites that best fit those criteria. This ability can be utilized to rapidly select sites in particular time periods or can demonstrate variation and uniqueness, as well as similarity, among sites. As noted, the frequency of Tusayan Corrugated in relation to that of Little Colorado Corrugated may have time control for the area of investigation. To test this idea further, a number of parameters, in addition to the two ceramic types, were selected, including time, vegetation, site facing, orientation, situation, size, and architecture. The search programs generated a matrix suggesting some interesting aspects:

1. Tusayan Corrugated appears in higher relative frequencies in sites dating A.D. 900–1050 and it diminishes between A.D. 1050–1325.

2. A general south orientation of sites exists throughout all time periods.

3. There is a general trend from early sites facing north to later sites facing south.

4. No correlation exists between vegetational zones and site situation; this inability to discern patterning may be due to the applied vegetation classification.

5. Site size, number of rooms, and site condition appear to have no correlation.

Modus Operandi

The modus operandi of the excavation was subjected to a new set of dimensions and some constraints created by the computer interface: (1) daily interaction between field, laboratory, and computer; (2) training and scheduling of personnel; (3) flexibility in initiating different tactical field procedures in light of the daily computer analysis of data; and (4) increased need for rigor in terms and definitions. The investigation demonstrated that modifications were necessary in many of these aspects in order to realize the potential of the computer.

To use computer results to affect daily decisions concerning field operations, it was essential that laboratory analysis keep abreast of data recovery. As a general rule, the use of a computer in this manner will require a greater number of laboratory personnel; in this investigation, involving 20 students, a full-time lab/field ratio of 1:4 proved satisfactory. A research design involving the use of a computer in the field should devise effective laboratory procedures and training of personnel in advance of the actual field implementation in order to ensure a successful application.

Since one of the objectives of our work was the evaluation of the ADAM programming system, access to it was more controlled than might normally have been the case. Students used the computer programs, thereby giving us a basis for evaluating the ease of use of the system by nonprofessional programmers and the training requirements. From the students' speed in data entry, kind of errors, and length of time they required to learn the system, we were able to identify the need for several changes in the operating procedures. Experience has shown that the individual supervising the field investigation should have a basic understanding of the potentials and limitations of the computer application.

Traditional methods of excavation needed modification. For example, data from the first feature of the excavation were subjected to computer analysis and the results suggested that the traditional units of excavation were not statistically significant. We found that the arbitrary 10 cm levels could have been combined and dug in larger vertical units such as overburden, fill, and floor. It is important to recognize that once data from a feature have been subjected to computer analysis and statistically significant levels have been defined, the archaeologist may wish to modify his operating procedures; in this instance horizontal excavation across entire segments of portions of the site, using the statistically defined vertical units, would have been of value.

In a computer application there is a propensity to change field forms and terms to make them more easily handled by the computer; this is an error. The human side of the question must be considered. Forms, records, and terms should be designed for ease of use by the field personnel, not for the computer. However, precise definition of variables is a cornerstone of any scientific approach, and the use of a computer to process the data requires a further degree of rigor in names and terminology. We cannot over-emphasize the need for explicitly defining all variables and standardizing the input codes or abbreviations. However, personnel cannot be depended on to be thorough; automatic verification of terms is essential. The amount of data available (6,423 entries for ceramics alone), was sufficient to test the procedures and programs, and support the above observations.

EVALUATION

Overview

By the very nature of archaeological data an excavation is a one time operation. It is difficult, if not impossible, to replicate the site or excavation unit in the laboratory, making it imperative that maximum value be gleaned from the material excavated. The importance of using the most effective methods of data description for the storage and analysis of information is unquestionable. However, before commitment to a computer approach, a number of factors should be considered. These factors are trade-offs the archaeologist must carefully weigh.

Factor 1. The decision to use or not to use a computer depends on the quantity of data to be processed, the number of statistical tests to be run, and the amount of information to be searched or compared. The nature and scope of the field operation and the time required for completion of the project should be considered.

Factor 2. Remote time-sharing or batch processing of data are alternative means of computer access. If the research is so designed that daily feedback from the fast response of an on-line time-sharing system in a remote location is valuable, then a remote terminal is needed. However, if the research can afford a time delay in obtaining results, one may transport data to the computer location and utilize batch processing.

Factor 3. Several types of telephone service from the remote terminal are available such as a dial-up service or a dedicated telephone line. Their cost must be viewed in terms of the amount of data, the distance involved, and the availability of the service.

Factor 4. Institutions often have available a time-sharing computer that can be used economically; this should be weighed against the usually better but more expensive commercial time-sharing service.

Factor 5. Restrictions in the use of standard computer programs in relation to the expense of developing more efficient programs for specialized field situations must be evaluated.

One goal of this investigation was to demonstrate that a computer application in a remote field location does make a significant difference in decision-making procedures. The research strategy employed involved the generation and testing of questions related to the excavation and survey data and, additionally, an evaluation of the field modus operandi. The modus operandi of the excavation was subjected to a new set of constraints that are the interface with computer technology. The impact of this approach suggests that modifications must be considered in terms of field-laboratory interaction, field tactical decisions, variable definitions and recording forms, and finally, personnel responsibilities.

The second major goal was to demonstrate the utility of computer technology in the field in terms of the following multiple aims: (1) to determine that on-line computer capability could be provided in an archaeological field situation that lacked support facilities; (2) to evaluate the field techniques in a real-time environment of providing data from excavation and survey on a daily basis and subjecting the data to immediate computer analysis; (3) to demonstrate that field personnel could successfully prepare input information, enter it, and isolate errors inevitable in such situations; (4) to develop a special language allowing field personnel to generate unique reports and formats, and to use relatively sophisticated computer techniques; and (5) to test and evaluate the computer programs developed for use under these conditions.

The usefulness of computer techniques to perform the various aspects of the project in terms of on-line computer capabilities, extensive use of file structures, and field personnel use of the developed archaeological computer language has been satisfactorily demonstrated. The on-line computer capability, in a remote field situation that lacked support facilities, functioned even more smoothly than had been expected. File structures, although limited in size, were adequate for the investigation. Field personnel (nonprofessional programmers) efficiently operated the entire project. The archaeological computer language that allowed field personnel to generate sophisticated reports and formats in a real-time situation was readily utilized by the investigator and students with only a minimum of error. Computer programs developed prior to field used functioned extremely well and only minimal changes were required.

Problems

Due to the uniqueness of this approach, certain problems could not be anticipated prior to actual field testing. Considering the substantial amount of data processed, the problems have been relatively minor, but some weaknesses have been identified.

Computer related problems can always be expected in remote processing. Computer malfunctions become extremely acute when on-line updating or analysis is in process. Although this occurred only rarely, a reliable backup approach, such as paper tapes, is indispensable. One must also consider the most efficient time of day to accomplish processing. As the investigator developed more familiarity with the system, it became possible to schedule time so as to minimize the impact on the data processing.

The capabilities and limitations of the computer system in use must be thoroughly recognized by the user. File structure constraints in this instance limited the Master Data file length and necessitated multiple linked files.

Problems related to telephone service can cause unforeseen delays in data processing schedules. Our standard telephone acoustical coupler had to be replaced during the season with a more sensitive type. Telephone lines on the reservation were of considerable age and not always reliable, although maintenance service was excellent. Static was a major difficulty, especially during the daily evening storms so common in that part of the country. Telephone service passes directly through Gallup, New Mexico, where operators occasionally experienced difficulties either obtaining terminal connection or losing the connection once it had been established. If one is sharing a telephone with other users, scheduling must be taken into account. Although we had a telephone at our disposal, the line was shared with the Bureau of Indian Affairs school office, which limited our use to some extent. Most on-line processing was performed during the noon hour or in late afternoons and evenings.

Only minor problems were encountered in the data base management system programs. It is strongly recommended that more automatic procedures to merge, index, and store updated information be designed for future applications. Somewhat limited editing capabilities of the computer system proved annoying when modifications of data were necessary, especially when data in the Master Data file had to be corrected or changed. Student errors in punching tapes and in formatting statistical tests were minimal. When errors did occur, our computer programs provided corrective diagnostics, so that the only problem was one of efficiency; additional time was required for correction of the tapes on which the errors occurred.

Another problem encountered concerned provenience level designations. In order to conserve computer file space the 10 cm excavation levels were combined into arbitrary levels such as fill, overburden, or roof fall, and assigned a computer designed level number. This operation required additional bookkeeping and it became an unnecessary and sometimes confusing procedure; such groupings should be generated by the computer. It is recommended that the finest division of excavation units be used for input and any additional modifications be carried out by the computer.

The process of entering the information from the excavation on a daily basis imposed a severe load on the laboratory personnel, one not usually experienced in a field situation. The problem can become acute as the excavation progresses and there is a shifting of personnel from laboratory to field as a training experience. A permanently staffed laboratory would have been a more efficient approach and would have provided the needed continuity for daily processing.

CONCLUSION

The test of a direct computer link to a remote terminal at a field location proved to be extremely successful. Application of the particular field methodology described requires a minimum of computer and programming knowledge and the technique is amenable to many archaeological investigations where the user has access to telephone service and a computer with time-sharing capabilities.

The total cost of the investigation was minimal. The daily telephone service cost approximately $400. We were not charged for the use of the time-sharing computer facility in Tempe. The design and development of the programming systems involved many hours of work by the investigator prior to the field session. Had this been done by a professional programmer, the cost of the project would have increased considerably.

The most significant contribution of the application of computer techniques was in "response time." The computer performed various routines and transmitted the desired information to the archaeologist in seconds. Requested information ranged from daily data report summaries and results of statistical tests to logical search of the data bank for sites with specific patterns. The computer freed the archaeologist from the tedious manhours needed to calculate or produce the information by manual techniques, and provided him with a tool for rapid evaluation of the hypotheses involved in field research.

Daily tactical procedures of the on-going excavation were dependent on the rapid response time. Hypotheses that were formulated were verified or rejected within a matter of minutes and the results were available to influence the excavation procedures for the following day. Similarly, for the survey data, the computer data bank was searched for cultural or environmental information requested by the archaeologist and it provided guidance for continuing field investigations.

Errors in field procedures or decisions are compounded rapidly in the course of an excavation and often are not recognized until after the termination of the field session. Cumulative errors resulting from statistical or mathematical calculations, biased judgments, or loosely structured terms and concepts can be reduced greatly in the field by both the discipline imposed by the use of a computer and the precision of the calculations.

The investigation described demonstrated that the use of a properly programmed computer accessed from a field location made a substantial contribution to daily tactical decisions and was of significant value as a research tool. The computer has tremendous potential as an adjunct to field research and it is hoped that future applications will expand on this pioneering effort.

REFERENCES

Gaines, Sylvia W.
1971   Computer applications in a field situation. *Newsletter of Computer Archaeology* 7(1): 2–4.
1973   A pragmatic approach to archaeological field problems. *Science and Archaeology* 8: 6–7. Stafford, England: George Street Press.
1974   Computer-aided decision-making procedures for archaeological field problems. *American Antiquity* 39(3): 454–462.
1977   Interactive data retrieval for archaeological field problems. *Revista Mexicana de Estudios Antropologicos* 22(1): 59–77. Mexico City.

9. Computer Graphics in the Analysis of Archaeological Data

Charles W. McNett, Jr.
American University

INTRODUCTION

The use of computer graphics for analysis and display of archaeological data did not develop until the 1970s, perhaps because its efficient use is dependent to some extent on the existence of the large scale data storage and retrieval systems of the last decade. One of the first uses of computer graphics in archaeology came in 1968 with the development of the MAPLO storage and retrieval system at American University (McNett, Gardner, and Kraly 1972), a small scale system based on the IBM 1130 computer. Even using the entire storage capacity of the disc, locational and other information on only about 200 sites could be stored, using a two-column code for each of a maximum of eight variables. Any or all of the variables could be used to search the data file and matches were output to a CalComp or similar pen plotter. Plotter output consisted of a map of specified scale on which the site number of each match was plotted at its proper location. In addition, register marks were drawn so that a transparent map could be overlaid on the distribution plot.

The MAPLO system proved invaluable in studying the distribution of artifact classes in the Potomac River drainage system. Application of the program was limited, however, not only by the special purposes for which it was designed but also by the small size of the available computer and the cumbersome coding required for data input and search.

In succeeding years, little was published on computer graphics, although a number of workers such as Redman and Watson (1970) were developing programs and applications. More recently, the state of the art was discussed at a combined symposium on photogrammetry and computer graphics in archaeology at the annual meeting of the Society for American Archaeology held in St. Louis in 1976 (Upham 1979). This chapter illustrates some of the uses of modern computer graphics in archaeology by describing the methodology used in the excavation and analysis of the Shawnee Minisink Early Man site in eastern Pennsylvania by the Upper Delaware Valley Early Man Project. It is by no means intended to be an exhaustive review of computer graphics in archaeology, but is intended to demonstrate how computer graphics can be an important part of a carefully thought-out research strategy.

Background

The Shawnee Minisink site is located at the confluence of the Delaware River and Brodheads Creek in eastern Pennsylvania about one mile north of the Delaware Water Gap. It was discovered in 1972 by Donald Kline, an avocational archaeologist, who, with his associates, conducted extremely careful excavations at the site in 1972 and 1973, ultimately exposing an area of 400 square feet. From this preliminary work, it appeared that the site was stratified to a depth of more than eight feet and that both Early Archaic and paleo-Indian components existed. Moreover, the paleo-Indian component seemed to be sealed by a thick layer of sterile sand. In his excavation, Kline carefully flotated the contents of a small scatter of charcoal that appeared to be the remnants of a hearth. Recovered were a small fish bone, wild hawthorne pits, and enough charcoal to yield a date of 8640 ±300 B.C. Recognizing the importance of his discovery, Kline asked American University to continue and expand excavation of the site.

American University personnel began excavations in 1974; they confirmed the existence of a sealed paleo-Indian level and observed that the Early Archaic zone was much thicker than had been revealed previously. Excavation continued until the end of the 1977 field season, resulting in the recovery of more than 55,000 artifacts ranging from a fluted Clovis point to thousands of waste flakes.

Research Goals

The chronology of the paleo-Indian and Early Archaic periods in the Northeast had never been adequately defined and researchers were dependent in large part on comparisons with successful efforts by Coe (1964), Broyles (1971), and Gardner (1974) in the Southeast. To accept a priori the existence of the same types in the Northeast was unwarranted, especially when the Shawnee Minisink site appeared to offer the possibility of working out the actual, not comparative, chronology if artifact provenience could be precisely controlled.

If the first goal were achieved, a fine-grained processual analysis would be possible, and that analysis should attempt to assess changes in culture as they relate to environment. Consequently, a second goal of the project was to recover paleo-ecological and geomorphological data as fully as possible from both the site and the area. Hence, the project took a multidisciplinary approach to the excavation.

The third goal of the excavation, based on environmental data and precise artifact provenience, was to define the settlement pattern for each period at the Shawnee Minisink site, including such items as activity areas, evidence for socio-political organization, group size, how the inhabitants utilized the environment, and other similar matters.

The fourth and final goal, unfortunately mainly unrealized by the project, was to study the community pattern—the way in which various types of settlements for a given culture articulated with each other. Obviously, data just from the Shawnee Minisink site was inadequate for this purpose, so other sites in the drainage of Brodheads Creek were sought as time and resources permitted.

FIELD METHODOLOGY

The methodology designed to meet these goals rested on the premise that the precise provenience of all cultural materials recovered should be controlled exactly. This decision was based on the results achieved at the Thunderbird site (Gardner 1974), where excavators drew each artifact found in each three-inch level at its exact horizontal location. How-

ever, this task is time consuming and it is relatively impossible to combine drawings if, say, a living floor occurs in the bottom of one level and the top of the next. We decided instead to follow the lead of Newell and Vroomans (1972); they took three-dimensional coordinate measurements that were adequate to pinpoint the location of each artifact both horizontally and vertically. In the past such a practice would be foolhardy for more than a few artifacts, since the labor involved in hand plotting would be prohibitive. Newell and Vroomans solved that problem by entering the data into a specialized computer storage and retrieval system, and we decided to follow the same course at the Shawnee Minisink site.

In practice, three-person crews excavate with trowels in arbitrary three-inch levels in a horizontal plane to the bottom of the Early Archaic level, since all of these deposits are essentially flat. In the paleo-Indian deposit, which has a rolling topography, levels conform to the surface of the particular stratigraphic zone. As each artifact is discovered, a nail marks the spot and trowelling continues. When the number of artifacts makes trowelling difficult, mapping takes place. All artifacts are measured for depth below the datum plane, and arc measurements from the two southern stakes are taken. All measurements are to 0.01 foot. Arcs were found to be more time efficient than X–Y coordinates and are easily converted by computer into X–Y form for plotting. Also recorded on the data sheet are a unique serial number assigned to each artifact, an assessment of the class of artifact, its material, and other items as needed. To minimize the amount of keypunching required, verbal data are entered in simple, easily remembered codes (EN for end scraper, for example) so that all data for a given artifact take only one card. Following a check of the data in the lab, cards are keypunched and entered into a conversion program that converts the arcs to standard Cartesian coordinates, looks up codes in a dictionary and translates them into full verbal data, and outputs in a form suitable for input to a storage and retrieval system. In addition, the program checks for unknown codes, impossible coordinates, coordinates that occur outside the particular excavation unit, and other data errors.

With this methodology, the excavation is conducted essentially in 0.01 foot levels, and the only purpose of the three-inch levels is as a control for the location of the relatively few artifacts that are recovered from the screen and the flotation samples (Struever 1968) taken from every level. The result is that artifact provenience is precisely controlled, it can be retrieved as needed no matter what the volume of data is, and the data can be recombined at will.

COMPUTERIZATION OF DATA

Selection of an Information Retrieval System

Choosing a data storage and retrieval system can be difficult (Scholtz and Chenhall 1976). Extreme care must be used to ensure that the system will give the results desired, since each system has its own advantages and disadvantages (Chenhall 1975). The large statistical routines such as the Statistical Package for the Social Sciences (Nie et al. 1975) may be all that are needed, since they provide for data reconfiguration, selective retrieval, and also make possible the derivation of all sorts of summary statistics on the data. Plog (see Chapter 5) discusses the use of SPSS as a storage and retrieval system, while its use for interfacing and simple plotting is described below. Given the capabilities of SPSS, it, or similar programming packages, may be adequate for many storage and retrieval applications in archaeology, including output suitable for use with more sophisticated plotting routines.

Other applications, however, such as the data gathered at the Shawnee Minisink site, require a larger and more sophisticated storage and retrieval system. The SELGEM system developed by the Smithsonian Institution was chosen for the Upper Delaware Valley Early Man Project for a number of reasons. SELGEM handled verbal data as well as numeric. It was thus possible for excavators to enter notes about artifact provenience and other items. In practice, for instance, all artifacts noted by the excavators at the time of recovery as from rodent disturbed areas could be easily eliminated from analysis using SELGEM. This same facility with verbal data also meant that a full description of each artifact could be entered if necessary, so that the researcher was not forced to use one of a relatively few codes as required with SPSS.

Another advantage of SELGEM, considering the cost of research today, was the ready availability of versions that could be installed on the American University IBM-370 computer at minimal expense. In addition, SELGEM was judged suitable for a wide range of other projects, planned or underway, including the conversion of the MAPLO verbal data into a large scale storage and retrieval system and a number of bibliographic projects made possible by the indexing routines.

Finally, a number of archaeologists using SELGEM were enthusiastic about its potential for our discipline (see Chapter 4). Consequently, versions of the basic storage (SELGEM) and retrieval (SELEXT) routines were secured from Eastern New Mexico University and an edit program (SELEPT) was obtained from Texas Tech University; these were installed at the American University computer facility.

It should be reiterated that because SELGEM best suited the purposes of analysis of the Shawnee Minisink material, it does not mean that it would be best for another project. The basic question to be asked should be: Is the system chosen the least expensive and simplest that will adequately do the job? Criteria useful in making this decision include the possibility that a suitable system such as SPSS already exists at the user's installation; the availability of a source code specifically adapted to the user's hardware; the experience of support personnel at the user's computer center; number of assistants available for coding, data checking, and program operation; possibility of using the system for other research projects both within and outside the archaeologist's department; and a host of similar considerations. After such an evaluation, it might become clear that hand plotting is a suitable alternative, or that a general purpose analysis routine like SPSS would suffice.

In the case of the Shawnee Minisink data, only a system capable of handling massive amounts of data, some of it verbal, was suitable. The fully developed master analysis tape is expected to have about 400,000 records relating to about 55,000 artifacts. The 1979 partial master list contained 240,000 lines on 4,760 pages and took nearly four hours to print on a high speed printer. Therein lies the crux of using a large system such as SELGEM—the computer will search through all those pages looking for a specific kind of artifact in about nine minutes of central processing time, and will not miss any.

Interfacing for Graphics

Having the data in a storage and retrieval system is but the beginning, however. Considerable time must be spent checking the data to ensure that they are correct, and then more time and effort must be expended in interfacing—getting the data into the form necessary for the available graphics routines. As an initial step, the Shawnee Minisink data were searched for known sources of error such as the words "rodent" or "disturbed" in comment categories and for association with intrusive pits. These "purified" data then were searched for the selected categories to be used in plots, including both material and artifact types such as end scrapers and utilized flakes.

A "purified" tape may be suitable for many analytic purposes. For instance, counts of artifacts by square or level and various statistical tables relating to artifact characteristics can be achieved through the use of appropriate selection and listing options, whether the data are stored in SPSS or SELGEM or any other adequate system.

Many graphic routines require rather specific formats for the input data, as do many other special purpose programs. If the data are in SPSS or a similar analytic routine, they can be selected as desired and written out in the proper format. But SELGEM and most storage and retrieval systems present certain problems. For instance, in SELGEM, missing data categories are simply omitted. As a result, there may be a variable number of data points for each item stored. On the other hand, most analytic and graphic routines require fixed field information, in which missing data are coded as missing, not simply omitted.

Fortunately, a special routine (SRPLTP) has been developed at Eastern New Mexico University solving this problem for SELGEM users. This procedure inserts at request a category filled with blanks every time missing categories are encountered so that the input always has the right number of data points for each item. In practice, to get any kind of interface desired, the "purified" SELGEM tape master is run through SRPLTP to produce only the categories. This interface tape is then input to SPSS without difficulty, and the data are analyzed as desired. If special purpose formats are required for other analytic routines or plotting, they are easily generated as output by appropriate SPSS control cards.

Interface thus may be the major problem faced by anyone desiring to use computer graphics and analytic routines on computer stored data. Depending on the storage and retrieval system used, it may require writing special purpose programs such as SRPLTP or it may only require a "write" statement in SPSS or a similar routine. Careful planning and creative use of available options in the software at the user's institution are once again crucial to the success of the research.

Punching original data in the format needed for the graphics routines, thus avoiding problems of storage and interface, is not recommended for any large scale application because recombination and selection of specific classes of data to be plotted may be impossible. The advantage of the storage and retrieval routines as a first step is the ability of the researcher to retrieve and plot only desired classes and combinations of data at any given step in the analysis. It would be the rare project, indeed, in which the exact combinations of artifacts to be plotted were known prior to the beginning of analysis. Also, few researchers want to apply graphics routines exclusively to their data; other analytic and data display routines are almost certain to be used. The problem of interfacing between the graphics data and the analytic display routines may be as major as the problems already discussed between data bank and graphics routines.

After all problems of storage and retrieval and interfacing have been solved, the resulting work tape will be in the format needed for the graphics routines described next. To reiterate, the data should have been

screened both for problems of provenience such as rodent disturbance, and for keypunch and recording errors. Often a listing of the work tape can be scanned and obvious errors removed.

COMPUTER GRAPHICS APPLICATIONS

Most of the illustrations of computer graphics presented here are derived from McMillan (1977) at American University. The data set involved Early Archaic artifacts from a 20-by-50 foot contiguous block excavated during the 1974 season of the Upper Delaware Valley Early Man Project. These data were used in a pilot project both to assess the effectiveness of graphics routines in archaeological analysis, and to solve the expected problems in using the routines, including interfacing. Results were encouraging and the routines will be used in the final analysis of the Shawnee Minisink site data.

Scattergram Routines

Perhaps the simplest solution to graphics display, available at virtually every institution, is the scattergram routine outputting to the printer. It is found in such general purpose statistical routines as SPSS. A scattergram plots in two dimensions on a standard set of X–Y coordinates. If the data are to be plotted with a top (plan) view, the X–Y coordinates of the artifact locations are used. Some experimentation with the input parameters may be necessary in order to get the two axes into the same scale so that both lines and spaces represent the same distance. The printout is a plot with the artifacts at their approximate location (examples are shown in Copp 1977). Such routines usually use an asterisk to indicate a single artifact located in the block represented by the particular printer line and space; numbers 2–9 signify the number of artifacts at a single location, and a plus sign indicates more than nine artifacts. This arrangement is obviously useful in allowing one to visually inspect the distribution of various classes of artifacts in the excavation.

In order to search for stratigraphy and look at the site from a side view, some juggling of the data may be required using compute commands to reconfigure the data. If the data are in the form of X–Y coordinates and elevations are above the bottom of the site, the coordinates specified to the scattergram routine are the X coordinate and the elevation (Z coordinate) instead of the Y coordinate, with no reconfiguration required. If the third coordinate (Z) is a depth measurement, however, it is necessary to insert a minus sign before each reading (thus forcing the plot down into the minus X axis), or to subtract each depth from the maximum depth in order to convert to elevations and then proceed as before. If one of these procedures is *not* followed, the resulting printout will be a mirror image of the actual site. In using scattergram routines, as in all computing, a little judicious use of small test files is highly recommended before the real analysis is attempted.

With some scattergram routines in powerful analytic packages, further steps in analysis may be taken. With the selective retrieval (SELECT IF) facility of SPSS, it is possible to plot through the site, either side or plan view, in "slices." For instance, suppose it is desired to plot in plan view the artifacts in each level as excavated or from one or a few contiguous levels. Then the user would specify the selection of all artifacts between the upper and lower boundaries of the level(s) desired for the plot. If multiple plots of successive levels are desired, the process would be repeated as needed.

Two problems with standard scattergram packages are immediately apparent in some archaeological applications. It may be very difficult to change the angle of view of the site without a mathematical expertise most anthropologists do not possess. Moreover, most, if not all, standard scattergram routines will not allow the use of special symbols for different classes of data so that it is difficult to locate, much less interpret, two or more classes of artifacts in the same plot.

BACKPLOT Routine

A special purpose graphics routine with these and many other features is BACKPLOT written by H. Martin Wobst. With this program, it is possible to automatically adjust scales and generate as many slices through the site as desired. The routine is much less cumbersome to use than a standard scattergram routine and with special input parameters we can specify the order in which the data will be input. In addition to the standard data we have been discussing, it is also possible to input the angle of the horizontal axis of an artifact in relation to a datum plane (i.e., the "dip"—upright, angled, and flat) and the serial number. With the serial number we can produce two kinds of indices to the plot as an aid in locating individual artifacts on it.

BACKPLOT, which outputs to the printer and is easily adapted for use at most institutions with the appropriate FORTRAN compiler, is an excellent two-dimensional graphics routine; it even has provisions for limited internal data modification. Figure 9.1 illustrates a typical plot of jasper artifacts from the Shawnee Minisink site, shown from the side. In addition to an Early Archaic component at the top of the entire plot, a lower component also appears to the right. This lower component had been tentatively identified

at the time of excavation; its existence is immediately evident in the plot.

Figure 9.2 is an illustration of the use of BACKPLOT with different symbols for each different artifact class. Identifying stratigraphically associated artifacts is easier using this kind of graphic display technique. In the illustration, the technique produces a plan view plot, although the program surprisingly lacks this feature. The production of it is possible with a little creative manipulation. To achieve it, the site must be turned on its side, as it were, and then the program may be operated as usual. The correction facility built into BACKPLOT makes this relatively easy to accomplish. In Shawnee Minisink applications, SPSS is used for the selection of artifacts to be plotted from the work tape, so it is more convenient and certainly more straightforward to use SPSS for the same purpose.

The slice feature of BACKPLOT is particularly effective since plan views of any depth may be generated easily. For instance, Figure 9.3 shows one such slice only 11 cm thick generated by the program. If living floors can be determined, this option allows them to be plotted without extraneous artifacts from other levels.

Care must be taken when generating plan views with this program because the plot labels will be incorrect, showing the information for a side view. Relabeling by hand is advised to avoid confusion.

BACKPLOT may be the only graphics routine that is needed for many analytic and display needs, and it is highly recommended. Indeed, by using both side and plan views, a pseudo-three-dimensional view of the site can be obtained. In some applications, however, a true three-dimensional view may be necessary.

BLOCK Routine

In compiling a three-dimensional view, the procedure becomes somewhat more complicated and expensive. For the Shawnee Minisink data, a program called BLOCK has been utilized. This routine, written by Jonathan O. Davis for research applications at Washington State University, has proven extremely flexible. It requires access to a CalComp or similar pen plotter and, in some applications, a large mirror stereoscope. Neither may be readily available at most institutions. If three dimensional plots are necessary, the expense may be well worth it.

Basically, BLOCK provides either a single or double view of any surface such as the topography of a site. Vertical exaggeration to maximize differences in elevation is possible, and any angle of view may be obtained by suitable parameters. Data input are the elevations of a regular grid over the surface to be displayed, plus a series of objects (artifacts, etc.) to be

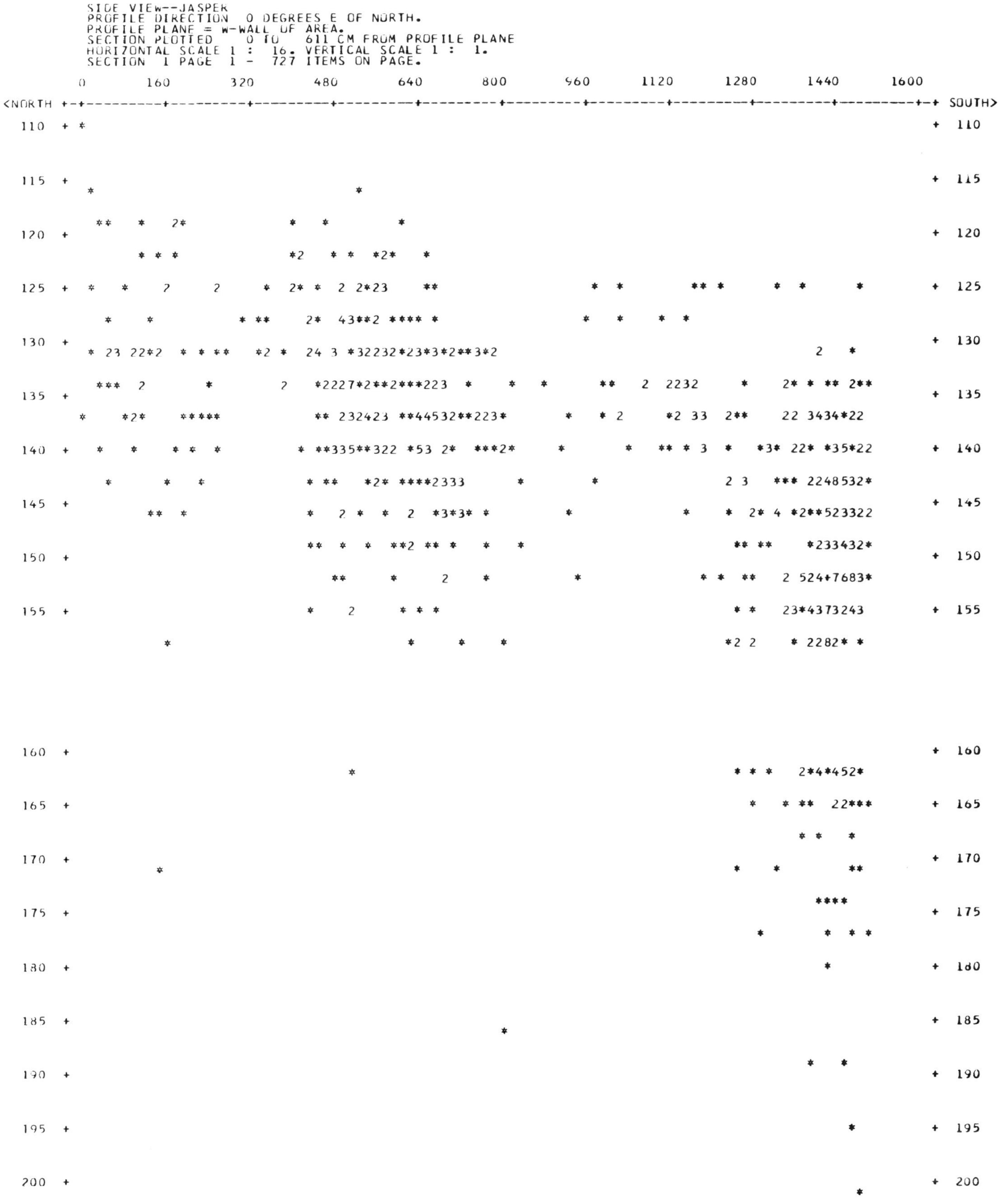

Fig. 9.1. Conventional use of BACKPLOT. A plot of all jasper artifacts from the Shawnee Minisink test file as seen from the side. A second lower component can be seen to the right (south) of the plot.

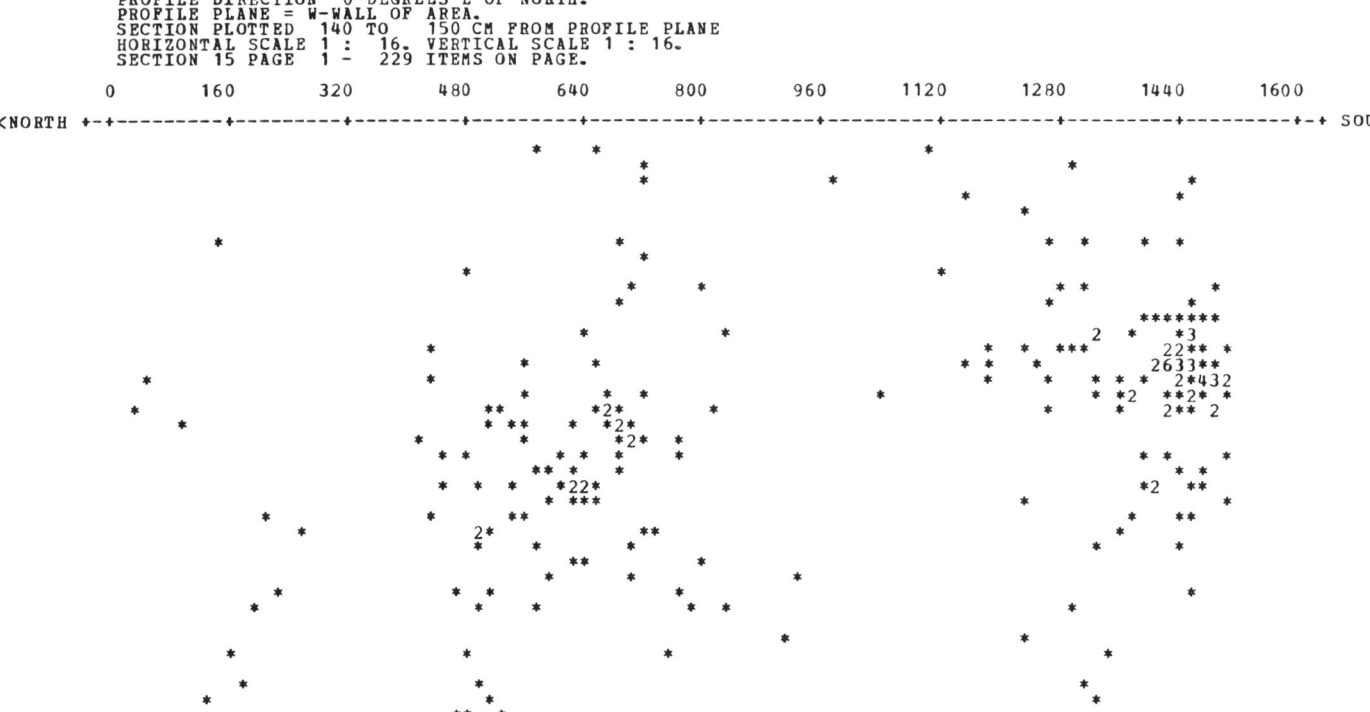

Fig. 9.2. The use of different symbols with BACKPLOT. A plot of all points (G) and endscrapers (H) from the test file, seen in plan view. All orientation information except north-south is incorrect, since the site has been turned on its side, but measurement data are accurate. Input plot label should be used in plot to indicate plan view.

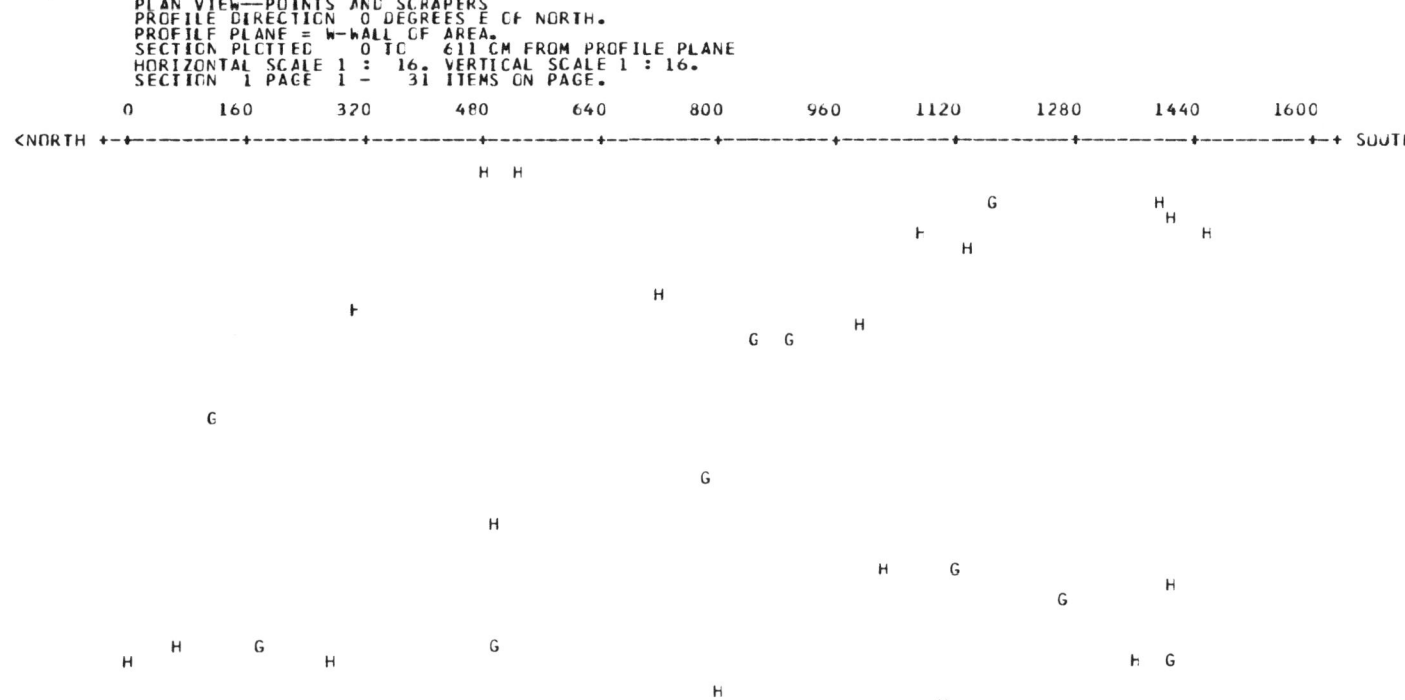

Fig. 9.3. Automated slice feature of BACKPLOT in plan view. A 10 cm slice through the site seen from the top. Shown are the jasper artifacts from 140-150 cm below site datum.

plotted in relation to the surface. In practice, a single view is adequate if only the surface is to be displayed; the major problem here is a "chicken wire view" (to use Davis' words) if too few elevations are entered. This is easily remedied using a surveyor's computer library routine to interpolate additional elevations between those actually read in the field. In fact, if enough elevations are used, the surface will have reasonably fair curves between elevation points.

For many archaeological purposes, we may wish to plot artifacts in relation to this surface, and all of the symbols available to the pen plotter may be used so that many classes of artifacts may be plotted simultaneously. In this application, the use of the double view and mirror stereoscope is absolutely necessary in order to determine where the artifacts actually are located. If no surface data exist, a flat plane may be drawn over the artifacts by specifying all elevations as the same.

This aspect of the use of BLOCK was developed in 1979 for the Shawnee Minisink data, and one problem became apparent. Using a flat-bed plotter, a plot about three feet square could be generated, but the cost of a mirror stereoscope to view a plot of that size was prohibitive. Using an 18-inch mirror stereoscope, a plot of about one foot square approaches the maximum usable size. Unfortunately, plotting a large number of artifacts to that scale may result in a generalized blob of ink over the more prolific parts of the output. The solution is to plot sections of the site (squares, for example), and examine them singularly. When a rare class of artifacts is plotted, however, the problem does not exist.

In the foregoing, real elevations and real artifacts are plotted. Figure 9.4 represents the 1979 surface of the Shawnee Minisink site and its environs output by BLOCK. This view is much more graphic in its depiction than the standard contour map, and minor differences in elevation have been brought into relief by using a five to one vertical exaggeration.

Unreal elevations may also be graphically displayed using BLOCK or the generally similar SYMVU program put out by Harvard University. In the SYMVU application, frequency counts or other numerical data are used as "elevations" so that the high spots in the surface represent greater counts, the low spots infrequent occurrence. For instance, at the Shawnee Minisink site Richard J. Dent discovered that high phosphorus readings corresponded with high frequencies of paleo-Indian artifacts. By taking samples on a regular grid with a three-inch bucket auger and analyzing them for phosphorus content, it was possible to delineate the exact extent of the paleo-Indian occupation without making extensive eight-foot deep test pits. The two pits that were dug confirmed the

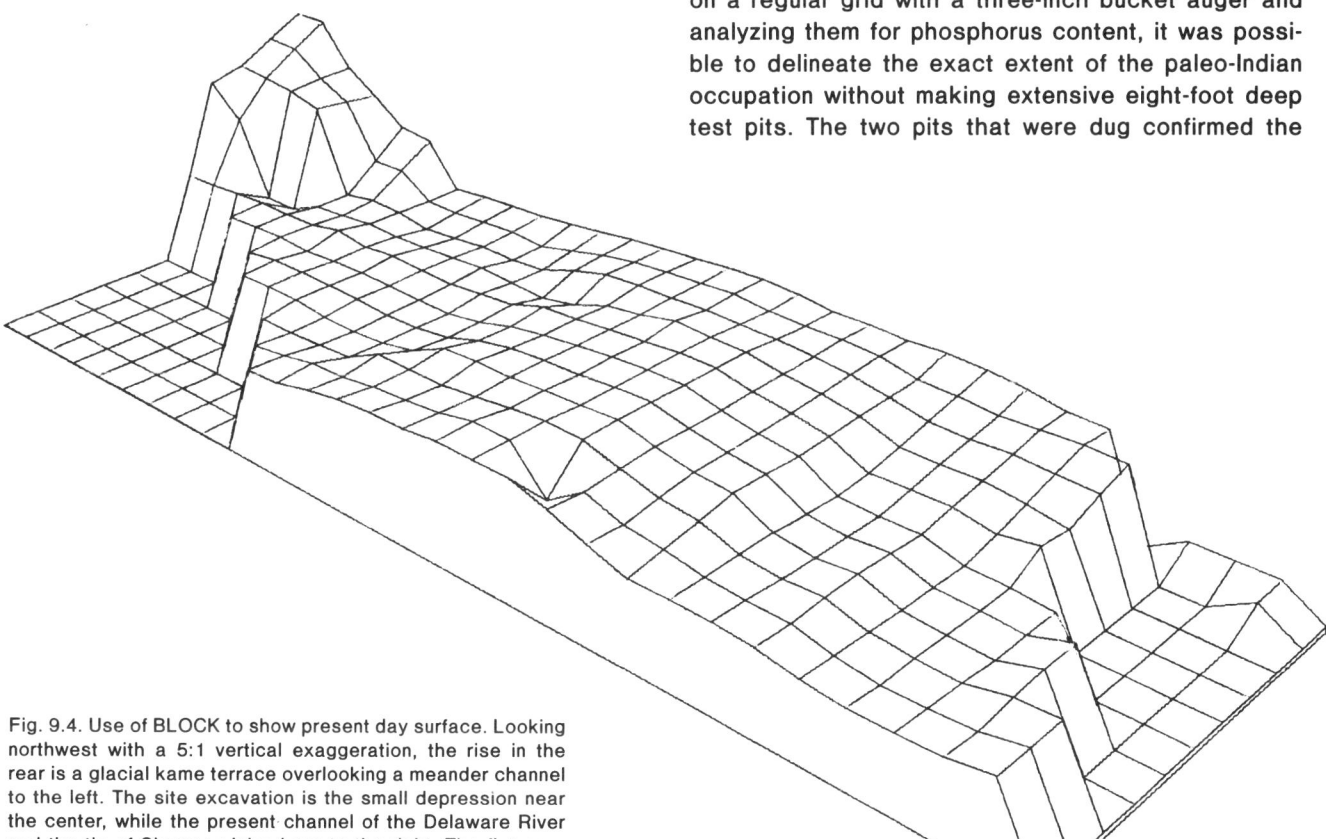

Fig. 9.4. Use of BLOCK to show present day surface. Looking northwest with a 5:1 vertical exaggeration, the rise in the rear is a glacial kame terrace overlooking a meander channel to the left. The site excavation is the small depression near the center, while the present channel of the Delaware River and the tip of Shawnee Island are to the right. The flat area with zero elevation to the left is an old railroad bed where elevations were not taken.

predictions from the soil chemistry tests. In this case, there were relatively few readings and so the results were readily apparent. With a great number of readings, however, BLOCK or a similar routine could be used to display the data for easier interpretation.

Another use of frequency data common in archaeology is the display of artifact counts, wherein the elevations are the number of artifacts per excavation unit under analysis. This application has been amply illustrated in Redman and Watson (1970), as has the use of SYMAP, another Harvard University program that displays frequencies on the printer, darker areas corresponding to higher frequencies.

A final illustration of the use of three-dimensional routines such as BLOCK should suffice to indicate the potential that computer graphics has for archaeology. Factor analysis and similar multivariate techniques are used frequently, but the graphic display of relationships is difficult in more than two dimensions. The usual solution is to plot the factors two at a time, but interpretation is hindered as it is with BACKPLOT because only two dimensions can be handled at once. If there are only three dimensions, there is another way to display the results. We can use BLOCK with a flat upper surface and input the coordinates of the variables (or cases, depending on the type of factor analysis) in the factor space as if they were artifacts. By assigning a unique number to each variable (case), the results of the factor analysis may be readily observed. In addition, some theorists are concerned with the validity of factor rotation as it is now practiced. Rotation is, of course, used primarily to make the factors more interpretable, but it is not necessary if the factors are plotted in three dimensions.

Furthermore, if an R–type factor analysis is undertaken (the variables are factored), the cases may still be plotted using the factor scores generated by the factoring program. In this instance, even if more than three factors are necessary, the cases may be plotted on the first three factors and, if principal components without rotation have been used, they will be the three most important factors for the data.

If plots require two or more dimensions, archaeologists frequently use factor or other multivariate techniques. In such cases computer graphics seems to have as much to offer in displaying and interpreting results of analysis as it does in conjunction with the archaeologists' concern with artifact patterning and other data in space.

SUMMARY

In this chapter I have discussed the ways in which an archaeological research project can utilize computer graphics for improved display and analysis of the data recovered. The uses described include graphic display of artifact provenience in both two and three dimensions, frequency tabulations ranging from artifact counts to phosphorus readings, a printout that can substitute for the conventional contour map, and interpretation of factor and other multivariate analysis. Obviously, there are more uses to which these powerful descriptive tools can be put; these are simply the ways in which the techniques are being used on data from the Shawnee Minisink site by the Upper Delaware Valley Early Man Project.

The need for careful planning cannot be overstressed. All too often researchers in anthropology approach me for advice on statistical analysis of their data *after* they return from the field. Usually the data are not suitable for computer analysis at all, or they are in such a form that a less efficient or informative set of analytic routines has to be used.

In using computer graphics as part of a research strategy, the following steps are suggested. The first step is to determine the research goals of the project. The second step is to decide on the excavation strategy and methodology necessary to meet these goals. The third step is to decide whether computer processing, including use of computer graphics, will be useful in handling the data. If this decision is reached after due consideration, the fourth step is to carefully examine the software available at the user's institution and to decide if some or all of it will meet the needs of the project. Only after a thorough investigation can the determination be made as to whether new software has to be secured or written for specific project purposes. Unfortunately, this fifth step will entail an additional, certainly time consuming and possibly expensive, sixth step of installing and debugging the new routines at the user's installation. A final step, whenever computer procedures are used, entails the testing of all routines with ideal data files invented by the user to ensure that they do what is expected and to develop the decks of control cards that will enable rapid processing of the data when the project begins.

Obviously, all of this work involves a large expenditure of time, effort, and money—knowing when *not* to use computer data processing is as important as knowing *how* to use it. Using the simplest and least expensive computer methodology congruent with the research goals of the project appears the most compelling criterion in these days of rapidly rising research costs and shrinking research funds.

ACKNOWLEDGMENTS

In addition to those persons cited in the text, the author would like to thank Sylvia Gaines for her patience and encouragement. Richard J. Dent, June Evans, and Barbara McMillan read an earlier version of this paper and offered valuable comments.

REFERENCES

Broyles, Bettye
1971 Second preliminary report: The St. Albans site, Kanawha County, West Virginia. *Report of Archeological Investigations* 3. West Virginia Geological and Economic Survey.

Chenhall, Robert G.
1975 *Museum Cataloguing in the Computer Age.* Nashville: American Association for State and Local History.

Coe, Joffre
1964 Formative cultures of the Carolina Piedmont. *Transactions of the American Philosophical Society* 54.

Copp, Stan A.
1977 A quick plotting program for archaeological data. *Newsletter of Computer Archaeology* 13: 17-24.

Gardner, William M.
1974 The Flint Run Complex: A preliminary report, 1971-73 seasons. *Occasional Publications* 1. Archaeology Laboratory, Catholic University.

McMillan, Barbara A.
1977 The Shawnee Minisink Site: A Technological Analysis of the Early Archaic. Unpublished Ph.D. dissertation, The American University.

McNett, Charles W., Jr., William M. Gardner, and Karen Kraly
1972 A computer program for mapping distribution of artifacts. *Newsletter for Computer Archaeology* 8: 2-3.

Newell, R. R., and A. P. J. Vroomans
1972 *Automatic Artifact Registration and Systems for Archaeological Analysis with the Philips P-1100 Computer: a Mesolithic Test Case.* New York: Humanities Press.

Nie, Norman H., C. H. Hull, J. G. Jenkins, K. Steinbrenner, and D. H. Bent
1975 *SPSS: Statistical Package for the Social Sciences.* 2nd Edition. New York: McGraw-Hill.

Redman, Charles L., and Patty Jo Watson
1970 Systematic, intensive surface collection. *American Antiquity* 35: 279-291.

Scholtz, Sandra, and Robert G. Chenhall
1976 Archaeological data banks in theory and practice. *American Antiquity* 41: 89-96.

Struever, Stuart
1968 Flotation techniques for the recovery of small-scale archaeological remains. *American Antiquity* 33: 353-362.

Upham, Steadman, editor
1979 Computer graphics in archaeology: Statistical cartographic applications to archaeological contexts. *Anthropological Research Papers* 15. Tempe: Arizona State University.

10. Information Retrieval Applications for Archaeology in Britain

J. D. Wilcock

Research Centre for Computer Archaeology, Stafford, England

MUSEUM APPLICATIONS

The IRGMA Contribution

From the middle 1960s the major effort in museum information retrieval in Britain was undertaken by members of the Information Retrieval Group of the Museums Association (IRGMA), renamed the Museums Documentation Association (MDA) in 1977. One of the chief workers, Geoffrey Lewis (1965, 1970/71; Lewis et al. 1967, 1969), formerly curator of Sheffield City Museum and later appointed curator of Liverpool City Museums, first called for a national lead to be taken in the organization of a standard museum index in a 1965 article. Several reports were presented at the 1967 colloquium on information retrieval at Sheffield Museum, including one by Renfrew on the requirements of the research worker in archaeology, and these papers were published in 1967, edited by Lewis (Renfrew 1967). The draft proposals for an interdisciplinary museum cataloging system were published by IRGMA in 1969 (Lewis et al. 1969), containing a full list of the categories used in the pilot scheme. A perusal of this document reveals that archaeology had been handled by IRGMA purely as a museum discipline up to 1969, for the proposed categories of information were suitable for museum records of finds but not at all suitable for archaeological site records nor for the routine cataloging of county and parish finds. Lewis (1970/71) stated in his summary of the IRGMA communication format that failure to appreciate the significance of the computer among museum staff, a profession concerned with the collection, processing, and dissemination of information, could only diminish the status of the museum as an information source. By the early 1970s pilot studies had been carried out in several museum disciplines, and it was known that preparation of data for computer input added only about one-twentieth of the cost to the existing cost of traditional cataloging. Nevertheless, IRGMA decided in 1971 that a national computer archive on a single central machine, with records from all museums in the United Kingdom, was unrealistic. Systems designed to meet *local* requirements, implemented on local computers, were felt to be more efficient, for the museum information on hand often orginated from a variety of sources outside the control of the museum, and the records were of variable reliability and completeness. A national standard designed to accommodate all possible local requirements would, it was felt, be most unwieldy and uneconomic.

But the IRGMA decision to decentralize meant that there would be hardware differences among the local computers of different manufacture. In the late 1970s the problem of hardware incompatibility still had not been solved, although interfacing and packet switching had progressed toward the goal of universal communication between computers. The chief problem is that each time a significant advance in computer hardware is made, the earlier equipment becomes obsolete rapidly. Truly efficient and economic communication between computers presupposes a common interface and standardized control and data codes, but this degree of compatibility had not been reached at the time of the IRGMA decision in 1971.

Having decided to decentralize, therefore, IRGMA was forced to propose communication between individual local computer records by some machine-independent means. Thus the "high-level communication format" proposed by IRGMA in 1969 was evolved, consisting of a defined series of categories of information. To ensure direct communication between n local, incompatible computers would require the writing of n(n−1) programs, for each of the n computers would have to communicate with n−1 others. Using the high-level communication format as an intermediary, the idea was that only 2n programs would be required (a much smaller number), each computer needing only two programs to handle transfer to and from the high-level format.

The IRGMA decision was probably correct under the circumstances prevailing at the time; the "state of the art" had not developed sufficiently for full hardware compatibility. Moreover, in view of Lewis's (1970/71) comments about the reluctance of some curators to employ computer methods, it should in fairness be pointed out that at the time some museums had not even acknowledged the need for a manual card reference file, adhering to the traditional method of recording each accession by a small sketch and handwritten comments in a collection of bound registers. A newsletter was issued in 1969 by IRGMA to publicize the proposals, but only a single edition ever appeared. Its place has been taken by instruction manuals issued with the various types of IRGMA cards (which are designed to be used both as conventional box file cards for manual reference, and as computer input documents), and also by the Museum Documentation Association periodicals *MDA News* and *MDA Information* (published by the Museum Documentation Association since 1977).

Thus we can see the IRGMA achievement in its true light as a high-level communication format that defined the information structures, but that was independent of any particular computer hardware. Naturally, specific computer implementations were carried out (the GOS program), notably on IBM 360 and ICL System 4 machines, by Cutbill (1973, 1974), the chief systems analyst for IRGMA. The data structure is hierarchical, employing several levels of sub-items, each kind of data corresponding to a specific box on a custom-designed index card. Several such cards have been printed for use in museums, and for fine art, geological specimens, history artifacts, mineralogical specimens, natural history specimens, scientific instruments, uniforms, bones, and general "museum objects," as well as for archaeology. They were designed by teams of museum curators, experts in the specific disciplines, and information scientists to meet museum cataloging requirements. All cards were subjected to a lengthy period of field trials followed by assessment and redesign where necessary, and they proved satisfactory in both manual and computerized reference systems.

Arising out of the Liverpool conference of the Information Retrieval Group of the Museums Association in October 1972, a subcommittee was set up to design a record card for archaeological objects. The subcommittee met through 1973, and the prototype card went to field trials in early 1974. An object group record card was also issued in prototype form in late 1974. As a result of field evaluation a modified object card was issued in early 1976 (see Fig. 10.1*a*, *b*). The group record card was still under evaluation in 1977, as was the whole philosophy of the recording of groups of objects.

The categories of information on the Archaeology Object record card were designed to fit the IRGMA software as developed by Cutbill (1973) and Williams. The card was intended primarily for museum use, but it was hoped that field archaeologists would also use it, in the interests of compatibility and communication. As an example, the York Archaeological Trust, a rescue unit with particularly strong links with the Yorkshire Museum, began to use a redesigned form of the IRGMA cards adapted to finds recording in 1975. The Archaeology Object card, redesigned as a result of field trials, contained boxes for the following categories of information:

1. Administration details
    1.1 Computer file name
    1.2 Institution (e.g., museum) and identity number (e.g., accession number assigned by the museum)
2. Identification
    2.1 Simple name (e.g., common term applied to object by the archaeologist)
    2.2 Materials
    2.3 Number of similar items found
    2.4 Full name or classified identification
    2.5 System of classification
    (Note. The last two headings are for use where an accepted classification system is in use; its name is placed in 2.5 and the class of the object under this system in 2.4.)
    2.6 Identifier (authority for identification) and date of the classification.
3. Dating
    3.1 Object period (a relatively vague term in common use; e.g., Palaeolithic, Mesolithic, Neolithic, Bronze Age, Iron Age, Roman, Migration and Early Medieval, Medieval, Industrial).
    3.2 Object date (numerical value in years with B.C., A.D., B.P.).
    3.3 Dating method
    3.4 Cross reference to result (laboratory number, etc.)
    3.5 Researcher and date
    (Note. The last three headings are for use where the object has been dated by some scientific method such as radiocarbon or magnetic dating.)
4. Collection or Excavation
    4.1 Site name
    4.2 Site number
    4.3 Grid location (National Grid Reference, or Global Reference Code based on Latitude and Longitude, with value, units, and accuracy)

a.

	FILE	CONTINUATION OF	ARCHAEOLOGY OBJECT RECORD CARD	

IDENTIFICATION

Simple name		Materials	Count
Classified identification		Classification system	

Cont

Identifier	Date	Unique/Pet name

DATING

Object period		Object date

Cont

Dating method	Dating authority		Dating date

COLLECTION/ EXCAVATION

Site name	Site number	Lat/long Grid ref	Co-ordinates value/units	Co-ordinate detail
Locality				
Site detail				

Context	Context detail		3-D co-ordinates
Context period (position dating)		Context date value/units	

Cont

Collection method	Collector/excavator	Collection cross-reference	

HISTORY

Acquisition method	Initial holder	Conditions	Transfer date

Cont

Storage location	Storage date

IDENTITY

Institution	Identity number	Recorder's name	Record date

b.

DESCRIPTION

Condition keyword	Condition detail	Completeness keyword	Completeness detail
Inscription mark	Position	Inscription/mark detail	
Dimension being measured		Dimension value/units	Reliability/accuracy/detail
Dimension being measured		Dimension value/units	Reliability/accuracy/detail

Cont

Dimension being measured		Dimension value/units	Reliability/accuracy/detail

PROCESS

Conservation process	Conservation cross-reference	Conservation detail	Conservation date
Conservation process	Conservation cross-reference	Conservation detail	Conservation date

Cont

Reproduction type	Reproduction cross-reference	Reproduction type	Reproduction cross-reference
Reference class	Author	Article title	

Cont

Journal/Book title	Volume/Edition	Date	Pagination	Page/Plate detail

UNDEFINED

Notes

Cont

Fig. 10.1*a, b*. The IRGMA Archaeology Object Card issued in early 1976.
(Reproduced by courtesy of the Information Retrieval Group of the Museum Association.)

4.4 Place name detail (incorporating elements such as Parish, District, County, Country)

4.5 Archaeological context (a *context* may be a depositional feature such as a layer, wall, foundation, or pit fill, or an "erosional" feature such as an erosion surface, foundation trench, robber trench, or pit outline)

4.6 Context period or date

4.7 Locality detail on site (3D grid, etc.)

4.8 Collection method

4.9 Collector or Excavator and Date (Site Director and date of excavation)

4.10 Find number allocated by collector or excavator

5. Acquisition (from the point of view of the museum)

   5.1 Acquisition method

   5.2 Person/Institution acquired from, and date of acquisition

   5.3 Price

   5.4 Conditions Yes/No (permanent loan, etc.)

   5.5 Valuation and date of valuation

6. Store

   6.1 Store and date of storage

   6.2 Recorder and date of recording

7. Description

   7.1 Condition keyword/detail

   7.2 Completeness keyword/detail

   (Note. Condition and completeness are sometimes confused; they are two essentially different concepts, since it is possible to have excavated only part of an object, but in an excellent state of preservation.)

   7.3 Dimensions (each in terms of dimension measured, value, units, and accuracy)

   7.4 Inscriptions, marks, and so on, with their transcription and description in terms of method used, position of feature, and detail

   7.5 Part descriptions, in terms of part being described, aspect, keywords, and detail; for example, handle (part), color (aspect), red (keyword).

8. Processes

   8.1 Conservation, reproduction, or other process (e.g., scientific determination of composition)

   8.2 Method with detail; operator; date; with laboratory numbers, results, and so on, where appropriate

9. Documentation

   9.1 Class of documentation

   9.2 Author

   9.3 Date

   9.4 Title

   9.5 Journal or Publisher (of book)

   9.6 Volume

   9.7 Detail (pagination, figure numbers, plate numbers)

   9.8 Drawing or photograph numbers

The above categories of information were structured, in terms of definition and position in the record, and readily retrieved by the computer. A further category (10. Notes) was appended for the insertion of additional comments. Since they are unstructured they cannot be retrieved, except as transcription in whole.

The prototype group record card released in 1975 had similar entries for administration, collection or excavation, acquisition, store, documentation and notes; the contents of the group were then to be described in terms of simple names, materials, number of items, identity numbers, and details. However, the pilot use of this card created numerous problems, and in 1979 the whole philosophy of group record cards was still under review.

Other Museum Applications

In the infancy of the IRGMA System, Renfrew (1967) commented on the need for information on the provenience of an object, its present location in the museum, and also the need for a national museum index. He emphasized that archaeologists researching in a particular field needed to be able to determine the museums containing items of interest to them, and he proposed that different sections of the catalog include biology, geology, archaeology, history, and art; the existence of marginal items belonging to two or more sections was inconvenient but inevitable. He made the point that archaeological codes of description could never have the finality, for example, of species names in biology. This raised the problem of archaeological "type," its advantages and disadvantages, and whether or not the concept of type could be abolished.

Roads (1968) described the use of 80-column punched cards in cataloging the collection of the Imperial War Museum. This museum also found a use for *aperture cards,* which are 80-column Hollerith cards with a space for insertion of a microfilm photograph of a document or object (Fig. 10.2). Aperture cards may be filed in the same way as normal punched cards, and may be punched in those columns not occupied by the microfilm aperture, thus providing some features of edge-punched cards or PEEKABOO cards. Roads also discussed the future transcription of cards onto magnetic disc for computer processing.

INFORMATION RETRIEVAL FOR ARCHAEOLOGICAL SITES

The second major application of computerized information retrieval in archaeology is the site file. The aim here is to record every item as it emerges from the ground, in sufficient detail to allow information retrieval to be performed while the diggers are still on the site, in order that decisions may be made on profitable and nonprofitable areas of the excavation. This mode of working is particularly useful for rescue digs where time is limited.

The application was still in its infancy in the 1970s, largely due to lack of equipment and financing. During this period the hard-pressed rescue units in Britain spent all their meagre resources on wages, digging

Fig. 10.2. Aperture card. A Hollerith 80-column card with an aperture for insertion of a microfilm photograph of a document or object. The left-hand part of the card may be punched with ISO card codes for retrieval purposes.

equipment, and publication, and had none left over for computer processing. Ironically, if only the capital equipment had been available, much money could have been saved in clerical assistance and publication costs. The urgency of rescue excavations in urban situations often prevents the production of site maps and context phase diagrams until well after the excavation; the complexity of such urban sites often means that skilled archaeologists are kept busy deciphering site records, just the routine kind of task in which the computer excels.

By 1978 a growing number of microcomputer installations were moved around to archaeological excavations for on-site data capture (Graham 1976; Jefferies 1977; Wilcock 1978). This equipment, with microprocessor, storage, video screen, keyboard, magnetic tape cassettes, floppy discs, and printer, will gain increasing importance in routine excavation data capture. Installed in a van, and with a small generator for supplying electricity, a microcomputer is a completely mobile and independent site office facility. Although experiments have been made in on-site retrieval and statistics using microcomputers, they are not really suitable for large data bases because of restricted storage and low-speed peripherals. Their use will probably develop for on-site data capture, followed by connection as a terminal to a large mainframe computer for large-scale information retrieval, statistics, and graphics use. Access to the computer may be gained from an archaeological site in two major ways—on-line mode or intelligent terminal.

On-line Mode

A teletype or character display video unit may be installed as a remote terminal in the site office, communicating with the computer by telephone line. The user lifts the normal telephone handset, dials the number of the computer center, and waits for a normal connection. After a few seconds the ringing tone is followed by a high-pitched note, the transmission tone sent out by the data transmission equipment in the computer center. The handset is then placed within an *acoustic coupler,* a special box that receives audio signals from the handset and converts them from serial pulses to character codes for the terminal. Similarly character codes from the terminal are recorded as serial pulses to be returned via the telephone line to the computer. Thus the remote terminal in the site office effectively becomes part of the computer that may be tens or hundreds of miles away. To gain access to the computer, a user number and password are necessary. This facility is expensive, for a normal telephone bill must be paid as well as capital costs or rental for the remote terminal equipment, and the costs of computer facilities for use of transmission lines, program running time, storage, and fast printouts. In certain rescue situations the cost may be justified, but if the archaeologist can wait a week for his results, the second method discussed below is preferable.

Intelligent Terminal or Microcomputer

A character display video unit, keyboard, printer, and magnetic tape cassette or floppy disc unit, all controlled by a minicomputer or microcomputer, are installed in the site office or in a vehicle for mobile use. Power supplies are normally from the AC mains of a generator, but if absolutely necessary battery power supplies may be used (although they are expensive and of limited duration). Such a set-up is called an *intelligent terminal* or *personal computer*. The computer displays one of several form layouts on the screen of the video unit. Each consists of a number of data category headings with blanks for the insertion of free-format text. A flashing cursor indicates to the operator where the next piece of information is to be inserted. The text may be edited using special keys; for example, if a spelling mistake has been made the operator repositions the cursor over any one of the available character positions using keys for "forward one line," "back one line," "forward one space," "back one space," and "beginning of page," then deletes or alters characters as appropriate. When the operator is quite satisfied with the text he presses a control key that repositions the cursor to the beginning of the next piece of text. Some workers use a repetitive question-answer scrolling message format rather than a static page format. Whichever is used, the operation is on a "question–answer" basis that precludes the omission of data. When the whole page has been satisfactorily completed, the depression of a transmission key causes the whole record to be written on the magnetic cassette or floppy disc and simultaneously a hard copy of the record is produced by the printer; this may be attached to the find. When full, the cassette or disc may be mailed or taken to the computer center where it is read into the main computer storage and perhaps transcribed to a larger magnetic disc or to magnetic tape. Comprehensive information retrieval and statistical analyses may be undertaken at this stage and the results returned to the site within a week. The capital cost of a microcomputer is comparable with that of an on-line terminal, and operating costs are much less than for telephone transmission. Finally, for long-term excavations input records may be prepared at the close of each season, and computer research undertaken on a nonurgent basis.

Some Examples of Site Information Retrieval

Probably the first use of a remote terminal on an archaeological site in the United States was by New-man (1969), followed by similar work by Gaines (1974). In Britain archaeological data was first transmitted in 1968 by Wilcock (1969a, 1969b) using the TELEX network to send computer-processed geophysical survey results for the South Cadbury excavation.

Buckland (1973) experimented with the use of a remote terminal at the Doncaster Roman fort site, communicating by telephone line with a computer at North Staffordshire Polytechnic, 60 miles away. Information retrieval programs were written in the BASIC language. Although the project was beset with transmission difficulties, sufficient experience was obtained to indicate the considerable potential of the method. A prototype coded classification scheme for Romano–British pottery was evolved, based on a hierarchical structure with decisions about fabric, form decoration, and other attributes at different levels.

A general review of the facilities used to transmit site data to a remote computer was given by Wilcock (1973), with a brief summary of experience gained on the Doncaster excavation.

The analysis by computer of long-term excavations was described by Shackley and his colleagues (Shackley and Wilcock 1974; Shackley et al. 1976; Shackley 1976). The 1974 paper referred to the initial design of an information retrieval scheme for the Iron Age hillfort at Danebury, Hampshire, using the hierarchical information retrieval facilities of the PLUTARCH System (Wilcock 1974a, 1974b). Each season of excavation yielded about 500 chalk-cut pits for study. By 1979 excavators faced the prospect of recording 5,000 pits, 100,000 bone fragments, 5,000 pots, and sundry items of metalwork, daub, and stone (Cunliffe 1971, 1977). It would be difficult to contemplate the analysis of such a large body of material without the help of a computer. Data were recorded in the field directly onto specially-designed computer data sheets (see Fig. 10.3), then punched on cards for creation of the file within the computer. Data recorded were site location; feature number; grid reference; relationships with other features; layer numbers within the feature; pit shape, depth, base dimensions, volume, fill type, and tool-marks; cultural phase; presence of animal and human bones; bone types and measurements; pottery; sediment analyses; mollusc; seed; charcoal; and small finds. Data types available in the PLUTARCH system further described by Duncan (Shackley et al. 1976) were alphanumeric, quantitative (integers, real numbers), and Boolean (presence/absence); the file structure was defined for each specific application by the user. In this same paper MacGregor also described the use of the PLUTARCH retrieval system by York Archaeological Trust to set up records using the IRGMA high-level format, a point that emphasizes the overall communication potential of the IRGMA System.

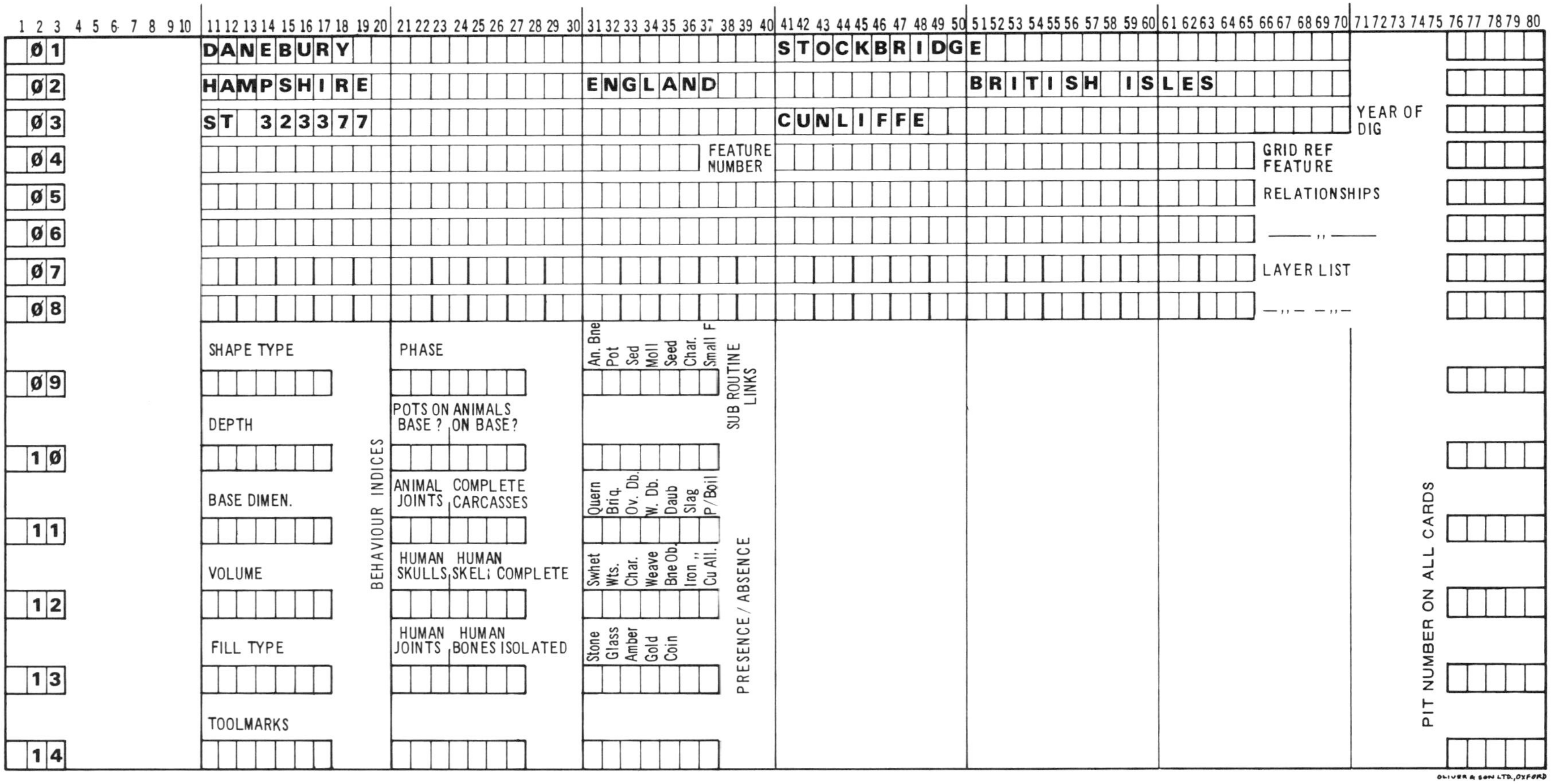

Fig. 10.3. Danebury on-site record sheet designed for computer input.

INFORMATION RETRIEVAL FOR LARGE BODIES OF SPECIALIST DATA

The third type of information retrieval application in archaeology concerns large sets of data on well-defined themes, and bibliographies. The British Library addressed itself to the problem of bibliographic retrieval for archaeology in 1976 (British Library Board 1977). Archaeologists do specialize, of course, and it is convenient for them to have all data on their particular specialty on one file. Many archaeologists keep private card-indexes of their work, and some of these have been inserted into computer files, but few have yet been made public. Some examples are given below of computer files implemented in Britain by the late 1970s.

Roman Inscriptions and the use of the PLUTARCH System

The Roman invasion of Britain and the occupation that lasted four centuries has left a wealth of inscriptions documenting the everyday lives and deaths of soldiers and ordinary people. The creation of a computer file containing this body of information provides the potential of discovering new facts concerning the movement of troops and individuals, the history of forts and civil settlements, and changes in epigraphic style. The prime reference work was published by Collingwood and Wright (1965), and there have been annual additions in the *Journal of Roman Studies* and *Britannia* (Wright 1939–1977). This raises yet another obstacle that is placed in the way of the information scientist, namely copyright law. Recording information on a computer file is regarded as publication and hence is subject to copyright; we are then left with the restrictive and highly artificial situation wherein the file is a "single copy for research purposes only." Naturally, the interpretative information in any publication must be protected, for example the translation and notes on the epigraphy of Roman inscriptions, as in Collingwood and Wright (1965). Archaeological facts, however, should surely be public property whatever their original source. Analyses derived by automatic means are essentially new information and cannot be regarded as subject to the original copyright.

It will be relevant to mention previous work on the recording of Roman epigraphic material, although it cannot be regarded as "information retrieval" in the usual sense. The first comprehensive publication of the Roman inscriptions found in the British Isles was published by Hübner (1873) as volume vii of the *Corpus Inscriptionum Latinarum* (*CIL*). It contained 1200 inscriptions on stone, about 100 on metal, 90 on pottery, and many potters' stamps. Hübner made some glaring errors in geography, placing the Mendips in Derbyshire and Denbighshire in Scotland, but despite these mistakes Hübner's work was a remarkable feat for its time. Hübner (1877a, 1877b, 1881) continued to publish additions in *Ephemeris Epigraphica* (*EE*) but the work never received a combined index to enable scholars to trace inscriptions easily. The fourth and fifth additions to *CIL* were continued by Haverfield (1892, 1913a) in *EE* until the termination of that periodical. Another reference work, *Inscriptiones Latinae Selectae* (*ILS*), appeared in five parts, edited by Dessau (1892–1916). Haverfield (1913b, 1914) published continuations of the additions to *CIL* and *EE* in British Academy supplemental papers, the prototypes of the summaries of inscriptions from Roman Britain edited by Collingwood (1921–1938) in the *Journal of Roman Studies* (*JRS*). Haverfield had decided that a new work, to be titled *The Roman Inscriptions of Britain* was to be prepared; the stones and their texts, whether clear or indistinct, were to be published as line drawings, and this task fell to Collingwood. Haverfield died in 1919, bequeathing his books to the Ashmolean Museum and making the University of Oxford his residuary legatee. The administrators of his bequest made the editing and publication of the future work a primary claim on their funds. Collingwood continued the work until 1938, when ill-health caused his partial retirement. Wright continued the annual summaries of inscriptions from 1939 in the *Journal of Roman Studies* and later in *Britannia,* bringing Volume I of *Roman Inscriptions of Britain* (*RIB*) to completion in 1965; it listed 2400 inscriptions, mostly on stone, although a few are on metal. An index to the work had not been published by the mid 1970s. The inscriptions include milestones, Roman inscriptions imported by travellers and collectors from other countries that have been mistaken for Romano-British stones, genuine inscriptions of other periods that have been mistaken as Roman, forgeries, and marked stones. The *RIB* deadline was the end of 1954 for inscriptions on stone and the end of 1956 for other items. There are concordance tables giving the correspondence between reference numbers in *CIL, EE, ILS,* Haverfield (1913b, 1914), *JRS,* and *RIB*. There is also an index of place names, but no other cross-indexes. The ordering of the inscriptions commences in London (*LONDINIVM*) and ends with Roman Scotland, but apart from a general south to north direction there seems to be no logical order. The lack of general cross-indexes is a severe disadvantage, and this is a problem the computer can solve easily.

Using a computer, Jory (Jory and Moore 1966; Jory 1968) has produced an index to *CIL* vi covering about 40,000 inscriptions originating in Rome. Problems were found in recording Greek letters, in identifying the different types of components of personal names, and in distinguishing Roman numerals from inscription letters. The goal was the establishment of a word index and analysis of dating criteria, and algorithms were developed for the recognition of features in the text.

The Conference on Roman Epigraphy, 1967, proposed that the coding for each inscription should be fitted onto a single 80-column Hollerith card. If this were done there would obviously be no room for natural-language phrases, and the result would be a jumble of numerals and other characters quite unintelligible without the code book. The suggested coding scheme went into great detail on some points such as occupation of the deceased and relationships within the family, while other important classifications such as grid reference of find site were omitted entirely. The scheme suffered from the disadvantages of all numerical coding schemes in that the codes must be learned or looked up in the code book, and the system is not attractive to archaeologists or epigraphists lacking computer training.

Chouraqui and other French workers (Chouraqui et al. 1972; Virbel 1973) have used the computer to process *CIL* viii, a volume containing 800 inscriptions concerning veterans in Roman Africa. Their purpose was to update and edit the data automatically, to produce indexes and tables, and to elaborate a documentation system. Codes were derived for the description of texts (reading interpretation), peculiarities of the language (morphology, linguistic particulars), present location of the inscription, material, size, ornamentation, conservation, and semantic studies of the inscription. The text was edited into three forms: raw (as it actually occurs), interpreted (with expansions and reconstructions), and canonical (with lexical units in the nominative case or other canonical form). The words of the texts were stored in a way that allowed generation of the interpreted and canonical forms from the raw text. The approach facilitated the segmentation of inscriptions and the identification of elements useful in the study of honorific titles for emperors.

Zarri (1974) has similarly studied *CIL* v, which deals with inscriptions found in Cisalpine Gaul. This work began in 1968. The epigraphic texts were broken into segments and each segment prefixed by the number of a corresponding index; for example, there are indexes covering gods, goddesses and mythology, nomina, praenomina, cognomina, geographical names, and so on. A system of delimiters was also developed to indicate such items as abbreviations, reconstructed letters, letters added or omitted by the mason, erasures, uncertain letters, ends of lines, or Greek characters. Instead of using the traditional punched card method, records were transcribed to magnetic cards; each card allowed 50 tracks of 100 characters, a total of 5,000 characters per record, as against 80 charac-

ters on the normal punched card. A golfball type head was used on the typewriter, enabling different fonts to be printed by interchanging type heads, and lower case was used for editorial additions, with upper case for inscription letters. The use of magnetic recording gave easy retrieval of any point in an inscription with editing by addition, modification, or erasure. With operator control via a terminal, the computer was used to process the records and detect formal syntactic errors such as unmatched brackets. Three files resulted from the analysis of the records: texts of inscriptions with notes and bibliographic references, citations ordered alphabetically for each index, and bibliographic and summary tables. These files were also the input to a photocomposition system that produced the publication plates for offset-litho printing. Photocomposition relies on projecting images of the required characters onto photographic emulsion, which is then pasted up to produce the offset plate, or the sensitized plate may be exposed directly. It reduces the time necessary for the preparation of printed reports considerably, and increases the reliability and accuracy of the entire transcription operation; it is, however, extremely expensive. Manual typesetting, galley proofs, and corrections to proofs are all superseded, and a copy may be kept on magnetic tape to aid preparation of revised editions.

Since 1968 the Roman Inscriptions of Britain have been the subject of computer information retrieval and analysis by Wilcock and Duncan. This ongoing project has been based largely on *CIL* vii and its successor *RIB* (Collingwood and Wright 1965) with addenda by Wright and Hassall. The technique uses plain-language entries in alphanumeric, quantitative entries in decimal, and Boolean (presence/absence) entries, each record using as many card-images as desired. All cards carry the *RIB* reference number. The retrieval system was designed to be suitable for *all* archaeological records, whether they concern the museum catalog, the excavation file, or a large body of specialist data; accordingly there are facilities for the data structure to be defined afresh for each application, giving great flexibility but retaining compatibility. Each card carries a type designator, specified by the archaeologist, to indicate what sort of information exists on the remainder of the card (also specified by the archaeologist in terms of alphanumeric, quantitative, or Boolean types, data field position on the card, and length in number of columns). For Roman inscriptions the data structure is presented in Table 10.1. A typical printout of a Roman inscription record is given in Figure 10.4. The Roman inscriptions were also produced in key-letter-in-context (KLIC) form to facilitate identification of fragmentary epigraphy on new specimens.

```
01      BREMETENNACVM               RIBCHESTER                      RIB  583
02      LANCASHIRE                  REGIO BREMETENNACENSIS           RIB  583
03      SD6535      24      51      20      JDW      691109          RIB  583
04      SHAFT OF RECTANGULAR PEDESTAL                               RIB  583
05      RIBCHESTER MUSEUM                                           RIB  583
51      RELIEF OF APOLLO            CLOAK                           RIB  583
151     PHRYGIAN CAP                QUIVER                          RIB  583
251     LYRE                        FEMALE FIGURES                  RIB  583
351     TURRETED CROWN              VEIL                            RIB  583
30      AELIUS          ANTONINUS                                   RIB  583
33                                          MELITENE                RIB  583
37      PRAEPOSITUS NUMERI ET REGIONISCENTURIO LEG VI VICTRICIS     RIB  583
39      M                                                           RIB  583
42      PRAEPOSITUS NUMERI ET REGIONIS                              RIB  583
47      WELFARE OF EMPEROR          WELFARE OF UNIT                 RIB  583
17      DOMINUS NOSTER                                              RIB  583
19      M                                                           RIB  583
27      APOLLO                      MAPONUS                         RIB  583
50      >GORDIAN                    NUM EQ SARMAIARUM BREM GORD      RIB  583
150                                 LEG VI VICIRIX                  RIB  583
127     RFGIO BREMETENNACENSIS      BRITANNIA INFERIOR              RIB  583
55      1                           1                               RIB  583
80      DEO SAN(CTU)/[A]POLLINI MAPONO/[PR]O SALUTE D(OMINI) N(OSTRI  RIB  583
81      )/[ET] N(UMERI) EQ(UITUM) SAR/[M(ATARUM)] BREMETENN(ACENSIUM  RIB  583
82      )/[G]ORDIANI/[A]EL(IUS) ANIONI/NUS C(ENTURIO) LEG(IONIS) VI/  RIB  583
83      VIC(TRICIS) DOMO/MELITENIS/PRAEP(OSITUS) N(UMERI) ET R(EGION  RIB  583
84      IS)/.../.../.../.../...                                      RIB  583
```

Fig. 10.4. Typical Roman inscription listing.

Up to 1975 data were input by means of punched cards and recorded on magnetic tape in serial form. In 1976 the PLUTARCH System was modified to record on magnetic discs and to use a *dictionary* in order to cut down the size of the files. When a dictionary is in use all *different* alphanumeric words are stored in the dictionary and allocated a number. As data are read the words are checked against the dictionary, then recorded on disc in numeral form, the dictionary numbers replacing the words. If a word is found that has not previously been encountered, it is added to the dictionary and allocated the next number available; then the process continues as normal. Using this method data may be reduced in volume by a factor of five, a considerable saving both in storage required and subsequent search time.

Such a system has a flexible data structure. The specification is largely the responsibility of the user, who must decide what kinds of data to record about each object; upon this decision will the effectiveness of retrieval depend. There are three possible approaches: (a) an existing local classification system may be transferred direct; (b) a well-known format such as the IRGMA Archaeology Object card may be adopted; or (c) a new recording system, tailor-made to individual requirements, may be devised by the archaeologist. The first approach has the advantage of requiring little or no reorganization of data; the second allows standardization on a national scale, and attendant expert guidance on recording methods; and the third applies to situations where no adequate data format exists, as in the case of Roman inscriptions above. The user should try to avoid proliferation of recording schemes. A search of existing schemes will often reveal a remarkable compatibility between concepts, and usually an existing scheme can be modified to suit individual requirements. When the data structure has been defined the user sets up a table defining each item of information; the table is stored and used to interpret input data. New fields may be added later if the need arises.

Certain categories of information may be designated as common to a series of consecutive records; for example, overall site provenience, site director, year of excavation and so on. These data are stored for all records until superseded with new information carrying the same type designator. This procedure allows hierarchical arrangement of data (layers belonging to the same pit will have common pit data), and also avoids duplication of punched cards in the data preparation stage.

The PLUTARCH system checked input for such errors as misalignment of data, and incorrect data types such as letters occurring within quantitative fields.

Cards with errors were listed, and correct cards stored on magnetic tape. Spelling mistakes can only be corrected by the user; the computer cannot "spell," and any sequence of letters, numerals and other symbols is accepted as a valid alphanumeric item. Rejected cards could later be corrected and re-input, and spelling mistakes could also be corrected by an amendment package that allowed insertion, deletion, and alteration of card images.

For a retrieval run, the user specified: (a) the Boolean search expression, (b) the modes of output, and (c) the fields to be output for records that satisfied the search expression, specified in the order they were to appear on the printout.

The Boolean search expression could be as complex as was desired by the user, consisting of one or more expressions of the form:

$$< field > \quad < relational\ operator > \quad < value >$$
or
$$< field > \quad < relational\ operator > \quad < field >$$

where the relational operator could be any one of:

EQ equal to
NE not equal to
LT less than
GT greater than
GE greater than or equal to
LE less than or equal to

(the above are arithmetic operators for quantitative variables)

SE string equal
SN string not equal
SI string includes
SX string does not include

TABLE 10.1
Data Structure for Roman Inscriptions

(Alphanumeric data unless otherwise specified)

Type Designator	Contents	Columns of field	Comments
Provenience and General Information:			
01	Roman name of site	11–40	
	Modern name of site	41–70	
02	Modern county	11–40	
	Roman grouping (e.g., HADRIAN'S WALL)	41–70	
03	NGR of site	11–20	e.g., ST 1234
	Width of stone	21–30	(quantitative)
	Height of stone	31–40	(quantitative)
	Depth of stone	41–50	(quantitative)
	Initials of classifier	51–60	e.g., JDW
	Date of classification	61–70	YYMMDD (e.g., 671205 for 5 December 1967) (quantitative, may be treated as a single number for purposes of testing whether a particular inscription was classified earlier than a given date; this is useful in the updating of records)
04	General description of stone	11–40	
	Material	41–70	
05	Present location	11–40	
06	Detailed location on site	11–40	
		41–70	
07	Associated finds	11–40	
		41–70	

Type Designator	Contents	Columns of field	Comments
n1x, n2x refer to the object of dedication (e.g., God, emperor, deceased person, etc.):			
10	Praenomen	11–30	
	Nomen	31–50	
	Cognomen	51–70	
13	Filiation	11–30	
	Tribe	31–50	
	Origo	51–70	
15	General Origo	11–30	e.g., Jewish
17	Status	11–40	e.g., Libertus, Augustus
	Occupation	41–70	e.g., Miles, Imperator
19	Sex	11	
	Social relationship to dedicator	21–40	
21	"Virtues"	11–30	e.g., Pientissima
		31–50	
		51–70	
22,23	Career details	11–40	e.g., Pontifex Maximus
		41–70	Cos, Trib. Pot., Caesar, Pater Patriae, Legatus
24	Age	11–16	YYMMDD (quantitative)
	General Age Term	21–30	e.g., child
	Military service (years)	31,32	(quantitative)
	Cos number	41,42	
	TRIB POT number	51,52	
	Name of deity, or DM, etc.	11–40	
	(not abbreviated)	41–70	

(the above are "string" operators for strings of characters forming alphanumeric variables)

Examples of the first type of expression might be:

height (of a pot) GT 20.0 cm

military unit   SE LEG XX VV

while an example of the second type might be:

height   GE maximum diameter
(of a pot)   (of the same pot).

Complex Boolean search expressions could be built up using the logical connectives AND and OR. Truth tables for these have already been given in Table 2.1. A "functionally complete set" of connectives would normally require the inclusion of NOT as well, in order that all possible Boolean expressions could be specified. The PLUTARCH System avoided this by treating Boolean fields as numerals (1 for logically *true* and 0 for *false*) and by including all possible negations in the

TABLE 10.2
Negation of Relational Operators

Relational Operator	Negation
EQ	NE
LT	GE
GT	LE
SE	SN
SI	SX

relational operators. The justification for this is given in Tables 10.2 and 10.3. The laws of Boolean algebra state that operators must be evaluated in the following order: (a) all NOT operators, in order left to right in the expression, (b) all AND operators, in order left to right, and (c) all OR operators, in order left to right. These are called the precedence rules for Boolean algebra.

TABLE 10.1 (*cont.*)

Type Designator	Contents	Columns of field	Comments
28	Cases following DM	11-20	Required for the study of the epigraphy
		21-30	
		31-40	
		41-50	
		51-60	
		61-70	

n3x, n4x serve the same purpose for the dedicator as n1x, n2x do for the object of the dedication:

Type Designator	Contents	Columns of field	Comments
30	Praenomen	11-30	
	Nomen	31-50	
	Cognomen	51-70	
33	Filiation	11-30	
	Tribe	31-50	
	Origo	51-70	
35	General Origo	11-30	
37	Status	11-40	
	Occupation	41-70	
39	Sex	11	
	Social relationship to object of dedication	21-40	
41	"Virtues"	11-30	
		31-50	
		51-70	
42,43	Career details	11-40	
		41-70	
44	Age	11-16	(quantitative)
	General Age Term	21-30	
	Military Service (years)	31,32	(quantitative)
47	Motive for dedication	11-40	e.g., V S L M
		41-70	

Type Designator	Contents	Columns of field	Comments
Other information:			
50	Date of inscription or generalized date	11-40	e.g., 112 (quantitative), < HADRIAN
	Military units	41-70	e.g., LEG XXVV
51	Motifs	11-40	
		41-70	
52	Curses	11-40	
		41-70	
53	Unusual spelling	11-40	actual (usual)
	Unusual punctuation	41-70	e.g., leaf
54	Unusual features	11-40	
		41-70	
55	Number of persons object	11-40	e.g., 2 (quantitative)
	Number of persons dedicating	41-70	(quantitative)
57	= 1 if fragmental	11	(Boolean)
	= 1 if the Emperor is the object of the dedication	21	(Boolean)
	= 1 if reused	31	(Boolean)
	= 1 if evidence of erasure	41	(Boolean)
	= 1 if authentication doubtful	51	(Boolean)
59	Formulae	11-30	e.g., H S E
		31-50	D D
		41-70	
63	Grandson of . . .	11-40	
	Place for freedman reserved (formula)	41-70	

n8x, in order 80-89, 180-189, etc.

Actual inscription on stone as in *RIB* or addenda, including omissions and reconstructions.

TABLE 10.3
Negation of Logical Connectives

Logical Connective	Negation	Explanation
AND	OR	$\overline{\text{(a EQ b) AND (P SN Q)}}$
		=
	(all relational operators must also be negated)	$\overline{\text{(a EQ b)}}$ OR $\overline{\text{(P SN Q)}}$ by de Morgan's Law = (a NE b) OR (P SE Q)
OR	AND	$\overline{\text{(a EQ b) OR (P SN Q)}}$
		=
	(all relational operators must also be negated)	$\overline{\text{(a EQ b)}}$ AND $\overline{\text{(P SN Q)}}$ by de Morgan's Law = (a NE b) AND (P SE Q)

where a and b are quantitative variables, and P and Q are alphanumeric string variables.

The first level of evaluation has been superseded in the above system as described. If the required expression cannot be evaluated according to the normal precedence rules—for example, if an OR needs to be evaluated *before* an AND—systems of brackets are used, as shown in Table 10.4.

The modes of output for the PLUTARCH System were *print, histogram, piechart, scattergram* and *map plot.*

In the print mode specified fields from the records that satisfied the search criteria were placed in a backing store file for subsequent tabulation in a specified format. The output file could also be sorted by any field so that catalogs could be arranged in various alphabetical and numerical orders. The results of a search are in themselves new data and the system allowed these results to be re-input to the retrieval program, allowing subsets to be created without the need to scan the complete main file each time.

TABLE 10.4
Evaluation of the Expression P AND Q OR R
where P, Q, and R are also Expressions

P	Q	R	Without brackets	With brackets P AND (Q OR R)
F	F	F	F	F
F	F	T	T*	F*
F	T	F	F	F
F	T	T	T*	F*
T	F	F	F	F
T	F	T	T	T
T	T	F	T	T
T	T	T	T	T

T = *true*, F = *false*.
*The asterisked values show that the expressions are different.

In the histogram and piechart modes one or more specified fields containing quantitative data could be extracted from records satisfying the search criteria, and placed in files suitable for later analysis by the histogram and piechart display segment of the system. Histograms and piecharts are intended to be used for continuous variables.

In the scattergram mode one or more specified pairs of fields containing quantitative data could be extracted from valid records and placed in files suitable for later plotting on two axes.

Finally, the map plot mode could extract grid references from valid records and place them in a file that could later be used to plot a distribution map wherein the points were plotted using a range of symbols on a map outline or site plan.

Suggested developments of such a serial-access system would be the conversion from serial access to an inverted file system, the specification of search criteria in an interactive fashion from the graphics console and not just by card input, and acceptance of synonyms and abbreviations so that retrieval is not affected by inconsistencies in the preparation of data.

Petroglyphs

Walker (1970a, 1970b) constructed a computer file of petroglyphs (rock carvings), mostly of Bronze Age date, with a highly-coded data structure specified by Walker. All records were identified by Walker's (1970a) reference numbers. The petroglyph data structure is presented in Table 10.5, and part of a typical petroglyph listing is shown in Figure 10.5.

The approach was partially plain-language recording and partially coding of information. Site names, bibliographical information, detailed location on site, and associated finds were recorded in plain language. But other information, covering the type of rock, type of site, age, height above sea level, distance from navigable water, class(es) of carving, and magnitude of site required a coding reference book for interpretation. Grid references were recorded for use in distribution maps, and classifier and date of classification for control of updating.

Pottery Records and the Work of the Medieval Pottery Research Group

The Medieval Pottery Research Group was instituted and financed by the British Department of the Environment. Arising out of a conference held in 1975, several subcommittees were set up to study Principles and Practice, Data Processing, Scientific Aids, and Publication. Meeting throughout 1975 these subcommittees drafted reports that were reviewed at a 1976 conference.

```
10      RS SC A    H1    D1    C6        M1            NR840907   JDW 691231        134
20      CARNBAN                          KILMICHAEL-GLASSARY                        134
30      SIMPSON (1867)           ASCC                  31-32,40                     134
130     CHRISTISON              PSAS     38            142-144                      134
230     BRUCE                   IMS                    PL. 28                       134
```

Fig. 10.5. Petroglyph listing.

The Data Processing subcommittee made many recommendations concerning the use of computers in the collection of data on the site and in the laboratory, the use of statistics, and the production of diagrams by computer. In particular, the recording of pottery was studied in great detail, in collaboration with IRGMA, and a prototype record card was proposed with headings as listed below. The order of the data was chosen to reflect the order conventionally used in archaeological reports of Medieval pottery, but it was intended that the card should be suitable for all pottery; also, several of the categories were identical with categories in the IRGMA Archaeology Card:

1. PROVENANCE
   1.1 Site name
   1.2 Site number
   1.3 Grid reference (NGR, Latitude/Longitude, etc.) with value, units, and accuracy
   1.4 Place name detail
      1.4.1 Parish
      1.4.2 District
      1.4.3 County
      1.4.4 Country
2. EXCAVATION DETAILS
   2.1 Context within site
      2.1.1 Identifier of smallest archaeological recording unit containing the find (context, feature, etc.)
      2.1.2 Cultural horizon
   2.2 Date of recording unit (period, numerical date with value, units, etc.)
   2.3 Three-dimensional co-ordinates to stated origin, with qualifier for the point of the feature referred to
   2.4 Excavator (site director)
   2.5 Numerical identifier allocated to object by excavator
3. TYPE
   3.1 Kiln site (Production place; with site name/number, place name detail, documentary reference, etc.)
   3.2 Type of pottery ("ware")
4. COMPLETENESS
   4.1 Completeness keyword (e.g., fraction of rim, fraction of base, etc.)
   4.2 Completeness detail
5. QUANTITIES
   Sherd weights/counts, number of vessels represented, equivalent number of vessels, as appropriate

6. IDENTIFICATION
   6.1 Form
      Form needs very careful objective definition, for the myriad terms used in the past are vague and show unsatisfactory overlaps (see Hardy-Smith 1974; Chantrey et al. 1975). It is best treated in a hierarchical manner, since terms used are often not of the same status. Possibly using subjective form, the following groupings may be devised:
         plate/platter/pancheon/charger
         dish/saucer
         bowl/basin/porringer
         cup/goblet
         mug/tankard/tyg/beaker
         chamber pot/posset pot/pipkin
         jug/pitcher/ewer/flagon
         jar/albarello/galley pot/vase
         urn
         food vessel
         amphora
         mortarium
   6.2 Form code or sub-type (an objective description of the profile of the pot as a series of numerical codes, from which the actual form of the pot can be regenerated)
   6.3 Form qualifiers (e.g., folded; aesthetic terms such as "well-proportioned"; and relative size terms such as "large," "miniature")
   6.4 Classified identification
      6.4.1 Ware group (earthenware, stoneware, etc.)
      6.4.2 Specific ware name (or number, see 6.5)
      6.4.3 Ware sub-type
   6.5 Identification system (e.g., Dragendorff, for Samian ware)
   6.6 Authority for classification
   6.7 Retrieval system reference number
   6.8 Date of classification
7. CONDITION
   7.1 Condition keyword
   7.2 Condition detail
8. PART DESCRIPTION
   8.1 Part described (might be "whole" of pot, body, internal or external glaze, handle, spout, neck, rim/lip, base, lug, foot, bung hole, etc.)
   8.2 Aspects of part described (might be texture, including "feel," materials; color; dimensions; inclusions—heavy mineral or clay analysis with composition, size of grains, quantities, variations, and origin of materials if known)

8.3 Description/keyword detail
(For example, possible combinations include: 8.1 body, 8.2 color, 8.3 Munsell 10 YR 2.5; or 8.1 glaze, 8.2 materials, 8.3 tin; or 8.1 "whole," 8.2 dimensions, 8.3 height 15.2 cm ± 0.1 cm, thickness 0.4 cm ± 0.1 cm; etc.)

9. PRODUCTION
9.1 Manufacturing technique (wheel-made, coil made, lump-made, segment joining, etc.)
9.2 Production Detail
9.2.1 Surface treatment (wet smoothed, compacted, polished, etc.)
9.2.2 Glaze/slip application (dipped, painted, trailed, combed, splashed, powdered, etc.)
9.2.3 Firing (oxidized/reduced, underfired, vitreous, etc.; orientation in kiln; kiln temperature if known; hardness in Moh).

9.3 Associated person
9.3.1 Person's role in manufacture (potter, designer, etc.)
9.3.2 Person's name
9.3.3 Person's characteristics (e.g., evidence for left-handedness, etc.)
9.3.4 Date of manufacturing process referred to in 9.3.1

10. DECORATION AND MARKS
10.1 Description of feature (decoration, inscription or graffiti, potter's mark, transcription, etc.)
10.2 Method (Glossary term, e.g., slip; incised; roulette; slashing; stabbing; combing; fingering/thumbing; stamps such as type swastika, circle, geometric, scroll, star, name of potter; corded; transfer printing; hand painting; applied relief; ribbed; boss/knob; etc.)
10.3 Position of feature on pot

TABLE 10.5
Petroglyph Data Structure
(Walker 1970a)

Data are alphanumeric unless otherwise stated.

Type Designator	Contents	Columns of field	Comments	Type Designator	Contents	Columns of field	Comments
10	R (for rock) plus one of the following: R (natural rock surface) S (slab) I (integrated rock) M (menhir) P (portable stone) Blank (uncertain)	11,12	Coded card		D (for distance) plus a single digit representing the distance from the nearest navigable water as follows: 1 (under ½ mile) 2 (½–5 miles) 3 (5–10 miles) 4 (10–30 miles) 5 (over 30 miles)	26,27	
	S (for site) plus one of the following: M (megalithic monument) S (stone circle) C (cist) B (barrow) O (occupation or industrial site) Blank (uncertain)	14,15			C (for class of carving) plus one or more digits, each specifying a class of carving, in the range 1–8 as follows: 1 (cup marks) 2 (cups and rings) 3 (spirals and labyrinths) 4 (crosses, swastikas, and segmented circles) 5 (rings, ellipses, hooks and loops) 6 (linear patterns) 7 (carreg saethau) 8 (weapons, feet, animals, and people) Q (questionable)	31–39	e.g., C1258
	A (for age) plus one of the following: N (Neolithic) B (Bronze Age) I (Iron Age) Blank (uncertain)	17,18					
	H (for height) plus a single digit representing the height above sea level as follows: 1 (0–250 ft) 2 (250–750 ft) 3 (above 750 ft)	21,22					

10.4 Color of feature (Munsell chart, etc.)

10.5 Feature detail (Glossary term, e.g., solid checker-board, hatched, cross-hatched, latticed, dotted, cables, chevrons, circles, angular or cursive line patterns, lozenges, plant motif, zoomorphic motif, etc.)

11. PROCESS

11.1 Name of process (conservation, reproduction, neutron activation analysis, X-ray fluorescence, X-ray diffraction, Beta-ray back scattering, petrological section, surface deposit analysis, etc.)

11.2 Cross reference to results

11.3 Operator or researcher

11.4 Date of process

12. DATING

12.1 Object period (e.g., Neolithic, Bronze Age, Iron Age, Roman, Migration and Early Medieval, Medieval, Post-Medieval, Unknown)

12.2 Numerical date

12.2.1 Earliest date

12.2.2 Latest date

12.3 Dating method (e.g., thermoluminescence, parallels)

12.4 Cross-reference to result

12.5 Researcher, laboratory number, etc.

12.6 Date of age determination

13. DOCUMENTATION

13.1 Documentation type (journal, book, microfilm, microfiche, etc.)

13.2 Author

13.3 Date of publication

13.4 Title

13.5 Journal name or publisher

13.6 Volume / edition

13.7 Detail

13.7.1 Pagination

13.7.2 Page / figure / plate details

13.8 Photograph number

13.9 Drawing number

14. STORAGE

14.1 Institution (Museum, etc.)

14.2 Accession number allocated to object by institution

14.3 Storage location within institution

14.4 Recorder (i.e., the authority for completion of the record, accession, or storage)

14.5 Date of completion of record

TABLE 10.5 (cont.)

Type Designator	Contents	Columns of field	Comments	Type Designator	Contents	Columns of field	Comments
	M (for magnitude) plus one of the following: 1 (single stone) 2 (multiple site)	41,42			Item classification number	71–80	
				30	Author and date	11–30	e.g., SIMPSON (1867)
	National Grid Reference consisting of two letters and six figures, or Irish grid reference consisting of one letter and six figures (in the latter case column 51 was left blank)	51–58	e.g., SJ123156	(Bibliography)	Journal (abbreviation)	31–40	e.g., ANT J
					Volume number	41–50	(Antiquaries Journal)
					Pagination OR	51–60	
					Book	31–60	
					Pagination OR, for Royal Commission on Ancient and Historical Monument literature	61–70	
	Initials of classifier	61–63	e.g., MJW		RCAM, RCAMS, etc.	31–40	
	Date of classification in format YYMMDD, allowing dates to be treated as numbers for ease of comparison. This enables records made prior to a certain date to be modified in the light of new information.	65–70	e.g., 680523 for 23 May 1968 (quantitative)		County	41–55	
					Number	56–60	
					Pagination	61–70	
					Item classification number	71–80	
				40 (Detailed site information)	Detailed location on site	11–70	
					Item classification number	71–80	
	Item classification number	71–80		50 (Associated finds)	Associated find	11–70	
20 (Site Names)	Name of site	11–40			Item classification number	71–80	
	Name of parish	41–70					

It was intended in 1977 that the above classification scheme for pottery would, after field trials, be published by MDA as a Pottery card, modified in the light of experience, but surprisingly this had not appeared by 1979, the majority of museum workers presumably preferring to treat pottery as art objects on their reference cards.

The late David Clarke (1962, 1970) recorded a data base covering British Beaker pottery on the first-generation computer EDSAC II at Cambridge; as a result he was able to define various types of Beaker on statistical grounds. These types have been accepted by Bronze Age specialists and have stood the test of time; his work is regarded as a classic study.

Sèvres porcelain was recorded on a computer data base by Williamson (Stones and Williamson 1970); data recorded were diacritical markings (names of artisans), colors, finishes, purpose and other attributes of the pottery, and names and addresses of the purchasers. Computerizing this information was possible because the Sèvres factory kept very careful records of payrolls and sales during the eighteenth and nineteenth centuries.

Orton (1970, 1971, 1973, 1974, 1975) recorded pottery wasters from the dumps of a Romano-British kiln site in Highgate Wood, London. Thereafter statistical models of the relationships between rim and base sherds were used to reconstruct the profiles of the vessels, thus producing useful data from fragmentary material. This project, which would have been an enormous task without the use of a computer, was aptly named the SHERD project (Sorting Highgate Excavations' Roman Debris) and was carried out using programs written in BASIC on a remote terminal.

Shannan and Wilcock (1975) created a data base for Central German Bell Beakers and used it to study variation in shape and style. Various statistical methods were used, and they all indicated that shape variation in the Bell Beakers could be explained in terms of the two simple ratios: height/maximum width and base width/maximum width. We also confirmed that shape and decoration were related: bell beakers decorated with two broad bands had a restricted range of shapes and were confined to Central Germany, while those with equal-zoned ornament had a *different* range of shapes and a more widespread distribution. This study showed the potential that even simple computer techniques have for bringing order to large quantities of data.

Stone Tools

In Britain several large data bases have been constructed for the recording of assemblages of stone tools. A comprehensive study of British Lower Palaeolithic handaxes was undertaken by Roe (1964a,

1964b, 1968), and later amplified and reworked by Graham (1970), McBurney (1973) and Callow (1976). Palaeolithic flint assemblages were analyzed statistically by Doran and Hodson (1966). European Palaeolithic "leafpoints" were recorded and analyzed by Allsworth-Jones (1975; with Wilcock 1974a, 1974b), and Celoria (with Wilcock 1975) similarly studied British Neolithic axes. The CBA Implement Petrology Survey, concerned with the typing of Neolithic axes by thin section analysis, had a card record in 1976, and had carried out a study for computerization of the records.

Sediments

The scientific study of sediments is becoming increasingly common on archaeological sites (Shackley 1972, 1973, 1976; Shackley and Wilcock 1974; Shackley et al. 1976). Computerized sediment records were reported in these studies. Typical data recorded were color, texture, pH, phosphates, particle size, shape of grains of corn found in deposits, X-ray diffraction results, heavy mineral analysis, spectrometry results, animal bone, pottery, molluscan data, microfauna, seed and pollen data, charcoal, and small finds. The usefulness of particle-size analysis has lately been questioned in a geological sense; whether it is still useful for archaeological studies remains to be seen, and computer recording of a large number of observations could resolve the question.

County and Regional Recording Schemes and the CBA Working Party on Archaeological Records

The Working Party on Archaeological Records was established by the Council for British Archaeology at the request and expense of the Royal Commission on Historical Monuments (England), following a meeting called by the Commission in January of 1974. The Working Party consisted of several archaeologists, museum officers, local authority planning officers, and information scientists, and they met throughout 1974 and the early part of 1975. Their report (Council for British Archaeology 1975) was presented to the Royal Commission in July of 1975, but has not otherwise been published.

The terms of reference of the Working Party were to survey existing archaeological records at regional and county levels, and to make recommendations designed to achieve maximum compatibility and standardization of data recording in such records, aiming for their eventual integration into a central national system; to consider existing national systems and to make recommendations on the most appropriate recording system and the most suitable location for an integrated national service; and to consider systems of automatic data storage and retrieval, including computers, and their suitability for an integrated national service.

The Working Party defined two distinct levels of data storage: the *intensive record*, containing all available information, and the *nonintensive record*, essentially an index to where the full information could be found, and containing only basic data on location and type of archaeological feature. The types of users of a central nonintensive archaeological record were considered to be local authorities (for planning applications, road building, etc.), central government (motorways, airports, etc.), central authorities and corporations (Forestry Commission, water authorities, gas, electricity, coal, and steel), industry, developers and consultants, rescue archaeological units, and research workers.

The Working Party was unanimously in favor of the computerization of records. It was recommended that the national nonintensive record should be established in the Archaeology Division of the Ordnance Survey at Southampton, England, using as a basis the 300,000 cards already held there (originally for the production of archaeological features on maps). The nonintensive record was to contain basic information about each recorded site, as indicated below.

1. Location
   Unique identification number
   National Grid Reference
   Accuracy of NGR and point on site referred to
2. Administrative
   Location of definitive (intensive) record
   County
   District
   Parish
   Legal status (scheduled, listed, SSSI, National
      Trust, etc.)
3. Description
   Hierarchical type (see below)
   Form (standing structure—complete/ruined; finds
      only; documents only; cropmark, including soil-
      mark; earthwork)
   Condition (complete; incomplete; destroyed;
      unknown)
   Period (Prehistoric, period uncertain; Palaeolithic;
      Mesolithic, Neolithic; Bronze Age; Iron Age; Ro-
      man; Post-Roman, period uncertain; Migration
      and Early Medieval; Medieval (1066–1485);
      Post-Medieval; unknown)
4. Control
   Date entered into system
5. Text (optional)
   Name
   Characterization
   Publication reference (usually only a single stan-
      dard work)

The Working Party was of the opinion that the description of the site should follow a hierarchical struc-

ture, enabling the relative importance of sites to be ascertained; moreover in a hierarchical scheme every type of site has a logical place in the data structure and can be found easily, and any additions can be slotted into the scheme without affecting previous classifications. The hierarchical position produces a "generic type" or unique code number for each type of site, thus forming an essential description of the site (see 3 above). An example of part of the hierarchy with its codes might be:

4. Defensive sites
   4.1 Military sites
      4.1.1 Castle

The Working Party also felt that the whole country should be covered by intensive record systems organized on a county or regional basis, and that these systems should be compatible with each other and with the central nonintensive system either directly (by means of a series of standardized outputs in standard order) or through a high-level communications format (such as the IRGMA format). Also, it was felt that the basic inputs to the national nonintensive record should be supplied from the intensive records at county or regional level, with the regional archaeological staffs responsible for the primary classification and authentication of input data.

The following data were recommended by the Working Party as the minimum information to be included in an intensive record:

1. Site reference number
2. Status of site (e.g., scheduled, listed, SSSI, National
   Trust, etc.) with reference number allocated by pro-
   tecting body.
3. Condition (evaluation of condition, with authority and
   date).
4. Completeness (evaluation, with authority and date).
5. Dimensions in m, area in ha.
6. Location
   Source (informant or site director, with date)
   National Grid Reference
   Height Ordnance Datum (in m)
   County (or Region)
   District
   Parish
   Site name
7. Associated finds
   Reference system, identification numbers.
8. Dating
   Period: Prehistoric (period uncertain), Palaeo-
      lithic, Mesolithic, Neolithic, Bronze Age, Iron
      Age, Roman, Post-Roman (period uncertain),
      Migration and Early Medieval, Medieval, Post-
      Medieval, unknown
   Numerical date (with authority, date of determina-
      tion, method, reference number—including ra-
      diocarbon and potassium-argon dating, palynol-
      ogy, etc.)
9. Bibliography
   Complete set of references

10. Further records
    Surveys, plans, and drawings
    Photographs
    Aerial photographs
    Transparencies
11. Archival material
12. Environmental data
    For example, site geology and soil type, climatic
    phase, river terrace or other erosional/
    depositional features
13. Cataloger (with date of entry)
14. Description (using a hierarchical scheme)

By 1976 most areas of Britain had intensive record schemes, although relatively few were actually computerized. The National Monuments Records of the Royal Commissions on Ancient and Historical Monuments were intensive, fully-researched documents relating to particular sites or areas, as well as manuscripts, plans, maps, photographs, air photographs, and ephemeral archaeological publications; many of these were held on microfilm. The National Monuments Record for Wales, in addition, had a nonintensive set of record cards for sites, while the other areas of Britain relied on copies of the 300,000 Ordnance Survey archaeological cards originally produced for the entry of archaeological sites on published maps. The Cambridge University Committee for Aerial Photography maintained an archive of several thousand aerial photographs of archaeological sites. By 1976 most museums had not progressed beyond the accession register or card index for their cataloging, but a few were actively using or preparing to use the IRGMA (MDA) cards for manual or computer operation. With regard to county records, the Northern Archaeological Survey had nonintensive computer records covering Northumberland, Durham, Tyne and Wear, and Cumbria. The County Archaeologists of most other English counties relied on duplicates of the Ordnance Survey cards, maps, registers organized by parish, and in some cases on optical coincidence indexes. Susan Laflin (1972, 1973) designed a fairly simple information retrieval system at the Computer Centre of the University of Birmingham, and by 1976 it was in use by local archaeological groups for county records in Shropshire, Herefordshire, Worcestershire, Hertfordshire, and Wiltshire on an experimental basis. The system used codes, by reference to a coding manual (e.g., "generic type" of find, four-letter parish mnemonic, county letters), and there was provision for serial number, national grid reference, bibliographical references, present location of find, and notes. While the system was adequate for small finds where the use of a coding manual was not a disadvantage, other County Archaeologists preferred to implement their own computerized systems to incorporate more elaborate data. Some of these were based on the IRGMA format

(e.g., Merseyside); others adopted a system developed by Benson at the Oxford City and County Museum (Warwickshire, Northamptonshire, Cambridgeshire, Berkshire, and West Sussex, as well as Oxfordshire itself); while yet others independently followed the computer recommendations of the CBA Working Party on Archaeological Records (e.g., Staffordshire).

In Scotland there were no county-organized records, but in addition to the Royal Commission on Historical Monuments (Scotland) records, there were card systems held in 1976 by planning officers, universities, museums, and archaeological societies at Renfrew, East Lothian, Dunbartonshire, Cowal, St. Andrews, Dundee, Aberdeen, Caithness, and Shetland.

In Wales no individual county records were held, but the National Monuments Record for Wales covered the whole principality on a National Grid basis.

Miscellaneous Private and Group Research Projects

Many other recording schemes have been undertaken in Britain by specialist research groups or private individuals, usually on a card basis but sometimes computerized. Within the Council for British Archaeology groups have created records for Medieval villages, moated sites, vernacular architecture, churches, industrial monuments and hillforts, as well as general Palaeolithic and Mesolithic records. Lilian Chitty kept her famous "indexes" to archaeological finds for many years. The British Cave Research Association undertook computerization of cave archaeological records in 1977 (see Wilcock 1970), and the British Museum (Natural History) was also preparing to computerize bones from archaeological sites, including caves, using an IRGMA card designed by Jewell. Laxton recorded collections of clay pipes on a computer for statistical study (Alvey and Laxton 1974). The coordination of dendrochronological studies in Britain was slower to develop than in the United States, but in 1977 Baillie proposed a computerized record of tree-ring measurements stretching over many thousands of years.

EVALUATION OF THE "STATE OF THE ART" IN BRITISH ARCHAEOLOGICAL RECORDING

Although it can be seen from the above catalog of applications that there has been no lack of initiative in the creation of archaeological data bases in Britain, it would be a mistake to assume that all British archaeologists were completely "sold" on the use of computers. In fact, most of the computer implementations were the work of persons not originally trained as archaeologists, for example, mathematicians and statisticians or computer scientists who also happened to be amateur or part-time archaeologists. We can discount here those studies where the archaeological data were used solely or mainly as a test-bed for the proving of multivariate statistical techniques—there have been a number of such studies carried on since the early 1950s where the statisticians involved had little or no interest in the archaeological implications, if any, except in passing. The remaining applications, in general, have produced significant or potentially significant archaeological results, and have been mostly the work of teams including at least one professional archaeologist and at least one expert computer scientist. Why have the techniques and even the results of this latter category of applications not received wider acclaim?

Some archaeologists see the computer as a threat to their authority because it would disseminate freely and widely the information which they have amassed over their lifetimes, and which is the basis of that authority. Fortunately such attitudes are in the minority. Another small group of archaeologists are almost pathetically eager to evangelize others with the newfound computer techniques. But the large majority are neither actively for nor against computers, wishing to be convinced that their advantages outweigh their disadvantages. While not requiring much mathematical knowledge, the preparation of computer data does require some logical ability. Normal archaeological training, however, does not usually include formal logic, and the "computer mentality" may be thought by some to be quite alien to the humanities-trained mind of the typical archaeologist. But the logical presentation and recording of categories of information is an asset to any archaeological study, whether or not it is ultimately computerized. Modern archaeology has already absorbed many scientific techniques drawn from the geological, physical, chemical, and biological sciences, and no publication would be complete without its specialist reports. Why should not computing science be similarly absorbed?

A second objection by the humanities-trained archaeologist may be that computer scientists with no archaeological background are trying to "muscle-in" to their discipline. But professional archaeologists have been involved in all the above-mentioned projects, and many of the computer scientists have studied in an effort to become archaeologically "respectable."

Another difficulty is financing the new techniques. Although governmental support for archaeology in Britain improved in the late 1970s, most of these resources went to fund rescue excavations made necessary by motorway construction and urban development. Faced with the need to allocate meagre reserves for the salaries of diggers, conventional excavation equipment, publication, and scientific aids, it was hardly surprising that unit directors chose an extra digger or a coveted piece of equipment, rather than expenditures on computing. Thus computer developments took place mainly under the heading of research in separately-financed institutions such as educational establishments and government-financed research centers. No archaeological unit in Britain could contemplate paying for computing at commercial rates. There was evidence in 1979 that the British government was making more resources available for archaeological computing. The Ancient Monuments Laboratory in London improved its computer facilities by using a satellite link to the United States computing network, a microcomputer for site work was made available to the Central Excavation Unit (Jefferies 1977), and computer-linked measuring equipment was installed to aid the measurement of animal bones and tree-rings.

The Working Party on Principles of Publication in Rescue Archaeology was set up by the Ancient Monuments Board for England Committee for Rescue Archaeology from among its own membership, and it consisted of leading academics. The Frere Report (Frere, ed., 1975) was published by the Department of the Environment in October 1975, and it gave formal encouragement for the use of the computer by British archaeologists. The recommendations were intended not only for the Department of the Environment but for academic and professional archaeologists and institutions. The report highlighted the crisis in publication of archaeological excavations, caused by larger and more numerous sites, more extensive scientific and specialist studies, and greatly increased printing costs. It proposed the following revolutionary and controversial system of publication, consisting of several distinct levels.

Level I	The site itself, general notes, old letters, previous accounts; excavated finds.
Level II	Site notebooks, recording forms, drawings, audio tapes; artifact records, X-rays, photographs, transparencies.
Level III	Full illustration and description of all structural and stratigraphic relationships; classified artifact lists and artifact drawings; all specialist analyses, including computer listings and computer-produced diagrams (e.g., of statistical analyses).
Level IV	Synthesized descriptions with supporting data; selected artifacts and specialist reports relevant to synthesis.

The report proposed that only Level IV should receive the glossy prestige publication treatment, but that Level III material should also be available on request, in duplicated form or microfiche. Levels I and II material should be housed in a museum, where it would be available for further study. Most excavations are recorded in the field on sheets of paper, and the site notebooks may only be intelligible to the Site Director. The report suggested that such problems would be overcome by the use of standard recording forms (e.g., the Danebury records, see Fig. 10.3) with a view to the preparation of data for the computer, and manipulation by computer program. The Working Party recommended that the use of computer records for the permanent storage of all types of quantifiable data in the archaeological record, especially for excavation data at Level III, should be encouraged. Cooperation with IRGMA was urged where possible, or, alternatively, the establishment of centralized computer services for excavation records in the National Monuments Record was recommended. Study of the whole field of possibilities for the use of computerized data for archaeological records was also recommended to the Department of the Environment, in consultation with the Royal Commission on Historical Monuments, and museum and other interests.

RECOMMENDATIONS FOR FUTURE APPLICATIONS

If financial support is forthcoming from the British government, it is recommended that those proposals of the Frere Report referring to computerization of records should be followed. The ideal would be a centralized nonintensive computer file for all British finds and sites, and a number of regional intensive computer files, eventually communicating with each other and accessible by remote terminal from anywhere in Britain. The creation of such files would be greatly facilitated by text analysis of archaeological reports, or "word processing." It is of interest that Biek (1974, 1976) has already suggested such techniques. Ideally, a research worker should be able to compare a find with similar finds in any collection in the country using the communications network. The advent of any such national archaeological computer system was in 1979 obviously far distant in time, for the financing was not available, nor had the archaeologists fully accepted the need for such a system. The ubiquitous microcomputer had begun to appear on archaeological sites, however, and systems for central recording were at least proposed, if not fully implemented.

REFERENCES

Allsworth-Jones, P.
1975   A cluster analysis of some Aurignacian and some Szeletian assemblages. *Computer Applications in Archaeology 1975*, pp. 81-92. Birmingham.

Allsworth-Jones, P., and J. D. Wilcock
1974a   A computer-assisted study of European Palaeolithic "leafpoints": Methodology and preliminary results. *Science and Archaeology* 11: 25-46. Stafford.
1974b   Palaeolithic "leafpoints"—an experiment in taxonomy. *Computer Applications in Archaeology 1974*, pp. 36-46. Birmingham.

Alvey, R. C., and F. R. Laxton
1974   Analysis of some Nottingham clay pipes. *Science and Archaeology* 13: 3-12. Stafford.

Biek, L.
1974   Progress with LERNIE. *Computer Applications in Archaeology 1974*, pp. 59-63. Birmingham.
1976   LERNIE—Phase III. *Computer Applications in Archaeology 1976*, pp. 65-72. Birmingham.

British Library Board
1977   Problems of information handling in archaeology. *The British Library Research and Development Report* 5329.

Buckland, P.
1973   An experiment in the use of a computer for on-site recording of finds. *Science and Archaeology* 9: 22-24. Stafford.

Callow, P.
1976   British and French handaxe series. *Computer Applications in Archaeology 1976*, pp. 33-40. Stafford.

Celoria, F. S. C., and J. D. Wilcock
1975   A computer-assisted classification of British Neolithic axes and a comparison with some Mexican and Guatemalan axes. *Science and Archaeology* 16: 11-29. Stafford.

Chantrey, D. F., J. D. Wilcock, and F. S. C. Celoria
1975   The sorting of archaeological materials by computer and by man: An interdisciplinary study in pottery classification. *Science and Archaeology* 14: 5-31. Stafford.

Chouraqui, E., M. Janon, J. Virbel, P. Corbier, and P-A. Fevrier
1972   L477. Automatic processing of the Corpus of Latin Inscriptions. *Computers and the Humanities* 6(5), in Directory of Scholars Active.

Clarke, D. L.
1962   Matrix analysis and archaeology with particular reference to British Beaker Pottery. *Proceedings of the Prehistoric Society* N.S. 28: 371-382.
1970   *Beaker Pottery of Great Britain and Ireland*, Volumes 1 and 2. Cambridge.

Collingwood, R. G.
1921-   Roman Britain in 19.., II. Inscriptions. *Journal*
1938   *of Roman Studies* 11, 12: 14-19, 21-28.

Collingwood, R. G., and R. P. Wright
1965   *The Roman Inscriptions of Britain I. Inscriptions on Stone*. Oxford University Press.

Conference on Roman Epigraphy
1967   Punching of cards: I. Data concerning the epitaph and the grave.

Council for British Archaeology
1975   Report of the Working Party on Archaeological Records made to the Royal Commission on Historical Monuments (England), July.

Cunliffe, B. W.
1971   Danebury, Hampshire: First interim report on the excavation, 1969-70. *Antiquaries Journal* 51: 240-252.

1977   Danebury, Hampshire: Second interim report on the excavations 1971–75. *Antiquaries Journal* 56(2): 198–216.

Cutbill, J. L.
1973   *Computer filing systems for museums and research.* Cambridge: IRGMA, Sedgwick Museum.
1974   Computer-based filing systems. *Computer Applications in Archaeology 1974,* p. 81. Birmingham.

Dessau, H., editor
1892–   *Inscriptiones Latinae Selectae,* 3 volumes in 5
1916   parts.

Doran, J. E., and F. R. Hodson
1966   A digital computer analysis of Palaeolithic flint assemblages. *Nature* 210(5037): 688–689. London.

Frere, S. S., editor
1975   *Principles of publication in rescue archaeology.* Ancient Monuments Board for England, Committee for Rescue Archaeology. London: Department of the Environment.

Gaines, Sylvia W.
1974   Computer-aided decision making procedures for archaeological field problems. *American Antiquity* 39: 454–462.

Graham, I.
1976   Intelligent terminals for excavation recording. *Computer Applications in Archaeology 1976,* pp. 48–52. Birmingham.

Graham, J. M.
1970   Discrimination of British Lower and Middle Palaeolithic handaxe groups using canonical variates (with a note by D. Roe). *World Archaeology* 1(3): 321–342.

Hardy-Smith, A.
1974   Post-Medieval pot shapes: A quantitative analysis. *Science and Archaeology* 11: 4–15. Stafford.

Haverfield, F. J.
1892   Additamenta quarta ad CIL vii. *Ephemeris Epigraphica* 7: 273–354.
1913a   Additamenta quinta ad CIL vii. *Ephemeris Epigraphica* 9: 509–690.
1913b   Roman Britain in 1913. *British Academy Supplemental Paper* 2. Oxford.
1914   Roman Britain in 1914. *British Academy Supplemental Paper* 3. Oxford.

Hübner, E.
1873   Inscriptiones Britanniae Latinae. *Corpus Inscriptionum Latinarum (CIL)* vii. Berlin.
1877a   Additamenta prima ad CIL vii. *Ephemeris Epigraphica* 3: 113–155.
1877b   Additamenta secunda ad CIL vii. *Ephemeris Epigraphica* 3: 311–318.
1881   Additamenta tertia ad CIL vii. *Ephemeris Epigraphica* 4: 194–212.

IRGMA Newsletter
1969   1, January 1969, Information Retrieval Group of the Museums Association, London.

Jefferies, J. S.
1977   *Excavation Records: Techniques in use by the Central Excavation Unit.* London: Department of the Environment.

Jory, E. J.
1968   S83. An index to Volume VI of the Corpus Inscriptionum Latinarum. *Computers and the Humanities,* in Directory of Scholars Active 1968/69(2): 318.

Jory, E. J., and D. W. Moore
1966   An index to CIL VI: Two aspects. *Revue* 2: 7–16. Organisation Internationale pour l'Etude des Langues Anciennes par Ordinateur.

Laflin, S.
1972   *Archaeological gazetteer for Shropshire.* Birmingham.
1973   Computer system for county gazetteers. *Computer Applications in Archaeology 1973; Science and Archaeology* 9: 26–28.

Lewis, G. D.
1965   Obtaining information from museum collections and thoughts on a national museum index. *Museums Journal* 65: 12–22.
1970/71   An interdisciplinary communication format for museums in the United Kingdom. (*UNESCO*) *Museum* 23(1): 24–26.

Lewis, G. D., et al.
1967   Information retrieval for museums. *Museums Journal* 67: 88–120.

Lewis, G. D., et al.
1969   *Draft proposals for an interdisciplinary museum cataloguing system.* Information Retrieval Group of the Museums Association, 23rd April. London.

McBurney, C. B. M.
1973   Measurable long term variations in some Old Stone Age Sequences. In *The Explanation of Culture Change: Models in Prehistory,* edited by C. Renfrew, pp. 305–315. London: Gerald Duckworth and Co. Ltd.

Museum Documentation Association
1976   *Introduction to the IRGMA Documentation System*
1977   *MDA News,* June. ISSN 0309-6661; *MDA Information* ISSN 0309-6653; MDAU, Imperial War Museum, Duxford, Cambridgeshire, UK.

Newman, S.
1969   Correspondence with R. G. Chenhall. In *Newsletter of Computer Archaeology* 5(2): 1.

Orton, C. R.
1970   The production of pottery from a Romano-British kiln site: a statistical investigation. *World Archaeology* 1(3): 343–358.
1971   On the statistical sorting and reconstruction of the pottery from a Romano-British kiln site. In *Mathematics in the Archaeological and Historical Sciences,* edited by F. R. Hodson, D. G. Kendall, and P. Tautu, pp. 453–459. Edinburgh: Edinburgh University Press.
1973   The tactical use of models in archaeology—the SHERD project. In *The explanation of culture change: Models in prehistory,* edited by D. Renfrew, pp. 137–139. London: Gerald Duckworth and Co. Ltd.
1974   An experiment in the mathematical reconstruction of the pottery from a Romano-British kiln site at Highgate Wood, London. *Bulletin of the Institute of Archaeology* 11: 41–73.
1975   Quantitative pottery studies: Some progress, problems and prospects. *Science and Archaeology* 16: 30–35. Stafford.

Renfrew, C.
1967   The requirements of the research worker in archaeology. *Museums Journal* 67: 111–113.

Roads, C. H.
  1968   Data recording, retrieval and presentation in the Imperial War Museum. *Museums Journal* 68: 277-283.

Roe, D. A.
  1964a   Statistics and archaeology: Metrical and statistical analysis of handaxe groups in the British Lower Palaeolithic. *Research Seminar on Statistics and Archaeology*. London: Institute of Archaeology.
  1964b   The British Lower and Middle Palaeolithic: Some problems, methods of study and preliminary results. *Proceedings of the Prehistoric Society* N.S. 30: 245-267.
  1968   British Lower and Middle Palaeolithic handaxe groups. *Proceedings of the Prehistoric Society* N.S. 34: 1-82.

Shackley, M. L.
  1972   The use of textural parameters in the analysis of cave sediments. *Archaeometry* 14(1): 133-145. Oxford.
  1973   Computers and sediment analysis in archaeology. *Science and Archaeology* 9: 29-30. Stafford.
  1975   *Archaeological Sediments, A Survey of Analytical Methods*. London: Butterworths.
  1976   The Danebury project: an experiment in site sediment recording. In *Geoarchaeology*, edited by D. A. Davidson and M. L. Shackley, pp. 9-21. London: Gerald Duckworth and Co. Ltd.

Shackley, M. L., and J. D. Wilcock
  1974   Pit sediments at Danebury and the computer. *Computer Applications in Archaeology 1974*, pp. 82-90. Birmingham.

Shackley, M. L., A. Macgregor, and J. M. Duncan
  1976   Information retrieval and graphics and Danebury and York. *Computer Applications in Archaeology 1976*, pp. 72-79. Birmingham.

Shennan, S. J., and J. D. Wilcock
  1975   Shape and style variation in Central German Bell Beakers: A computer-assisted study. *Science and Archaeology* 15: 17-31. Stafford.

Stones, C. J., and J. B. Williamson
  1970   Sèvres porcelain and its incised marks. *Science and Archaeology* 4: 15-18. Stafford.

Virbel, J.
  1973   Methodological aspects of the segmentation and the characterization of textual data in archaeology: applications to the mechanized processing of the Corpus of Latin Inscriptions. In *The explanation of culture change: Models in prehistory*, edited by C. Renfrew, pp. 141-148. London: Gerald Duckworth and Co. Ltd.

Walker, M. J.
  1970a   An analysis of British petroglyphs. *Science and Archaeology* 2/3: 30-61. Reviewed by I. Scollar, 1972, in *Computers and the Humanities* 6(3): 191.
  1970b   An analysis of British petroglyphs. Note in *Science and Archaeology* 4: 26-29, N4/1. Stafford.

Wilcock, J. D.
  1969a   Computer analysis of proton magnetometer readings from South Cadbury 1968—a long-distance exercise. *Prospezioni Archeologiche* 4: 85-93. Rome.
  1969b   Computers and Camelot: South Cadbury, an exercise in computer archaeology. *Spectrum, British Science News* 60: 7-9. London: Central Office of Information, H.M.S.O.
  1970   Information retrieval for cave records. *Transactions, Cave Research Group of Great Britain* 12(2): 96-98.
  1973   The use of remote terminals for archaeological site records. *Science and Archaeology* 9: 25. Stafford.
  1974a   The facilities of the PLUTARCH System. *Science and Archaeology* 11: 16-24. Stafford.
  1974b   The PLUTARCH System. *Computer Applications in Archaeology 1974*, pp. 64-68. Birmingham.
  1978   The Automated Archaeologist. *Computer Applications in Archaeology 1978*, pp. 49-52. Birmingham.

Wright, R. P.
  1939-   Roman Britain in 19. ., II. Inscriptions. *Journal of*
  1977   *Roman Studies*, latterly in *Britannia*.

Zarri, G. P.
  1974   A project of a new and updated edition of the fifth volume of the *Corpus Inscriptionum Latinarum*, with automatic preparation of indexes. *Association for Literary and Linguistic Computing Bulletin* 2(3): 7-15.

11. SOFIA: A Data Base Management System Applied to Archaeology

Jacques Le Maitre

Centre de Recherches Archéologiques, Valbonne, France

INTRODUCTION

Computerized data bases in archaeology, history of art, and related fields are extremely varied. According to a survey on this subject (Le Maitre 1977), they can be classified in the following way.

1. Data bases dealing with material objects or monuments: (a) records of archaeological excavations and surveys—material data recovered from a given geographical area (site, county, region); (b) records of museum collections or national inventories; and (c) serial data bases of given types of objects or monuments such as ceramics, cylinder seals, mosaics, and so on.

2. Data bases dealing with written documents: (a) records of ancient texts (e.g., a corpus of Latin inscriptions, of manuscripts, and the like); (b) bibliographical data bases—data bases wherein only the titles of documents are recorded, and those in which the content of documents is also indexed.

The information systems used to manage these data bases are themselves extremely varied. They consist of general systems like data base management systems, or, more often, of documentation systems like SATIN (see Chapter 12), STAIRS, and GOLEM, or of ad hoc systems like GRIPHOS (see Chapter 3) and SELGEM (see Chapter 4) for the management of museum collections and PLUTARCH (see Chapter 10), for the management of records of archaeological excavations.

One way toward a compromise in this field is to design a general system capable of managing all the above mentioned categories of data bases. With that aim in view, we made a comparative study of a number of systems with respect to the data description languages (Le Maitre 1977) involved in each case. We

observed that most description languages have a considerable number of properties in common; their differences mainly concern: (a) the authorized types of attribute values, (b) the fact that entity types are declared or not declared, and (c) the type of structure (hierarchical, etc.) of each data base. We were then able to design a canonical exchange format into which data expressed in other input formats could easily be translated. Next we needed a system that could process any data described according to this exchange format, that is, a general purpose system (Le Maitre 1977).

In this chapter we attempt to show that SOFIA is a system of this kind. SOFIA is a French acronym meaning "System Operant sur Fichiers Inversés en Archéologie." The system is used at the Centre de Recherches Archéologiques (C.N.R.S., Paris and Valbonne) for management of several archaeological data bases.

The first section of this chapter is devoted to a description of the proposed exchange format. The development and use of a general system raises two kinds of problems; one of them concerns performance. It is well known that the generality of a processing system is usually attained at the cost of efficiency, inasmuch as processing time and costs are considerably greater than they would be if one used ad hoc systems for every data base. The second problem concerns the actual adaptation of a general system to the users' needs, since input data and required outputs may be very different from one data base to another. It is never desirable to impose on users constraints such as a standard input format and standard output products.

The way in which the SOFIA system offers solutions to these problems is the subject of the second section; however, no detailed description of the system itself is provided here (see Le Maitre 1977, Chapter 5). Examples of current and future applications of the system are given in the third section.

Throughout the first section, our examples refer to a *fictitious* data base (a collection of paintings; Heller 1974: 14); the data consist of information about the paintings themselves (identification by title, author, date, and some iconographical indications), about the museums where they are exhibited, and about the artists who painted them.

DEFINITION OF THE EXCHANGE FORMAT

A data base is a set of elementary values linked by a set of relationships. An elementary *value* is a string of characters such as a number, a name, or a text. Examples are "1935," "Picasso," "the three musicians." Elementary values are classified by one or several attributes (for instance, DATE, AUTHOR, TITLE). An *attribute* is defined by its name and several parameters characterizing its values (e.g., type of value, range of validity). In our fictitious data base, the attributes are: TIT (title) and DC (date of creation), for *paintings;* CNM (code number), MUS (name of museum), ADR (city), for *museums;* and CNA (code number), NAM (name), CN (Christian name), DB (date of birth), DD (date of death), for *painters.*

Relationships

A distinction is drawn between two types of relationships: relationships within an entity and relationships between entities. An *entity* consists of a set of relationships linking one or several *descriptive terms,* each formed by an attribute-value pair, which make up its *description.* For instance, the description of the "Picasso" entity is:

CNA : 15 & NAM : Picasso & CN : Pablo &
CN : Ruiz & DB : 1881 & DD : 1973

The characters ":" and "&" are separators. The order of descriptive terms within an entity is indifferent; several descriptive terms may be associated with a common attribute (e.g., CN : Pablo & CN : Ruiz, in the above example).

Relationships between entities, as their name would indicate, are relations that hold between entities irrespective of their description. In a given data base one or several types of inter-entity relationships may exist: (a) An R attribute, or, if the R relationships are oriented, an R1-R2 attribute pair, is associated to each R relationship. (b) A descriptive term "R : r" is added to each entity description in which the r relationship is found; or, if r is oriented, a descriptive term

"R1 : r" is added to the description of the entity that is the origin of r, and a descriptive term "R2 : r" is added to the description of the entity that is the extremity of r. Consider, for example, the following descriptions of three entities that respectively refer to a painting, its author, and the museum in which it can be found.

TIT : the three musicians & DC : 1935 &
A : IS & M : 20 / CNA : 15 & NAM : Picasso
& CN : Pablo & CN : Ruiz & DB : 1881
& DD : 1973 / CNM : 20 & MUS : The Museum of
Modern Art & ADR : New York /

The character "/" is an entity separator. The pair "CNA : 15" "A : 15" represents the "author" relationship and the "CNM : 20" "M : 20" pair represents the "location" relationship. The set of inter-entity relationships of a data base defines what we call its *structure.* We can say that the above representation accounts for any type of structure whatsoever: n-ary relations, hierarchical structures, networks, are shown in Figure 11.1 in which each entity is described by its number N.

To summarize, a data base described according to the exchange format is a sequence of descriptions of entities, each description consisting of a sequence of descriptive terms. Thus, we have (in BNF, Bacchus normalized form):

<BD> : = <description of entity> Fb | <description of entity> Fe <BD> <description of entity> : = <descriptive term> Fv | <descriptive term> Fv <description of entity>

<descriptive term> : = <attribute> Fa <value>. Fb : = character (end of DB), Fe : = character (end of description of entity), Fv : = character (end of value), Fa : = character (end of attribute name).

<attribute> : = string of characters ($\neq$ Fa), <value> : = string of characters ($\neq$ Fb, Fe, Fv).

GENERAL PROPERTIES OF THE SOFIA SYSTEM

Physical Organization of a Data Base Managed by SOFIA

Much thought had to be given to an optimum physical organization of a SOFIA data base in order to achieve high standards of performance. The main characteristics of this organization are implicit relationships between entities and partitioning of files by attributes, each partition containing three possible kinds of files: (1) an indexed sequential file, (2) an inverted file, and (3) a coding file.

Implicit relationships between entities

In the physical representation of a SOFIA data base, relationships between entities are not denoted by means of flags, as is the case for most systems

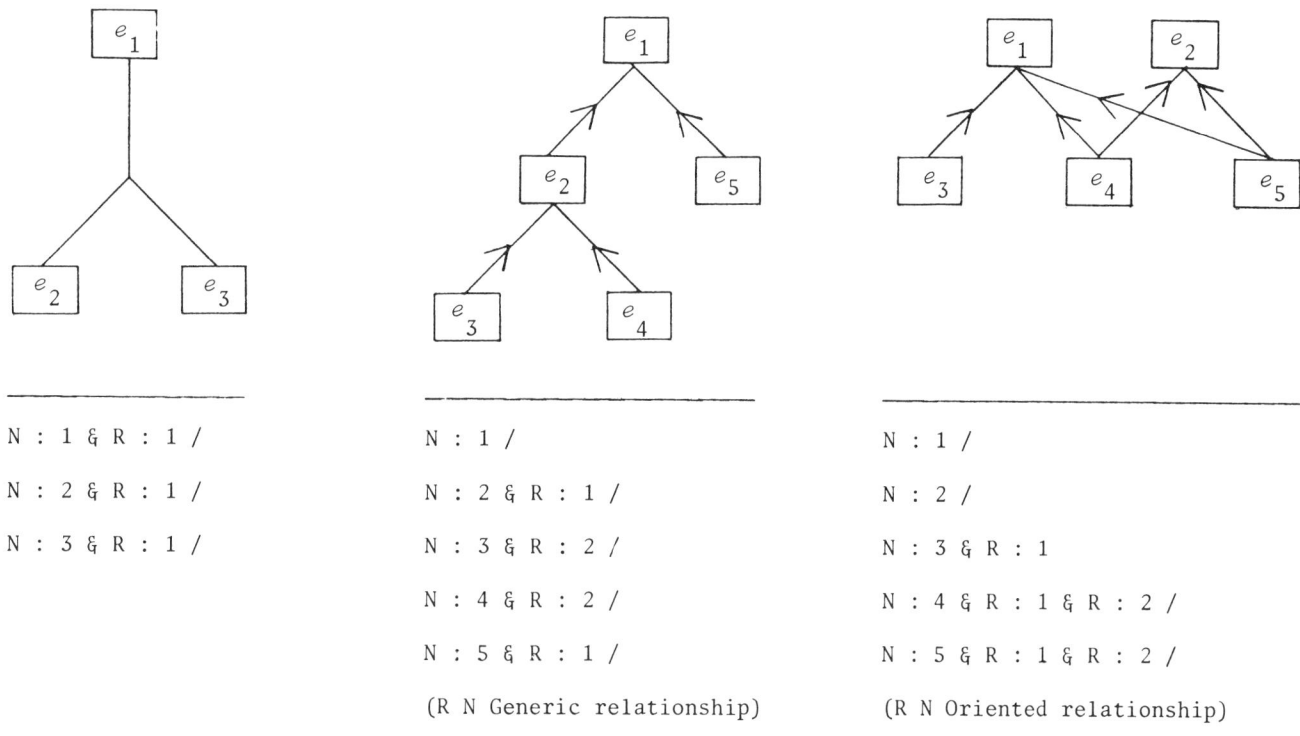

N : 1 & R : 1 /

N : 2 & R : 1 /

N : 3 & R : 1 /

N : 1 /

N : 2 & R : 1 /

N : 3 & R : 2 /

N : 4 & R : 2 /

N : 5 & R : 1 /

(R N Generic relationship)

N : 1 /

N : 2 /

N : 3 & R : 1

N : 4 & R : 1 & R : 2 /

N : 5 & R : 1 & R : 2 /

(R N Oriented relationship)

Fig. 11.1. Structure of entity, hierarchy, and network relationships.

whenever certain attributes possess identical values. In the course of retrospective searches, this linkage between entities is achieved by a special routine that detects entities with identical values for the same attribute(s). We must point out that, as a consequence, the updating of the data base is an easier task than in the case when flags are used, since the latter impose a rigid structure that cannot be modified easily. A drawback, or at least what is usually considered as such by specialists, is that retrospective searches, in this case, have lower performance, since the system has no defined access channels. In our view, this deficiency can be alleviated by using ad hoc search techniques (we have done this in the present case), and also by appropriate choices of the attributes that support the relationships between entities.

The physical organization of files

In most cases, queries only bear on selected subsets of attributes, rather than on all attributes in the file. Selective access to all values for a given attribute should therefore be advantageous. For that reason a SOFIA data base is physically organized as a sequence of partitions, each partition being accessed through the name of an attribute. Each partition can contain an indexed sequential file, an inverted file, and a coding file.

The indexed sequential file for a given attribute contains the list of entities described by this attribute, and the corresponding values; in addition, it contains a table indicating the locations of entities inside the file. This table provides a quick access to values since it saves scanning the entire file for a given entity.

The inverted file indicates, for each of the values of an attribute, all entities described by this value. With this kind of file it is possible to make a quick selection of the entities described by a given value. However, an inverted file takes up much storage space, which is why SOFIA users are free to decide whether or not this file is to be created for each attribute.

When the values of an attribute are names or texts, and if each value occurs fairly frequently, it may be convenient to save storage space by replacing each of these values by a code (an integer number, the value of which may not exceed the maximum number of values to be coded). In such cases, each attribute can be associated with a coding file containing a "value-code" correspondence table, which ensures the automatic coding and decoding of values for input and output. Figure 11.2 illustrates the physical organization of the files.

Data Handling

SOFIA is a modular system in the sense that any kind of data handling can be done by means of a combination of a number of elementary routines. These

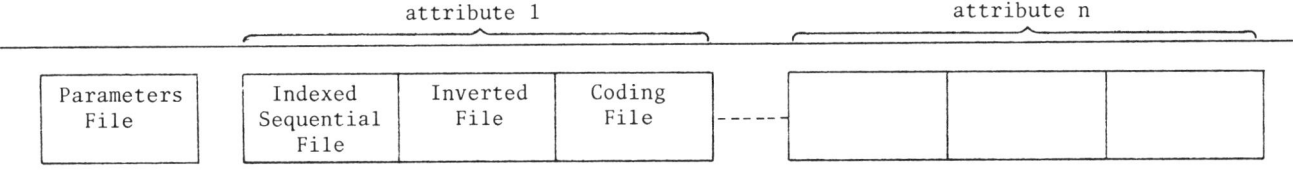

Fig. 11.2. Physical organization of files.

elementary routines have been devised so as to answer two kinds of requirements. First, performance should be high, and programming easy. Secondly, facility of use is essential—data handling operations that occur most frequently should require only the use of a minimal number of basic routines, and routines should be sequentially linked in such a way that no intermediate results have to be manipulated by users. These routines carry out three categories of operations: file management operations, retrospective search operations, and transition operations. This classification, however, is proposed only for the sake of our presentation; any sequence of linked operations belonging to different categories can be used in actual programs.

File management operations

With file management operations the user can create new data and modify or delete existing data, including: (a) attribute management—creation, change of name, addition, deletion; (b) entity management—creation and updating of entity descriptions; and (c) coding file management—creation, management, and codification of "value-code" pairs.

Retrospective search operations

A retrospective search operation is a scanning process that does not modify the content of the data base. These search operations can be divided into three categories: procedural operations, nonprocedural operations, and search operations in a coding file. According to the physical organization of a SOFIA data base as previously described, each of these operations can apply only to files associated with a single given attribute (a given attribute is called A; a given list of entities is called D).

An operation is called *procedural* when it applies to data and results wherein each value is associated with the entity described by it. The operations are *extraction* (i.e., extracting the value of A for all entities of E) and *selection by reference* (i.e., selection of all entities linked by an A relationship to all entities of E).

An operation is called *nonprocedural* when it applies to data or results that are sets of entities or values. Nonprocedural operations are: *inverted selection* (i.e., selection of all entities in which a given value

for A occurs); *extraction,* when all the values of A for all entities of E are to be extracted; and *selection by reference* (i.e., selection of all entities linked by an A type relationship to one or several entities of E).

Search operations in a coding file include: *search by value* (i.e., extraction of the code number of a given value) and *search by code number* (i.e., extraction of a value corresponding to a given code number).

Transition operations

Transition operations do not apply to the files, but to the results of retrospective search operations. With them, users are able to link operations of different kinds sequentially. They can be divided into three categories: (a) Boolean operations (i.e., union, intersection, or difference of two given sets of entities); (b) transition from a procedural operation to a nonprocedural operation, and vice-versa; and (c) transition from a procedural operation to a file management operation when the user wants to create new entities, or modify the descriptions of given entities, on the basis of the results of a procedural extraction operation.

Utilization of the SOFIA System

Input formats vary with each particular field of application (prehistory, history of art); it would not be fair, and often it is impractical, to ask every single creator of a data base to describe his data in terms of a canonical exchange format. For instance, excavation data are often first recorded on exercise books, or loose leaves, and recording formats are different from one excavation to another. When such data are prepared for computerization, archaeologists have good reason to insist on an input format as close as possible to what they actually write in their books in the field. Also, output products, even though they may be formally quite similar from one data base to another (e.g., printed indexes, selective dissemination, occasional queries), may legitimately be presented in different formats according to local needs. Although it is meant as a general purpose system, for all these reasons SOFIA has been designed to function jointly with what we call a "user system," one that takes care of exchange and communication tasks (see Fig. 11.3).

The main function of the user system is to ensure a

translation of the user's input format into SOFIA's input format on the one hand, and of SOFIA's output format into the user's output format on the other. In addition, the user system is entrusted with various kinds of operations necessary for the "understanding" of the data in their original form: the control of syntax and semantics in the input data, the selection of entities in the course of retrospective searches (according to constraints that are verified by their description), and lastly, computing operations performed on these descriptions.

Implementation and Performance

The SOFIA system is written entirely in FORTRAN IV. It consists of a set of subroutines:

GESATT: Attribute management,
GESENT: Entity management,
GESCOD: Coding file management,

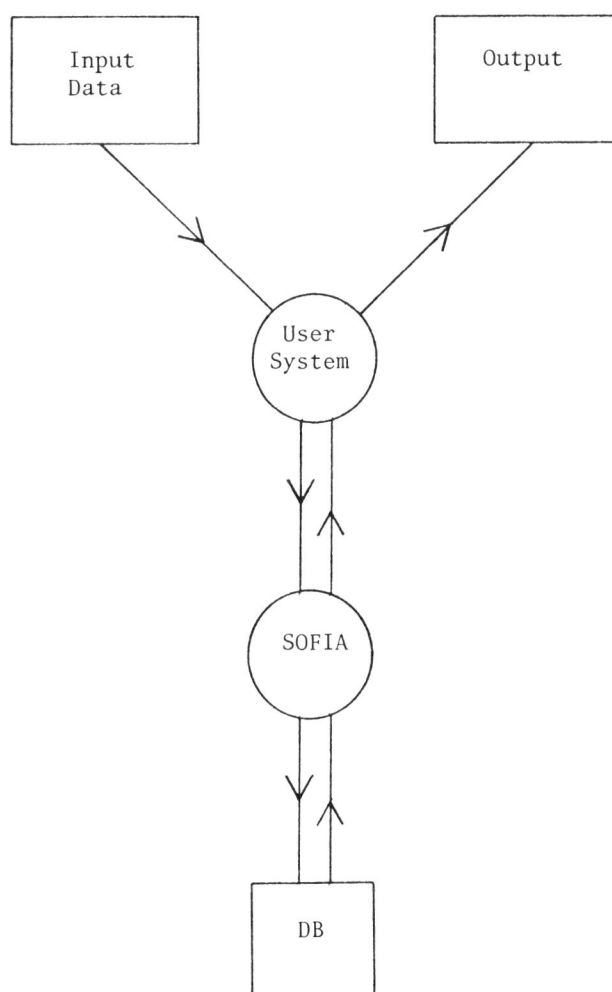

Fig. 11.3. User system interface with SOFIA.

RECPRO: Retrospective procedural search,
RECNOP: Retrospective nonprocedural search,
OPBOOL: Boolean operations,
TRTCBE: Transition between procedural and non-procedural operations,
TRTLDE: Transition from a procedural operation to a file management operation.

The whole set contains around 1500 FORTRAN instructions. Performance measurements have been made in the course of the initial applications of SOFIA. It would be too long to describe them here, but they have shown that computing time is indeed very small (see Le Maitre 1977).

APPLICATIONS

A special user system, SOFIADOC, has been designed to deal with what we call documentary data bases that are often used in archaeology and related fields. Although we cannot describe SOFIADOC in detail here, we can summarize a SOFIADOC application. The data base consists of a *thesaurus,* one or several *record files,* and one or several questionnaires, each applying to a given record file.

The thesaurus contains all necessary descriptive terms. It is divided into separate parts, each associated with an attribute, and it is hierarchically organized. A *record* is a tree of nodes of *subrecords* that are entities composed of a set of descriptive terms. The query language provides Boolean operations and tree structure search (within the thesaurus and within records). Lastly, a printout module can produce four kinds of different outputs.

SOFIADOC is used at present to manage two data bases: "Le Répertoire Analytique des Cylindres Orientaux" (Digard 1975) and the "Bibliographie analytique de Préhistoire et Protohistoire" (DeMoule and Werner 1976). Other applications of SOFIA include the management of a collection of Hellenistic ceramics recovered at Aï Khanoum in Afghanistan (Gardin 1973), and the management of the bibliographical catalog of archaeological periodicals of the Centre de Recherches Archéologiques (C.N.R.S.) in Valbonne.

The Analytical Index
of Oriental Cylinder-seals

The cylinder-seal data base consists of a collection of about 4800 engraved cylinder-seals from the Near East (3000–1000 B.C.) described in terms of an analytical documentary language (Digard 1975) containing about 1700 descriptors. The data base was derived from a manual file on "peek-a-boo" cards, structured as an inverted file, each punched card corresponding to one attribute-value pair. For this reason we designed an ad hoc input program instead of rearranging the data in a sequential form as they should be for input to SOFIA.

The initial purpose for creating this data base was the need to retrieve and print out all possible relevant references (to cylinders) in reply to a number of iconographical searches (1800 queries). We were not able to use the printout format in SOFIADOC to meet the printing requirements, so we used a printout module devised at the Centre de Documentation pour les Sciences Humaines (C.N.R.S., Paris). This data base can be searched at a low cost by any user.

The Bibliographical Data Base on French Protohistory and Prehistory

The bibliographical records consist of the titles and indexed representations of articles or monographs published every year in the field of French Protohistory and Prehistory. A record is divided into two sections: an identification section (author, title, etc.), and an analytical section, where the content of articles is indexed in terms of a documentary language (DeMoule and Werner 1976). Records are hierarchically structured with one, two, or three levels. The root subrecord contains information concerning the whole article (bibliographical references, natural environment of archaeological sites, technology, etc.). The second and third level subrecords contain an analysis of the sites described in the article. Each second level subrecord contains the identification of an archaeological site, and the subrecords attached to it contain a description of structures and objects associated with this site. An example of a record (in SOFIADOC input format) reads:

D / A : A1 / A2 & TIT : T & ANP : 1978 & TP : P
& V : 1 & P : 10 - 15 & (L : VAR & C : C1
& S : S1 & (M : HACHE & D : BRONZE))
& (L : VAUCLUSE & C : C2 & S : S2 &
(M : COUTEAU & D : OS))*

The record concerns an article published in 1978, from page 10 to page 15 of the first volume of periodical P, the authors are A1 and A2, and the content describes two objects—a bronze axe discovered on site S1 situated in the commune C1 of the Var Department, and a bone knife discovered on site S2 situated in commune C2 of the Vaucluse Department.

A sample of 500 records was used for this application, which illustrated various possible forms of output. In this application, SOFIADOC was only one of the components of a broader information system—the "Bibliographical system of French Protohistory and Prehistory."

The Data Bank on Aï Khanoum Ceramics

This ceramic data bank deals with a collection of potsherds excavated at Aï Khanoum in Afghanistan (Gardin 1973). Each record contains detailed information about the location of a sherd according to a horizontal cross-section of the site (excavation sector, square), and a vertical (stratigraphic) axis (layers, levels). Sherds in each location unit are described in terms of a detailed typology. The number of sherds is indicated for each type. All sherds in a given location unit form a "lot." The structure of a "lot" defines the input format of the data base. A lot is composed of several categories: horizontal location, vertical location, label identification, and the description of all types of sherds thus located. The description of a type includes category, genus, group, series, variant, detail, annotation, and number. The input format uses a set of separators to identify each category. This format was chosen primarily because it was close to the initial records in the archaeologists' notes, and secondly, because it allowed us to reduce the volume of input data considerably. No fixed space was required for each category, since separators indicate the beginning and end of each value. In addition, if a category is not used, there simply is no corresponding separator.

Description of a "lot":

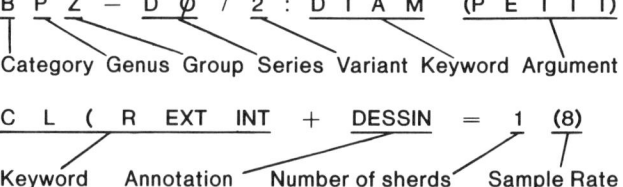

Description of a type:

In this application, the user system consists of a set of FORTRAN subroutines which in turn call SOFIA routines. This set is "open-ended" in the sense that new subroutines can be added everytime they are needed for new applications.

Three SOFIADOC subroutines are already available. CREBAC creates the data base from parameters defined from sampled data. GESBAC adds new entities to the data base, and modifies or deletes them. The core of this set of routines is a syntactical analyzer by which data are validated and translated into SOFIA's input format. TRIBAC sorts data by values of all or part of the attributes, using a CII sorting software.

The ceramic data base was completed in 1979 (about 25,000 entities have been registered), and various sortings have been completed. In the future, statistical processing will be applied by connecting SOFIA to an already available string of statistical programs such as the STRADES system (Guenoche and Le Maitre 1977).

The Union Catalog
of Archaeological Serial Publications

SOFIA is also used at the Centre de Recherches Archéologiques (C.N.R.S. Valbonne) for the management of a Union Catalog of Archaeological Serial Publications (called CCA, Catalogue collectif d'archéologie). The CCA contains the bibliographical descriptions of collections of archaeological serial publications available in the main French libraries (about 3,000 different titles have already been recorded). This catalog will enable archaeological teams belonging to the Centre de Recherches Archéologiques to obtain information on the places where any given volume in a serial publication can be consulted, borrowed, or reproduced. Indexes, printed periodically, will be the first output of this data base. Further facilities will be off-line queries as well as on-line access to the data base, through an interface between SOFIA and a time-sharing system developed at the Marseilles computing center.

CONCLUSION

The variety of applications we have described explains the qualification of SOFIA as a general purpose system. Such a system is especially useful for the creation of an information network, within a scattered scientific community, made up of different research units working in different areas such as the Centre de Recherches Archéologiques. Its main advantages are: (a) exchange facilities between data bases using different input formats through a user system; (b) an easy and flexible use of modular sets of routines; and (c) relatively high performance rates.

REFERENCES

DeMoule, J. P., and B. Werner
   1976   *Bibliographie Analytique de Préhistoire et Proto-histoire.* Centre de Recherches Archéologiques. Paris and Valbonne: C.N.R.S.

Digard, F.
   1975   *Répertoire Analytique des Cylindres Orientaux.* Paris: Editions du C.N.R.S.

Gardin, J. C.
   1973   Les céramiques. In Fouilles d'Aï Khanoum, I, edited by P. Bernard et al., pp. 121–188. *Mémoire de la Délégation Archéologique Française en Afghanistan* 21. Paris: Klincksieck.

Guenoche, A., and J. Le Maitre
   1977   *STRADES: Manuel d'utilisation.* Rapport du Laboratoire d'Informatique pour les Sciences de l'Homme. Marseilles: C.N.R.S.

Heller, J.
   1974   On logical data organization, card catalogs, and the GRIPHOS management information system. *Museum Data Bank Research Report* 3. Rochester, New York: Margaret Woodbury Strong Museum.

Le Maitre, J.
   1977   *La rationalisation des systèmes de traitement de l'information documentaire en archéologie.* Report of the Centre de Recherches Archéologiques. Paris: C.N.R.S.

12. The SATIN I System

Louis Bourrelly and Eugene Chouraqui
Laboratoire d'Informatique pour les Sciences de l'Homme, Marseille, France

PROBLEMS ARISING FROM ARCHAEOLOGICAL DATA DESCRIPTION

Defining a Reference Framework

An important part of archaeological activities is devoted to the derivation and characterization of data. Artifacts are raw materials constituting the basis from which the data must be defined. They may be items of various kinds, including pottery, coins, weapons, statues, paintings, tools, garments or texts. Data derivation is the first step in an experimental process that leads to a deeper knowledge of the investigated fields. Since a well established theory is lacking in these fields (Borillo 1977, Soudsky 1970), we have to define a precise and coherent methodological framework that will show, in an explicit way, the various steps involved in such processes (Chouraqui and Virbel 1976).

1. Definition of aims: (a) types of problems that are to be solved (bibliographical, cognitive, etc.); (b) formulation and construction of hypothesis relative to the problem; and (c) types of results that may be expected.

2. Raw material collection and corpus construction. Explicit criteria must be established to enable us to associate without any ambiguity an object to a corpus. These criteria may be internal (i.e., semantic, syntactic), or external (i.e., spatio-temporal, social, historical).

3. The artifact analysis must be conducted under conditions of regularity and replication inherent to all scientific approaches. Such analysis leads us to the construction of models that may be used to represent key parameters of the raw materials during the ongoing investigation. By necessity, these models are incomplete representations of the full information contained in the original artifact. The models reflect the objectives of the analysis and the investigation.

4. Data base construction.

5. Data processing and manipulation of the data base, including document retrieval, information extraction, statistical calculations, classifications, and seriations.

It must be noted that the first step (i.e., the definition of the objectives) governs all the following steps of investigation and that there exists no generic or exhaustive descriptions likely to solve all problems (Borillo 1971; Chenhall 1976).

Various Levels of Information Representation in the Experimental Process

In most cases, the archaeologist does not actually work with the artifacts (i.e., raw materials), but with descriptions. The representation of these descriptions is expressed in terms of specific use of the Natural Language (NL). In handling such representations, any treatment that does not constrain the Natural Language is bound to carry the ambiguities of that language. These ambiguities may be of a semantic or syntactic nature such as problems related to synonymy, polysemy, periphrases, or groups of words (Gardin 1974; Hesnard and Virbel 1973). In order to avoid this problem, it is necessary to construct a classificatory system to describe the artifacts in a consistent way. To accomplish consistency we use a relational network and a vocabulary that are controlled and defined by the objectives. This system is given the status of a language and is called Indexing Language (IL) (Bourrelly and Chouraqui 1974a, 1974b; Gardin 1974). The Indexing Language is composed, on the one hand,

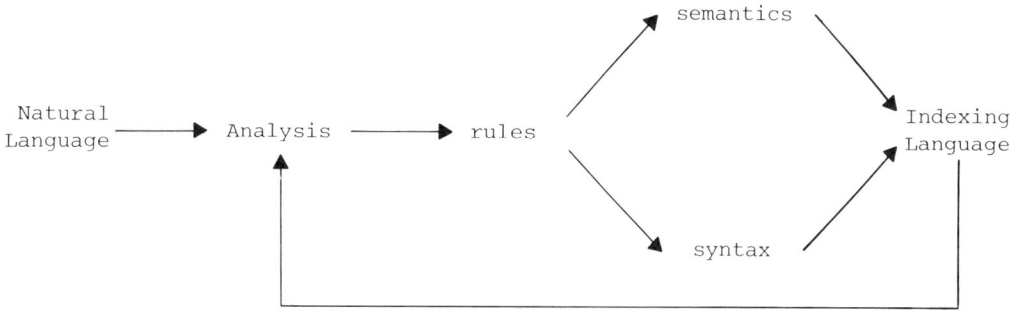

Fig. 12.1. Diagram of the formulation of an Indexing Language.

of a set of words or symbols expressing the semantic content of the studied artifacts (i.e., the vocabulary), and, on the other hand, of a set of rules allowing us to point out the possible links between the various concepts describing a similar artifact (i.e., the syntax; Figure 12.1). The codification of the vocabulary and syntax elements may be quite different in nature depending on the applications. In particular, this codification may be expressed by character strings borrowed directly from the natural languages. Nevertheless, it is critical that such codification does not lead to a confusion between Natural Language and Indexing Language (Bourrelly and Chouraqui 1976).

Processing related to the data base construction and management may be mechanized only if the artifact representations (the Indexing Language), are considered as the input data of the algorithms. The types of data structures defining these representations are derived from a set of rules with which we can manipulate the Indexing Language. The syntactic and semantic organization of these rules give them a status of formal language called Data Description Language (DDL). The executable statements used to activate the various processes are also translated into

specific language called Command Language (CL). The Command Language accepts Data Description Language elements as input data. These languages (Natural, Indexing, Data Description, and Command) bear relationships that point out the progressions the artifact information undergoes throughout the experimental processing (Fig. 12.2). Any system that handles and manages the data expressed in Data Description Language by means of a Command Language is called an information storage and retrieval system.

Archaeological Basis for SATIN I

The methodological framework we have just described developed from experience with a set of archaeological investigations aimed at the creation of data bases for scientific purposes (LaGrange 1968). Using these as our models, we developed the specifications of the SATIN I information storage and retrieval system. The first experimental materials we applied were "L'Inventaire Général des Monuments et Richesses Artistiques de la France" (Chouraqui 1973) and materials related to a prehistoric bone industry

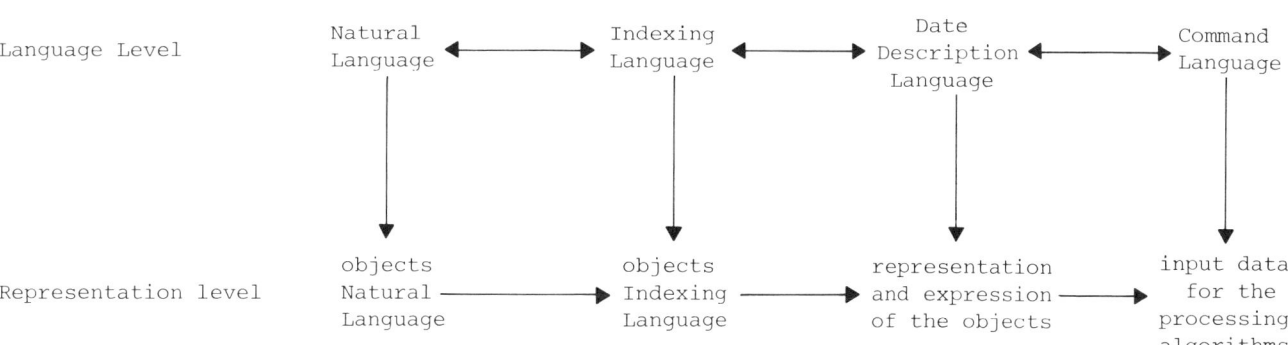

Fig. 12.2. Relationships between representations and languages.

(Bourrelly and Camps-Fabrer 1974). We were able to improve and increase the system capabilities by further studies performed on other materials such as cadastral cartography (Borillo et al. 1975), urbanism data (Daumas and Raby 1976), an archaeological map of France (Buchenschutz et al. 1976), and Roman and Greek mosaics (Guimier-Sorbets 1976). These studies resulted in further refinements made in order to satisfy the scientific requirements of the wider audience using the system.

SATIN I is an information retrieval system that performs various functions associated with automatic documentation such as archaeological data input and updating, retrospective search for information, and printing of reference sheets selected or not selected by topics. Additional functions more specifically adapted to aims of scientific research are the description of complex and diversified archaeological data, construction of Boolean or numerical matrices with a view to using them for scientific calculations, and storage and reutilization of intermediate research results. This kind of approach leads to the construction of a data base composed of a number of items relevant to the objectives of the study and requiring a sophisticated Indexing Language.

DATA DESCRIPTION LANGUAGE IN SATIN I SYSTEM

With the SATIN I Data Description Language we are able to express both the semantic and syntactic aspects of a class of Indexing Languages. Both aspects are used for the description of archaeological artifacts. The Data Description Language specifications presented here relate to iconographical documents belonging to classic mythology (Ginouves and Guimier-Sorbets 1978). In order to illustrate the possiblities offered by the system we give a brief descriptive representation of the "Exekias Amphora."

The Exekias Amphora was painted by Exekias about 540 B.C. in the black-figured Attic style, and it is now exhibited at the Vatican Museum. Both sides are decorated and the designs represent a game of dice between Achilles and Ajax, and the return of the Dioscures. One side shows Achilles holding two spears, Ajax holding two spears and wearing a helmet, a table, a stool, and two shields. The other side shows the gathering of Tyndare, Leda, Kastor (holding a spear), Polydeukes, a slave who is holding a stool and an aryballos, a horse, and a dog.

This description in natural language must be translated into Data Description Language terms. The translation must point out, on the one hand, the vocabulary and its organization, and, on the other hand, the syntactic relationships between the elements of

this vocabulary. With this example we illustrate the concepts that constitute the basis of SATIN I formal organization.

Vocabulary Organization

Definition of the thesaurus

Considering our objectives only some of the terms in the preceding description are significant in expressing the descriptive content of the Exekias Amphora. Two types of significant words are distinguished, the fields and the descriptors.

The fields. Elementary information items expressing the theme of the artifacts are called fields, and this type of analysis is referred to as thematical analysis. In this level of analysis occurs the first partition of the semantic domain into *categories of information.* These categories are of the TEXT type and are composed of fields defining a free vocabulary that the system does not control.

Categories	Fields
- DESIGNATION	: EXEKIAS AMPHORA
- AUTHOR	: EXEKIAS
- STYLE	: BLACK-FIGURED ATTIC STYLE
- PLACE OF CONSERVATION	: VATICAN MUSEUM
- DATING	: 540 B.C.

The descriptors. According to our objectives, the *descriptors* are elementary information items expressing the content of the artifacts. This analysis is called *descriptive analysis.* In this example the content analysis deals with certain aspects of the description of both sides of the amphora.

Categories	Descriptors
- TYPE OF SUPPORT	: AMPHORA
- PERSONS	: ACHILLES, AJAX, TYNDARE, LEDA, KASTOR, POLYDEUKES, SLAVE
- ANIMALS	: DOG, HORSE
- REPRESENTED OBJECTS	: STOOL, TABLE, SPEAR, SHIELDS, HELMET

In this level of analysis occurs a second semantic partition into *categories of information.* These categories are of the DESCRIPTOR type and are composed of organized descriptors defining a vocabulary that is controlled by the system. This organization is a tree-structure and with it we can establish generic/specific relationships between the descriptors (Figs. 12.3, 12.4, 12.5). The descriptor positions in the tree-structure are indicated by the level-numbers. Each descriptor may have one or many synonyms. The various forms representing these synonyms are then associated with the same concept.

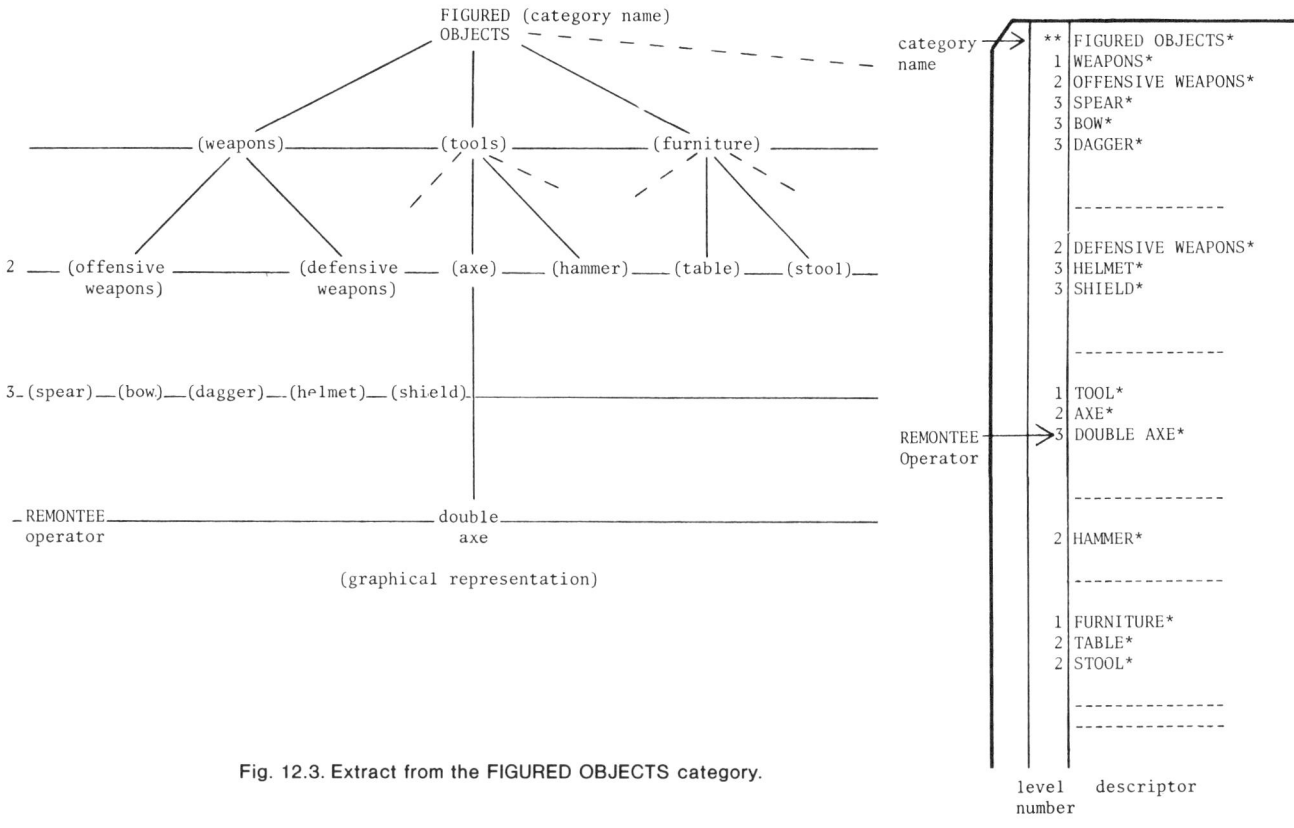

Fig. 12.3. Extract from the FIGURED OBJECTS category.

Representation in SATIN 1
D.D.L. terms

Each category has a specific name that defines the semantic partition of the investigation and individualizes the descriptors or the fields within the study. Each category defines a homogenous conceptual domain, and the descriptors or fields constituting this category are connected to this domain (Bourrelly and Chouraqui 1974a, 1974b). All of the TEXT and DESCRIPTOR type categories define the thesaurus. The thesaurus constitutes the Data Description Language vocabulary.

Thesaurus access mode

In the information retrieval process, the DESCRIPTOR type categories are automatically scanned by the SATIN I system, using four lexical operators.

1. REMONTEE operator. This implicit operator automatically associates each specific descriptor with its "father" descriptor. In Figure 12.3, we automatically substitute the descriptor AXE for the descriptor DOUBLE AXE if the latter does not appear in the studied document.

2. CHEMINEMENT operator. This explicit operator associates each descriptor with its descendants in the tree structure. In Figure 12.4, we associate the term DIOSKOUROS, with the terms POLYDEUKES and KASTOR.

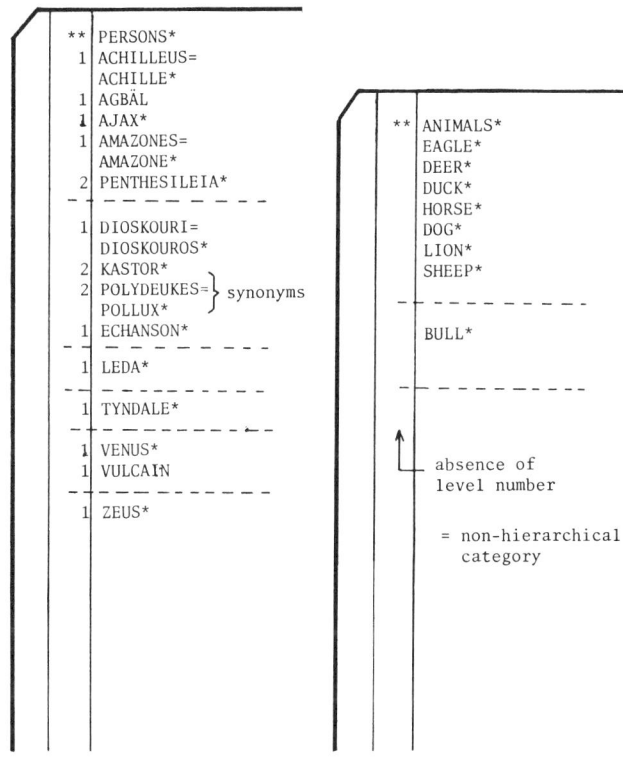

Fig. 12.4. Extract from the PERSONS category.

Fig. 12.5. Extract from the ANIMALS category.

3. GENERALISATION operator. This explicit operator associates each descriptor with its ascendency in the tree structure. In Figure 12.3, we associate the term SPEAR with the terms OFFENSIVE WEAPONS and WEAPONS.

4. COINCIDENCE operator. This explicit operator forbids any scanning of the category structure.

It is possible to modulate both CHEMINEMENT and GENERALISATION operators by controlling the depth of the tree-scanning.

Thesaurus updating

The Thesaurus is a finite vocabulary, but it may be modified as required by updating operations. SATIN I offers two updating levels: (a) addition or deletion of categories, and (b) modification of the category contents by addition, deletion, or replacement of the descriptors or their synonyms and, under certain conditions, modification of these category structures.

Syntactic Relationships

Introduction to the relationships

The significant words that we examined throughout the foregoing paragraph do not provide a satisfactory description of the Exekias Amphora if we consider that our aims are more ambitious than purely bibliographical objectives (the latter are expressed by keyword systems). In the example, the content analysis of the amphora points out two things: (1) the relationships between the persons, the animals, and the objects painted on the amphora, and (2) the properties that characterize them. As examples, we chose a few relationships between these elements, and Figure 12.6 shows the nature of these relationships: (a) the BELONGING relationship to a scene painted on the artifact; (b) the MANIPULATION relationship existing between a person and an object such as to hold, to carry, to brandish, to grasp, and so on; and (c) the DRESSING relationship existing between a person and an object such as hatted, dressed, gloved, shod, and so forth. Moreover, some descriptors are characterized by certain additional properties.

1. OCCURRENCE NUMBER. For example, it is important to note that two scenes are represented on this amphora. Similarly, in each scene, a descriptor may appear several times.

2. ORNAMENTS. If Ajax's helmet had been topped by a shaft, the shaft would be considered as a property belonging to the helmet and not as a descriptor.

3. ATTITUDES. In the same way, the animals could be characterized by their attitudes such as sitting, standing, or lying down.

There may be two types of characterization—one of numerical nature (such as occurrence-number, dimension, weight) and a second of nonnumerical nature (such as attitude, color, clothing detail).

Syntactic components

The Data Description Language in the SATIN I system manipulates the foregoing relationships by using the notion of syntactic components. These compo-

Nature of relationship		Actants	
belonging to scene 1	manipulation	Achilles	spear
		Ajax	spear
	dressing	Ajax	helmet
belonging to scene 2	manipulation	Kastor	spear
		Slave	stool
		Slave	aryballos

Fig. 12.6. Relational description of the Exekias Amphora.

nents are associated with the various descriptors involved in the relationship (Bourrelly and Chouraqui 1974a, 1974b). Each syntactic component is formed by three elements: (1) the syntactic group expressing the logical characterization in the relationship, (2) the syntactic class 1 expressing the semantic characterization in the relationship, and (3) the syntactic class 2 expressing the syntagmatic characterization or a property.

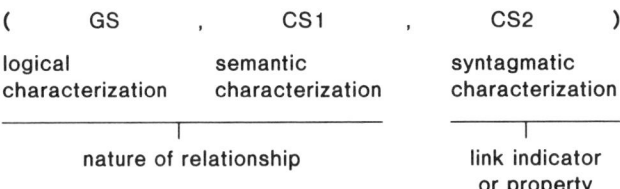

The relationships in Figure 12.6 are then expressed as shown in Figure 12.7.

It must be noted that with SATIN I we can arrange the properties in a tree structure; this structure is then automatically scanned by the system.

With the SATIN I Data Description Language we can handle two kinds of relationships. One kind links two or more descriptors of a same lexical category or of different categories. These relationships are composed of two parts called syntactic components; they are associated with each descriptor as shown in Figure 12.8. The second relationship links a descriptor to a property that characterizes it. These relationships are then reduced to a unique syntactic component associated with the descriptor.

Thus, we can build descriptions that fit our aims by using the descriptors and the relationships that link them. In SATIN I we call descriptive analysis the operation that produces these descriptions by means of a semantic network (thesaurus) and relational network (syntactic components).

Operations performed on syntactic components

SATIN I Data Description Language provides us with two kinds of operators involving the syntactic components. One kind includes the numerical comparison operators that we can apply to class 2 of the syntactic group "number":

.EG. (equal),
.GT. (greater than),
.GE. (greater than or equal),
.LT. (less than),
.LE. (less than or equal)

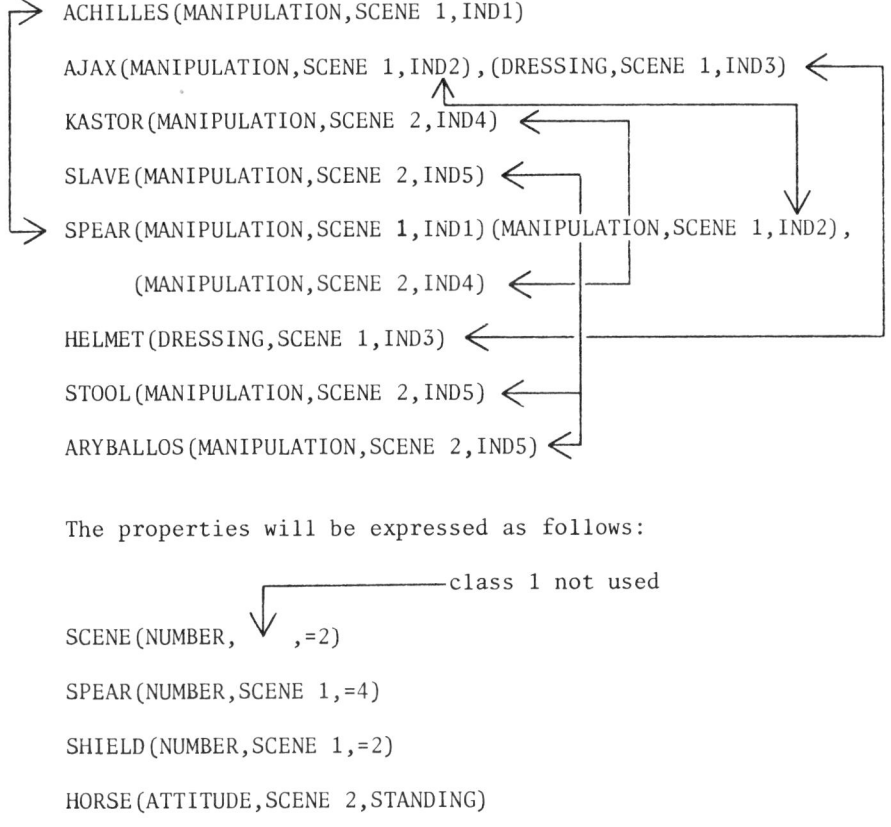

Fig. 12.7. Diagram of relationships expressed in Figure 12.6.

The second kind involves the identity operator of syntactic classes denoted "MEM=" used to assure that the values of two or several syntactic classes (considered as variables) are effectively identical.

DATA BASE

The Documents

Using the concepts introduced in the foregoing paragraph, we may represent the artifact "Exekias Amphora" in SATIN I Data Description Language terms. This representation constitutes a document. The modes of the artifact analysis determine the structure of the documents. A document is composed of two parts that respectively use the two types of analysis we have already defined: thematic and descriptive.

The thematic part carries information resulting from the thematic analysis. This part is mainly used by output editing routines. Nevertheless, it may be used on the fields without employing the possibilities offered by the thesaurus or the relational network.

The descriptive part carries information resulting from the descriptive analysis. This part is used for information search and extraction operations that are based on the thesaurus structure and on the relational network structure. Thus the document—Exekias Amphora—will have the following representation.

```
THEMATIC PART
DESIGNATION            : EXEKIAS AMPHORA
AUTHOR                 : EXEKIAS
STYLE                  : BLACK-FIGURED ATTIC
                         STYLE
PLACE OF CONSERVATION : VATICAN MUSEUM
DATING                 : 540 B.C.
------------------------------------------------
------------------------------------------------
DESCRIPTIVE PART
SUPPORT : AMPHORA-SCENE(NUMBER,  ,=2)*
PERSONS : ACHILLES(MANIPULATION,SCENE 1,IND1)-
          AJAX(MANIPULATION,SCENE 1,IND2),
             (SUPPORT,SCENE 1,IND3)-
          KASTOR(MANIPULATION,SCENE 2,IND4)-
          SLAVE(MANIPULATION,SCENE 2,IND5)-
          ----------------------------------------- *
OBJECTS : SPEAR(MANIPULATION,SCENE 1,IND1),
             (MANIPULATION,SCENE 1,IND2),
             (MANIPULATION,SCENE 2,IND4),
             (NUMBER,SCENE 1,=4)-
          HELMET(SUPPORT,SCENE 1,IND3)-
          STOOL(MANIPULATION,SCENE 2,IND5)-
          ARYBALLOS(MANIPULATION,SCENE 2,
          IND5)-
          SHIELD(NUMBER,SCENE 1,=2)*
ANIMALS : HORSE(ATTITUDE,SCENE 2,STANDING)-
          DOG(ATTITUDE,SCENE 2,STANDING)*
------------------------------------------------
------------------------------------------------
END*
```

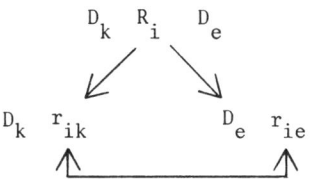

where: D_k = descriptors
       D_e

       R_i = relationships

       r_{ik} = syntactic component associated with D_k

       r_{ie} = syntactic compoent associated with D_e

Fig. 12.8. Descriptor relationships.

Document Organization

The documents constitute the system reference units. They are organized in partitions and are bound by three criteria. The first criterium always constitutes the dates of creation or updating. A total or fractional combination of these criteria defines a semantic access to the partitions used in the document processing operations.

We again find the documents thematic/descriptive dichotomy in the organization of two separate document files: the THEMATIC partitioned file and the DESCRIPTIVE partitioned file.

Data Base Updating

The data base updating may apply to the thematic as well as to the descriptive parts of the documents. It may be performed either on a document or on a set of documents selected by an interrogation. SATIN I offers two levels of updating: (a) addition or deletion of documents, and (b) modification of the contents of the documents by means of addition, deletion, or replacement of descriptors, fields, or syntactic components.

DOCUMENT PROCESSING

Interrogation

We may interrogate the data base by means of questions written in Data Description Language terms and activated by Command Language orders. A set of questions dealing with either the thematic or the descriptive file constitutes a SATIN I query program. With SATIN I we can manipulate the operators: (a) Lexical operators—COINCIDENCE, CHEMINEMENT, and GENERALISATION; (b) Syntactic components operators—Comparison (EG, GT, GE, LT, LE), and Syntactic classes identities (MEM=); and (c) Boolean operators.

The Data Description Language elements arising in a question are interrelated by Boolean connectors: AND, OR, NOR, NAND, YES, NOT. We illustrate the interrogation language with a few questions concerning our example Exekias Amphora.

Example 1

Search for artifacts that are amphorae representing two scenes.

QEST		AMPHORA WITH TWO SCENES	
G1	100	AMPHORA*	AND
	100	SCENE*(number, , =2).	
EXPR		(G1 YES)	
RPON		QSVP EXP	
FORM		(10X,'DESIGNATION :',25X,(101,1))	
	****/		

CL QEST declarative statement introduces the wording of the question.

G1 is a label that spots Data Description Language information related by the same Boolean operator (AND).

100 is the code generated by SATIN I for the category "TYPE OF SUPPORT."

EXPR declarative statement relates labels by Boolean operators. (Here, we ask for the unique G1 label by the affirmation operator YES). This declarative statement ends the question.

RPON is an executable statement that defines the nature of the results and QSVP is a key-word that asks for the printing of references according to the format introduced by the declarative statement FORM.

****/ are the signs showing the program end.

Example 2

Count the artifacts in which Ajax is wearing a helmet OR one of the Dioscures is holding a spear.

QEST		AJAX WEARING A HELMET *OR* DIOSCURES HOLDING A SPEAR	
H1	102	AJAX*(SUPPORT, MEM=HAT).	AND
	106	HELMET*(SUPPORT, ,MEM=HAT).	
H2	102	DIOSCURES*CHEMINEMENT, (MANIPULATION, ,MEM=WEAP).	AND
	106	SPEAR*(MANIPULATION, ,MEN=WEAP).	
EXPR		(H1 OR H2)	
RPON		CPTG	
	****/		

In this question, MEM= operator establishes the identities of the link indicators for which the value is not given. The variables HAT on the one hand, and WEAP on the other hand, establish the operator-scope. The lexical operator CHEMINEMENT automatically associates KASTOR and POLYDEUKES descriptors with

the DIOSCURES descriptor (see Fig. 12.4). CPTG is a key-word asking for the numbering of relevant documents.

Example 3

Among the Attic Style Amphorae, dated between 600 and 400 B.C., which are the ones (a) representing Achilles AND Ajax in the same scene, (b) representing at least two shields and no spear, and (c) showing a slave holding an aryballos and a stool?

THEM		ATTIC STYLE AMPHORAE DATED BETWEEN 600 AND 400 B.C.	
T1	100	AMPHORA*	AND
	108	ATTIC*	
T2	110	DATE*(VALUE, ,GE-600).	AND
	110	DATE*(VALUE, ,LE-400).	
EXPR		(T1 AND T2).	
QEST		ACHILLES AND AJAX IN A SAME SCENE	
A	102	ACHILLES*(MANIPULATION, MEM=SCEN).	AND
	102	AJAX*(MANIPULATION,MEM=SCEN).	
EXPR		(A YES)	
QEST		NUMBER OF SHIELDS GE-NO SPEAR	
B1	106	SHIELD*(NUMBER, ,GE2).	YES
B2	106	SPEAR*.	NOT
EXPR		(B1 AND B2)	
QEST		SLAVE HOLDING AN ARYBALLOS AND A STOOL	
C	102	SLAVE*(MANIPULATION, ,MEM=OBJT).	AND
	106	ARYBALLOS*(MANIPULATION, ,MEM=OBJT).	
	106	STOOL*(MANIPULATION, ,MEM=OBJT).	
EXPR		(C YES)	
RPON		GRIL EXP	
FORM		(10X, 'DESIGNATION',25X,(101,1),/,; 'AUTHOR',25X,(103,1),/,; 'STYLE',25X,(108,1),/,; 'DATING',25X,(110))	
	****/		

The declarative statement THEM introduces a question aimed at selecting a set of documents (Attic style amphorae dated between 600–400 B.C.). The following QEST questions deal exclusively with this set.

The keyword GRIL provides us with a result in a matrix form. The matrix rows correspond to the documents selected by the THEM type question. The columns correspond to QEST type questions. At the row/column intersection, the Boolean value 1 or 2 indicates the relevance or irrelevance of the document with respect to the question (Fig. 12.9).

Output Products

SATIN I output products have been established in order to satisfy the demands of (a) diversity, (b) reutilization of results and updating, and (c) user selected format for output printing. SATIN I supplies nine output products.

QSVP: references output for relevant documents issued from a retrieval operation.
CPTG: counting of relevant documents.
GRIL: creation of a Boolean matrix and references output associated with a research theme.
CPTH: counting of the documents selected according to a theme.
IDEX: references output in index form.
FREF: references output without previous retrieval.
EXTR: extraction of descriptors of algebraic values with references output.
EXTG: extraction of descriptors of algebraic values without reference output.
-***: counting of the relevant documents and storage of a file for future use (*dynamic secondary file*).

Some output products may constitute intermediate results for further processing (statistical calculations, classifications, graphs, and the like). The -*** dynamic secondary file is reused by SATIN I to define a sub-set of relevant documents associated with the study in process, and to operate updatings. The operations (i.e., output products and -*** files reutilizations) are made possible by cataloging the output products library managed by SATIN I.

The printing format is extremely flexible concerning vertical and horizontal margin, spacing, literal data, and so on. If it is possible to choose a standard format for the whole processing operation, this format may be cataloged and used again without the need for further definition.

SATIN I SYSTEM ORGANIZATION

The various concepts that have been presented concerning the Exekias Amphora analysis demonstrate some of the SATIN I Data Description and Command Language specifications. On a more general level, we must note that SATIN I is a machine-independent system entirely written in FORTRAN. It is composed of programs that perform the following functions: creation, recording, printing, updating, and processing of documentary data (Bourrelly and Chouraqui 1978).

The processing corresponding to each function consists of two consecutive phases. The first one corresponds to the syntactic analysis of the Data Description Language; with it we can spot the formal errors associated with the data formulation and organization. The second one corresponds to the execution phase, the result of which depends on the type of function used. These various functions are organized as shown in Figure 12.10.

RESEARCH THEME:

Attic style Amphorae dating from 600 to 400 years B.C.

Number of relevant documents: 125

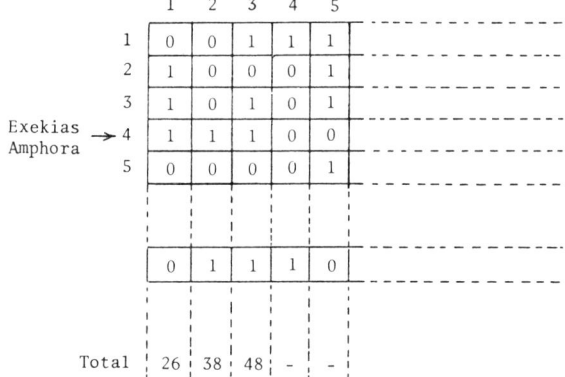

COLUMN REFERENCES:

Column 1: Achilles and Ajax represented in same scene

Column 2: Number of shields GE2. No spear

Column 3: Slave holding an aryballos and a stool

ROW REFERENCES:

1. ----------------------

2. ----------------------

3. ----------------------

4. DESIGNATION: The Exekias Amphora

   AUTHOR   : Exekias

   STYLE   : Black-figured Attic

   DATING   : 540 B.C.

5. ----------------------

Fig. 12.9. Example of a GRIL type output product.

RECOMMENDATIONS FOR FUTURE APPLICATIONS

SATIN I is mainly intended for archaeologists who utilize their data bases for scientific investigations. For such applications, the system offers the following properties.

1. It is provided with a Data Description Language that allows a manipulation (under a flexible format) of complex and diversified data that essentially express a content analysis.

2. It can provide output products in a form suitable

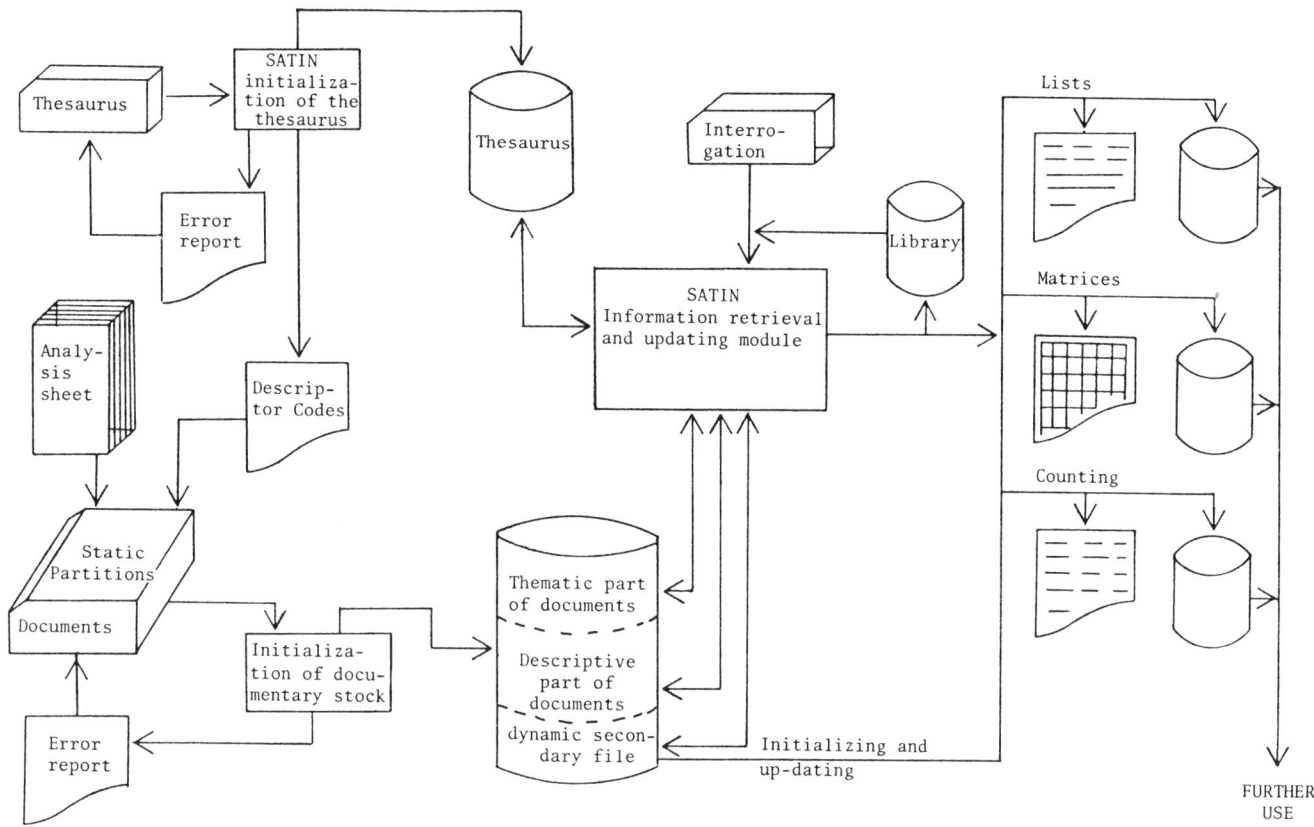

Fig. 12.10. General organization of the SATIN I system.

for use in scientific calculations (statistical, cartography, sorting, automatic classification, etc.).

3. It allows an extremely well detailed updating of the stored information.

4. It offers the user the opportunity to conduct a study of a subject in stages. The system allows storage of the result of the previous step for use in each subsequent step. Thus, we may obtain a better defined and more selective data search.

This type of approach leads to the construction of a data base composed of a number of documents limited only by the aim of the study but requiring the use of a sophisticated Data Description Language.

REFERENCES

Borillo, M.
1971   Formal procedures and the use of computers in archeology. *Norwegian Archeological Review* 4: 1–27.
1977   Raisonner, Calculer. *Raisonnements et méthodes mathématiques en Archéologie.* Paris-Marseille: C.N.R.S.
Borillo, O., M. P. Chiavari, P. Donati, and P. Jervis
1975   Analyse sémiologique de la cartographie cada-

strale. Communication au Colloque international DGRST–CNRS "Informatique et Sciences Humaines." Marseille.
Bourrelly, L., and H. Camps-Fabrer
1974   Premiers résultats concernant le traitement en ordinateur des objets en os de quelques gisements du midi méditerranéen. Exposé des méthodes et résultats obtenus. *Table Ronde sur l'industrie de l'os dans la préhistoire.* St. Germaine.
Bourrelly, L., and E. Chouraqui
1974a   Le Système documentaire SATIN I. Description générale et manuel d'utilisation. Paris-Marseille: C.N.R.S.
1974b   Description générale du système documentaire SATIN I. Communication au premier congrès national sur la documentation automatique. Paris.
1976   La représentation des données documentaires—Structure du Métalangage SATIN I. Communication EURIM 2. Amsterdam.
1978   Le système documentaire SATIN I. Génération et aide à la mise au point. Paris-Marseille: C.N.R.S.
Buchenschutz, O., J. Dorion, and A. Querrien-Mansuy
1976   Cartographie et analyse descriptive des sites archéologiques du department du Cher. Communications au IX Congrès de l'U.I.S.P.P. (Colloque no. IV). Nice.

Chenhall, Robert G.
  1976   The theory and practice of using data banks in archeological research. Communication au IX Congrès de l'U.I.S.P.P. (Colloque no. IV). Nice.

Chouraqui, E.
  1973   The index and filing system used by the Inventaire Général des Monuments et richesses artistiques de la France. *Computers and the Humanities* 7(5): 273-285.

Chouraqui, E., and J. Virbel
  1976   Construction d'un dispositif expérimental pour la représentation et le traitement des données textuelles sur un exemple en histoire. Communication au 6ème Congrès International de linguistique computationnelle. Ottawa.

Daumas, J. C., and E. Raby
  1976   Documentation automatique et urbanisme. Adéquation et Validation d'un language documentaire par rapport au système documentaire SATIN I. Communication à l'Atelier "Analyse et expérimentation dans les Sciences de l'Homme par les méthodes informatiques." Congrès AFCET "Panorama de la nouveauté informatique en France." Paris: Gifsur-Yvette.

Gardin, J. C.
  1974   Les projets de banques de données archéologiques. Problèmes méthodologiques, technologiques, et institutionnels. *Les banques de données archéologiques*. Paris: C.N.R.S.

Ginouves, R., and A. M. Guimier-Sorbets
  1978   *La constitution des données en archéologie classique*. Paris: C.N.R.S.

Guimier-Sorbets, A. M.
  1976   Code pour l'analyse des mosaïques romaines. Thèse de 3ème cycle. Université de Paris X.

Hesnard, A., and J. Virbel
  1973   Analyse sémantique d'un champ lexicologique se rapportant à des objets en vue d'une traduction automatique dans un langage formalisé. Communication au 5ème Congrès international de linguistique computationnelle. Pise.

LaGrange, M.S.
  1968   *Code pour l'analyse des monuments civils*. Paris: C.N.R.S.

Soudsky, B.
  1970   Le Problème des propriétés dans les ensembles archéologiques. *Archéologie et Calculateurs. Problèmes sémiologiques et mathématiques*. Paris: C.N.R.S.

Index